ADVENTURES IN
MISPLACED MARKETING

ADVENTURES IN MISPLACED MARKETING

Herbert Jack Rotfeld

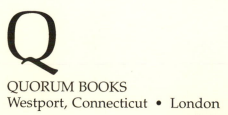

QUORUM BOOKS
Westport, Connecticut • London

Library of Congress Cataloging-in-Publication Data

Rotfeld, Herbert Jack, 1950–
    Adventures in misplaced marketing / Herbert Jack Rotfeld.
      p.   cm.
    Includes index.
    ISBN 1–56720–352–3 (alk. paper)
    1. Marketing. 2. Consumer behavior. I Title
    HF5415.R635   2001
    658.8—dc21   2001019869

British Library Cataloguing in Publication Data is available.

Library of Congress Catalog Card Number: 2001019869
ISBN: 1–56720–352–3

First published in 2001

Quorum Books, 88 Post Road West, Westport, CT 06881
An imprint of Greenwood Publishing Group, Inc.
www.quorumbooks.com

Printed in the United States of America

The paper used in this book complies with the Permanent Paper Standard issued by the National Information Standards Organization (Z39.48–1984).

10 9 8 7 6 5 4 3 2 1

Contents

Preface

It began because I had a problem. I wanted to teach a graduate course on "marketing and society" and I needed to encourage our M.B.A. students to enroll. I could only get so far on my adorable personality.

My problem had some academic history. Many years ago, in the wake of some major business scandals of the early 1980s, business education programs were directed by the major accrediting organization to require the study of business ethics. At first, most universities added a new course to the list of requirements; at Auburn, the M.B.A. course was titled "Legal Social Ethical Environment of Business." Unfortunately, discovering that many students were concerned only with pragmatic directives on how to be financially successful, many schools (including Auburn) responded by dropping the course requirement, claiming that the basic material was integrated into other courses in the program.

Whether such "integration" actually occurs at any school is questionable. But regardless of whether my colleagues performed as they claimed, the course was changed from a degree requirement into a department elective. I thought an unofficial course title of "misplaced marketing" would generate student interest.

It seemed intuitively obvious that marketing's social issues easily fit dictionary definitions of "misplaced" in that a marketing perspective had either been lost or misdirected. Other times, marketing tools were abused. After all, many criticisms of business involve firms that do not use or apply a marketing perspective when they should. Other critics attack what they perceive as marketing's failure to consider the societal impact of business decisions. I also noted, with growing fascination, that marketing—and especially advertising—is often attacked as undesirable when, in reality, the critic's real desire is to restrict, ban, or outlaw the product or service marketed.

Writing about misplaced marketing started with a phone call in early 1996 to Gregg Cebrzynski.

"Hi. This is Herb Rotfeld. You still having fun as managing editor?"

"Herb, how are things in Auburn? It's been a while since you've sent me any new essays for *Marketing News*. We haven't received a letter of complaint for months."

"Actually, I was wondering if I could write a regular ongoing column for you."

"Well, you know our columns are all dedicated to certain topic areas and we're pretty much committed to the current roster of columnists. Did you have something special in mind? A new topic?"

"Something new and different. 'Misplaced marketing.'"

"Sounds interesting just by the title. What is it?"

Okay, so this wasn't the exact conversation. We had talked before on the phone, I wanted to be a columnist and Gregg hadn't heard of "misplaced marketing," but, then, no one had, except for my students.

Anyway, my general description got Gregg interested and, after he reviewed some sample columns, "Herbert Rotfeld on Misplaced Marketing" started running once a month beginning July of that year.[1] Toward the end of 1998 I sent several other misplaced marketing commentaries to an academic outlet, *Journal of Consumer Marketing*, where they were reviewed and accepted by the editorial board, with an additional request that I serve as a special section editor for the journal to encourage other people to submit papers on the subject. And when I visited a school in Melbourne, Australia, marketing faculty member Colin Jevons encouraged me to turn my attention to writing a book.

Like the magazine and journal commentaries, this book presents my personal perspective on past and current marketing practices, as well as many nonmarketing activities that could be aided by a marketing view. And this format allows me to present my original thinking on the subject. With short magazine columns or research notes, people read a series of seemingly eclectic essays and they might think "misplaced marketing" is only a collection of weakly related stories on bad customer service. This book restores the tapestry initially envisioned when I started using misplaced marketing as a basis for my class.

The downside of writing a book is that I lose any pretense of timeliness. Some of the firms that were the basis for these stories might have corrected some or all of their unfortunate practices. A business once noted for its positive marketplace role might have changed and could now serve as an exemplar of negative practice. Decisions in legal cases could have been reversed or altered on appeal. Since it is impossible to follow every up-to-the-minute change, the examples and personal experiences are presented herein to explain, not to castigate or praise.

Most companies described in this book are not directly identified. Others have fictitious names. Identifying details of many people mentioned in the stories are changed to protect their privacy. Of course, with the names disguised or removed, people who never talked to me or business employees I never encountered might see themselves in the stories. Perhaps more people will feel guilty because they'll think I am talking about them.

Kim Rotzoll has endured and supported my writing for almost three decades as my teacher, doctoral advisor, and friend. He once explained that "Essay writers put themselves on a limb. They are, after all, expressing thoughtful opinions, often in short supply among many [academic writers]." While I have acquired a degree of fame (or maybe I should say "infamy") from my essays in magazines and academic journals, even some people who enjoy reading my articles have said that they are "provocative." They apparently view this as a negative label for a scholar or educator.

It is an unfortunate commentary on modern education that being provocative is now seen as something a faculty member should avoid. Instead of pushing new ideas or perspectives, we are encouraged to provide the intellectual equivalent of a day at the beach for our students and colleagues. An M.B.A. class does not provide a forum for discussion of education philosophy, but the application of misplaced marketing that interests me most stems from the conflict between what education *should* do and what students want from classes. Chapter 12 explains how the marketing *of* education is not only misplaced, but is also a destructive force for education itself. I restricted the comments on this topic to one chapter, but I barely scratched the surface of my concerns.

Many people inspired and encouraged my work, both now and in years past, such as Colin, Kim, and Morris Holbrook. Colin, Morris, and especially my graduate school classmate Lory Montgomery all gave me crucial help with editing notes and comments on preliminary drafts of chapters.

The opinions expressed herein are my own. And to borrow from comedian Mort Sahl, if there are any readers that I haven't insulted, I apologize.

NOTE

1. Gregg left the organization in mid-1997 and the series of short-term replacements had me recall Thomas Sowell's statement: "The fact that I have never killed an editor is proof that the death penalty deters." Some editors inserted errors into my columns and I ran disclaimers on my Web page. In this book I re-create parts of those columns with my original perspective intact. The last column for that magazine ran in February 1999, though I am still writing new and original commentaries for *Journal of Consumer Marketing*.

Acknowledgments

Portions of the material for this book develop and significantly expand stories and ideas that were published in various issues of *Marketing News* and *Journal of Consumer Marketing*, plus a book review published in *Journal of Marketing*. Any material that appeared in *Marketing News* from July 1996 to January 1999 and in *Journal of Marketing*, volume 63 (January 1999), is reprinted by a license from the American Marketing Association. Material from *Journal of Consumer Marketing* is reprinted by permission of MCB University Press.

Included below is a full listing of the *Marketing News* columns:

Volume 30, 1996: July 15; August 12; September 9; October 7; November 4; December 2.

Volume 31, 1997: January 20; February 17; March 17; April 28; May 26; June 23; July 21; August 4; August 18; September 15; October 27; November 24; December 8.

Volume 32, 1998: January 19; February 16; March 16; April 13; May 11; June 8; July 6; August 3; August 31; September 14; October 12; November 9; December 7.

Volume 33, 1999: January 4; February 15.

Included below is a full listing of the *Journal of Consumer Marketing* commentaries:

Volume 15, 1998: issue #6.

Volume 16, 1999: issues #1, #2, #4, and #5.

Volume 17, 2000: issues #5 and #7.

1

Myths and Legends of the Modern Marketing Concept

Marketing is a very difficult topic to discuss with people working in other fields, since everyone seems to be a self-proclaimed expert on the subject. After all, they're experienced shoppers, exposed to advertising their entire lives. They see it and therefore they "know" it. And they're all critics.

Even at social gatherings, marketing people find the introductions followed by all sorts of virulent complaints. I am reluctant to say I am a professor of marketing or that I teach advertising courses. Total strangers quickly blame me, as if I were personally responsible for the television advertising they don't like.

"Where do I work? I'm a faculty member at the university."

"Really? What department?

"Uh . . . business."

"Oh, I'm interested in business. What do you teach?

[Pause. Reluctant response.] "Marketing and advertising."

"I hate those panty shield commercials."

"I'm sorry, but I have nothing to do with those. They weren't my fault."

When I visited New Zealand, even bus drivers or the clerk at the souvenir store asked me what I thought of a then-current commercial for Toyota trucks in which the characters repeatedly say "Bugger." (That word is of questionable and profane etiology for many Kiwis and the commercial recently had been the basis for complaints before their national self-regulatory Advertising Standards Association.) In the United States, people have followed the introductions by grabbing my lapels and complaining about cigarettes targeting children, as if I personally had designed the campaign.

As one of the most visible of business practices, marketing is criticized by almost everyone, from social critics to government lawmakers to political pundits. Audience manipulation, offensive products, and cultural destruction are among the social ills often laid at the feet of the marketing business. Some students in my classes say they enrolled because they wanted to learn how (not "if") advertising manipulates people's behavior. In keeping with this popular view of the business, *Time* magazine's cover story in a mid-1999 international edition "reported" various tricks and tools of marketing used to manipulate consumers, illustrated by a metaphorical picture of a consumer dancing on a marketing man's puppet strings.[1] Supposedly, consumers are controlled by the mind manipulations of marketing planners, or so many people believe.

Admittedly, this near-paranoid view of marketing power fit with the beliefs held by leading scholars and business people a half century ago under their own views of marketing theory and practice. At that time, firms pursued what is now called a "production orientation," producing what the managers personally believed was a good product; marketing was the job of selling it. If the product wasn't selling, the marketing people were not doing a good job. In mass communications, everyone believed that political propaganda drove the citizens of every nation. In the 1930s, the first widespread scholarly and professional efforts to study how and why mass communications and persuasion might influence the public were impelled by a widespread perceived need to find ways to inoculate the vulnerable citizens of free nations against the much-feared powers of Nazi propaganda. After the war, the fear was communist influences in mass communications.

Today, marketing people know better, or so we hope, since research consistently reveals that people are very resistant to the persuasive efforts of marketing tools. It is generally realized that marketing practitioners can only wish they had the power business critics presume they possess. In reality, they don't. As it says in a once-popular song performed by Paul Simon and Art Garfunkel, people hear what they want to hear and disregard the rest.

Twenty-five years ago, a documentary interviewer asked noted advertising man George Lois how it felt to have so much power over consumers' minds. But his response was that advertising is *not* mind bending because, as he put it, "No one is that good."[2] The fact is that no one can be that good.

The criticisms might be voiced by people with limited knowledge or understanding of marketing theory and practice.[3] And yet, since marketing practice is not a guild—the business doesn't require any training or education programs for people making marketing decisions—many business practitioners also share these mistaken beliefs. I often tell students that just because they see a big-budget advertising campaign doesn't mean it is a good idea. Years ago, an executive at a major advertising agency insisted that, with a large enough budget, he could persuade men to start wearing dresses to work, a statement that was obviously ignorant of the large and unsuccessful advertising efforts to persuade women to wear dresses of lengths dramatically different than current general tastes.

Therefore, another way of viewing various issues and criticisms of marketing is to think of them as being generated by what I have come to call misplaced marketing: People who could or should be making marketing-based decisions are misplacing their focus, ignoring, misusing, or abusing some basic perspectives that should be followed.

THE MARKETING CONCEPT

A microbiologist I knew years ago always liked to describe the latest research problem in his laboratory or research dead end by saying that, "Under carefully controlled conditions, organisms behave as they damn well please." What was sarcastically true for his microbes is more true for people. Successful marketing planning and tactics have to take consumers' behavior tendencies into account.

An oblong piece of plastic on my desk with a curved bottom and a flat top can be spun on its axis. But because of the way it is weighted, curved, and balanced, you can only spin it counterclockwise. Even though it is a plain looking piece of plastic, as complicated as a common thumb tack, it inexplicably will resist spinning in the other direction. If it is shoved clockwise, it starts to spin, then wobbles, hesitates, and reverses direction. Similarly, with free-willed consumers in the marketplace, as long as a marketing planner knows the way people want to go and understands why, he or she can try to encourage them to go faster or slower, or try to start them moving in the first place. Trying to get them to move in ways they don't want to will only result in failure.

Some people might believe that marketing people pull consumers' strings. Many people think consumers are controlled by marketing or advertising, but they're not. At best, marketing people try to find those "buttons to push"; they want to understand, explain, and predict exactly how those potential customers will jump when exposed to various aspects of marketing decisions.

The widely accepted "modern marketing concept" has become common and repeated ad nauseam in literature for our trade associations and textbooks. It presents an approach for all product and service planning that takes into account a world in which people have more in common with my obstinate piece of plastic or my friend's unicellular lab organisms than they do with puppets on strings. In short, marketing people can't sell a product unless there is some underlying initial consumer interest or inclination. In theory, the modern marketing concept combines all facets of the product design, price decisions, where the product is available for sale, personal selling and mass communications with an orientation to "satisfy consumer needs and wants."[4] (That's their mantra: "satisfy consumer needs and wants.")

At its core, it shifts the basis of planning from what would otherwise be production-then-sales efforts. Instead, it directs marketing planners to first assess how and why people make various decisions and to use those assessments as the basis for designing products amd setting prices. Then, it uses those same assessments to decide how to inform and persuade consumers. A marketing plan can't set a goal to significantly alter consumer beliefs because such changes can't be made. Top-notch marketing efforts failed to sell Edsel cars, the original mididress, or other products that interested no one; no marketing plan could impel Auburn University men to start wearing skirts to class.

Some critics might reluctantly admit to this limit to marketing power, but then blithely assert that all-knowing marketing managers have studied people and know exactly which of consumers' mental buttons to push to get the desired response. And yet, even this supposed power is intrinsically limited. The best available predictions are very difficult, weak, and uncertain. After decades of studies of consumer and market analysis, the most heavily researched predictions are still providing only weak correlations with actual outcomes. Even among the most successful firms that regularly use extensive research as a basis for making marketing decisions, the majority of new products or service innovations fail to entice customers to make a purchase.[5]

In theory, the marketing concept as a planning perspective increases the likelihood that a firm will be successful, but it is far from a promise of certainty. This is not to overstate the power of the marketing concept: It is not a guarantee of marketing success, but it does offer a basic perspective that recognizes the limits of marketer power and, at the same time, a focus for analysis of marketing problems.[6] Making business decisions based on consumer interests does give anyone a clear way to view customer–firm relations.

Unfortunately, the language of the modern marketing concept can be misleading. It could be read to imply values that it does not possess. Marketing trade associations and college textbooks say that marketing is a matter of satisfying consumer needs and wants, making it seem as if "real" marketing is above reproach and positive. Since this was the predominant worldview of marketing theory and practice when the United States started the modern wave of business criticisms thirty years ago, many educators and practitioners did not understand the problems the critics were raising. Many still don't. Marketing experts (both practitioners and educators) were heard to say, "The marketing concept says that we should 'satisfy consumer needs,' so since we are satisfying consumers, 'consumerism' [as consumer protection was called in the 1970s] isn't really a problem for us."[7]

Unfortunately, saying that "We are just providing a service that people want," at best sounds the same as a drug dealer, a prostitute, or the Prohibition-era gangster, Al Capone.

Irony notwithstanding, even the best reading of such a view presumes that all firms follow this marketing orientation. Many don't. The often-ignored fact is that many firms fail to ask basic marketing questions of "how," "why," or "if" people might be interested in the planned product features or advertising messages. Instead of considering audience views of the world, the managers practice ethnocentrism. Instead of trying to anticipate customer problems, systems are put in place for the convenience of employees. And (more dangerously), while doing a good job using marketing tools to focus on key customer groups, they ignore potential critics' complaints.

Even if all businesses did adhere to the marketing orientation for every decision, it would not necessarily be true that many firms satisfying consumer needs would also serve the interests of society at large. From a societal point of view, what many consumers "want" are not necessarily what they should be getting. So while some organizations do a good job of marketing their goods or services or ideas, many business critics wish that they weren't doing such a good job (because we do not want corporations to do a good job of selling, say, cigarettes).

WHAT IT MEANS TO MISPLACE MARKETING

Apparently, there is strong disagreements as to how to define marketing. When someone on an Internet discussion line for marketing educators and professionals raised the issue, participants tossed out all sorts of lengthy arguments. Some definitions turned on a variety of

arcane terms and few had any pragmatic implications. Some definitions were the "official" statements of national or international trade
associations, while one or two writers claimed that the "best" definition was in the latest edition of their textbook. Yet, through it all, there
seemed little disagreement about the marketing concept's customer
orientation as a business philosophy, and the basic tools used by marketing, such as communications, are intuitively obvious.

Fortunately, the definition of misplaced marketing does not require
a definition of marketing. Starting with the marketing concept, the
definition of "misplaced marketing" consists of two prongs that are
both broad and simple.

First, marketing can be misplaced in the sense that it is "lost" or
missing when a business, government agency, nonprofit organization,
or other group could (or should) follow the basic dictates of a marketing perspective but does not. In these instances, marketing tools or
tactics are used without reference to a strategy or customer-based perspective that a marketing orientation would require. Second, marketing can be misplaced in the sense of that it is being used in the "wrong"
place. In these instances, it may be "properly" used and applied for a
product or service, but its use is still amoral, in that the context or
products or marketing benefits for consumers may be detrimental to
a societal interest or, at the very least, detrimental to the interests and
values posed by critics of business practices.

In other words, marketing activities may be "misplaced" because a
marketing perspective or the basic tools of the business are misused,
misapplied, abused, or simply the source of social criticisms of business activities. In every instance, the firms that misplace marketing
may be financially successful while some present or potential customers are dissatisfied. Social groups that use marketing tools rarely discover how (or if) their public information campaigns fail. Government
agencies often don't ask marketing questions, to the detriment of the
public groups they are expected to efficiently serve.

The modern marketing concept may call on businesses to "satisfy
consumer needs," but misplaced marketing shows that marketing practice does not always put the concept to its best use. And, in the end,
consumers or society are not "satisfied."

SUCCESS WITHOUT THE MARKETING CONCEPT

Based on textbook and trade association literature, conventional
wisdom holds that some "smaller" or unsuccessful firms still look at
marketing in terms of selling, but the modern marketing concept's
acceptance and use is virtually universal among successful firms.[8] Yet
there exist many examples of products or services that do not follow
the "marketing concept," but, instead, provide features in terms of

what designers or engineers say they can produce. While it is seldom discussed in the textbooks, many modern businesses still follow a production or selling orientation.

In these cases, marketing can be misplaced in the sense of "lost." Since they are making marketing decisions simply because the manager finds it interesting, or if the product has a feature because the company "can" add it, but the business decision makers don't ask if they "should," marketing remains just selling. Often, marketing gets "misplaced" because the planners or managers don't ask how the product or service could meet consumer needs.

Everyone has at some time or other looked for a product with certain features and "settled" for something short of what was desired. It is not uncommon to hear store managers state that they "know" the customers, so certain products are never stocked. "My customers aren't interested in that kind of thing," the inquiring customer is told, though the manager never tried stocking it, never even tried to buy one or two and see if they sold, and never sought other opinions.

Some examples are bad service. Sometimes it is a manager or owner seeing rules as more important than service, as when customers of retail stores test doors a few minutes before opening and walk away, while employees mill about inside the store waiting for the clock to chime on the hour for the posted opening time. Sometimes features are added to a product mix because an engineer thought it would be simple and inexpensive to do, not because anyone thought it made the product more desirable for consumers. And some examples are just plain corporate or engineering stupidity: Expensive electronic items often have simple parts like batteries or lights that are expected to die but are nigh impossible to replace. Many service hotlines are always busy and not very helpful. Some offensive ads are just bad messages, the result of business stupidity or ethnocentrism.

Of course, a product is more than the sum of its physical features and a good sales job changes the product itself. And maybe the people who can't find exactly what they want are just out of step with the rest of the marketplace. There might not be enough of them to be considered a viable target market segment—maybe virtually all potential purchasers want the commonly bundled features of, say, stereos that also include AM radios, portable digital radios with clocks, wristwatches with several alarms, and minivans that fill every inch of space with seats, even if a purchaser's primary purpose in buying it is to carry cargo.

Misplaced marketing does not mean a business will fail, especially if all its competitors engage in the same activities. Yet the business is wasting money when advertising is done without any idea or direction of what it can or should accomplish. And all examples of this form of misplaced marketing make for unusual perspectives of businesses toward their customers.

People from the United States are notoriously bad at this, as many of our domestic companies try to ram our products down the throats of the rest of the world and claim "unfair trade practices" when they aren't bought. Using misplaced marketing, these firms are more ethnocentric than international.[9] U.S. companies often send products to other countries with features designed to satisfy customers in the domestic market without considering the special concerns of consumers in other nations, as if what satisfies consumers in the United States meets the needs of people around the globe.

WHEN MARKETING SHOULD HAVE BEEN USED

In another sense, marketing gets lost as a result of arrogant ignorance. As I noted at the outset, everyone is a marketing expert, or so they like to believe. Many times, marketing tools are used without any understanding of how or why they should do the job. There are so many efforts in which marketing perspectives could be used, but aren't.

A fellow student in my graduate school classes saw a massive advertising campaign as the solution for almost every social or cultural problem. Public television stations are facing a funding shortage? An advertising campaign would get more viewers for the shows which, in turn, would generate more funding. Too many people not wearing seat belts? An advertising campaign would convince them to change their habits. Too many children in schools trying drugs? Advertising would convince them not to. The space program is facing problems getting funding from Congress? A public information advertising campaign would show everyone how important the program is for U.S. prestige and new product development.

Beyond my fellow student's simplistic solutions, from someone who should have known better—she had worked in the business for several years before entering the graduate program—she never really said how or why advertising could or would persuade people to change their habits. She misplaced the basic marketing perspective that would first ask if the advertising could serve a role in changing consumer views and, if so, what type of appeals should be used.

What she recommended fits an all-too-common practice. In many cases, marketing tools are used because some official thinks "something" should be done. But without understanding just how or why marketing could do a job, they often waste money on ineffectual and unnecessary advertising.

There exist numerous examples of cases when people decide to use advertising to "sell" a social idea without any consideration of how or why marketing tools would do the job. In many instances, the term could be "misplaced social marketing," referring to marketing campaigns that are myopically seen as the solution to social problems.[10] Many public information campaigns fail because they are created around what the managers want to say instead of an understanding of what would persuade or change the behaviors of a target audience. Arrogant ignorance outweighs marketing planning to the detriment of the campaign's ability to accomplish anything.

National and local government agencies in several countries have been running very strong television commercials describing the dangers of drunk driving, speeding, failure to use seat belts, and other unsafe driving behaviors. The advertising messages all say, "Do these things and you will die, or be so badly injured you will be sorry you survived." The advertising images are often very graphic. Reductions in fatal crashes are credited to the campaigns and increases in the death toll are blamed on bad advertising, yet a failure to ask marketing questions means the actual role or value of the advertising is questionable at best.

In New Zealand, city school districts no longer require children to attend the nearest neighborhood school. Instead, parents could send them to whatever public school they think might be doing a better job of providing a quality education. Since each school is funded based on the numbers of students that enroll, the school administrators believe that they must advertise to attract students. Just what those ads should say, or if advertising should be used at all, is never really questioned, but the schools feel they must do "something" to attract students. So they advertise. Comparable situations are also found in places such as Australia or parts of the United States where local schools or universities feel they are competing to attract students.

Under this same category, we should include the unfortunate story of trade associations that seem more bent on serving internal needs than those of dues-paying members. If the association is old, large, and influential, it may lose touch with members and retain its position by use of power instead of marketing. It may lose members and incur the eternal enmity of many who stay by failing to consider how to satisfy member wants and needs. People quit, but the organization is so large that no one notices.

All these failures—to not use marketing or to use it poorly—are clearly lost opportunities. The results are unfortunate and frustrating.

NOT ALL CONSUMER NEEDS
"SHOULD" BE SATISFIED

The most vexing problem for marketing people comes from those instances when marketing is accused by pundits, activists and public policy makers of being misplaced when it is properly used and applied. Politicians, movie or music producers, cigarette companies, distillers, gun companies, and pornographers often do a good job of following the dictates of thorough strategic marketing, while many people might wish that, at least for them, marketing was not used.[11] In practical terms, marketing is not necessarily misplaced in the sense of "lost," but, to critics, its power is misused or abused or misdirected.

Politicians should be leaders, using marketing theory and practice to, at most, sell their ideas to the public, instead of using marketing to adapt to a marketable image, as dictated by current public opinion polls. No "leader" should base policies on a marketing plan, since "leader" should not mean "good reader of polls." Cultural artifacts should grow from the populace, not be designed according to a marketing strategy, or so we are often told. In addition, to critics of these products in various nations where they are legal, guns, cigarettes, pornographic movies, and gambling games should not be efficiently and profitably delivered to "satisfy consumer needs," no company should be allowed to maximize its profits with these products, and *never* should these products be marketed to children as a target segment.

It should also be noted that, from a social or societal point of view, not all things customers "want" are what they should be getting. Marketing might also be misplaced in the sense that satisfying consumer needs might be contrary to those of the greater society. More than two decades ago, when the first oil shortages forced car companies to offer more efficient products, the solution was to produce smaller and lighter vehicles. But one U.S. company tried to delay, offering a downsized version of its luxury car line but strongly promoting the still available "original," full-sized, gas-guzzling version (clearly for the U.S. market, I often say, complete with rotating gun turret). The affluent consumers who cared little about rising gas costs might have been served, but not the social goal of oil conservation.

Of course, even if critics believe that marketing is misplaced, that does not necessarily mean it should be banned, but it could be a source of "problems" (or, at least, a basis for criticisms of various aspects of marketing practice). Calling the problem "misplaced marketing" provides a context for understanding mistakes or unintended consequences (though it does not account for events such as heads of American cigarette companies appearing before the U.S. Congress—as they did a few years ago—and swearing their belief that nicotine was not addictive and that there was no link between smoking and cancer).

And, sometimes, what might be seen as good marketing could be harmful to both the "product" and society. The "product" should not be deformed just to serve the dictates of a marketing plan, especially if those changes reduce product quality while not better serving customers or society. In the marketing of education, schools and universities have often focused on "benefits" other than education, such as sports teams or jobs graduates might try to fill. These might be reasons why some people choose a school, but by presenting these benefits as important, the marketing of education has caused harm to education itself, as both parents and students lose sight of the basic values of education itself. There exists some valid basis to blame marketing for education's deterioration when educational leaders distort their school's priorities in order to meet what they see as the needs of a marketing plan.

WHY "MISPLACED MARKETING"

When I coined the term "misplaced marketing," it was intended to encompass a broad perspective for all the times that marketing could be misplaced because it is misapplied, misused, abused, or simply the focus of social criticisms. These are not all marketing mistakes, though it makes it easy to see where some products failed. The creators of the Apple Newton misplaced marketing and totally misunderstood consumer views for that type of product, while the makers of the successful Palm Pilot did not. But many firms can be (and are) successful by following a production orientation, depending on either market power or luck. Government and nonprofit organizations do not need to be successful in the business sense, but the public might be better served if they did not misplace marketing perspectives in planning activities. And in many cases, firms might be better off (at least in the public relations sense) if they did not use all the marketing tools at their disposal, since the marketing could readily become the focus of public criticisms or products or services that various activists do not like.

Some readers might see an intrinsic problem with misplaced marketing in that what is "misplaced" is the marketing concept. Does it really define marketing? There have always existed some criticisms of the concept's pragmatic utility, with some saying that it tends to be removed from the reality of marketing practice.[12] It even seems limited in marketing education. Many textbooks use it as the starting point of a "history of marketing thought," then seem to ignore it when giving more details on concerns of research or practical activities.

By accepting the marketing concept herein, I am not endorsing it as much as using its basic view of the limits of persuasion power as a way to assess various marketing activities.

On the other hand, misplaced marketing is also an oblique response to a survey of marketing educators in the United States, Australia, and New Zealand that found little agreement as to whether there exist any core perspectives on marketing as an academic discipline.[13] Since the marketing concept provides a general basis for viewing marketing perspectives or problems, I often thought it could have been that core of the discipline. Misplaced marketing is just my own idiosyncratic twist.

Misplaced marketing offers a perspective for analysis, a basis for studying problems and situations. If the marketing concept doesn't give us a way to deal with these ideas, then all we have in marketing is a collection of obvious generalities and wishful thinking with limited apparent business value (plus terms that you won't find in any dictionary). After decades of research, the academic discipline and the realm of business practice should be more than that.

NOTES

1. *Time*, August 2, 1999, pp. 39–43. This prominent cover story only appeared in the international edition, while the North American covers focused on the then-recent death of John F. Kennedy, Jr.

2. "Adland: Where Commercials Come From," 1974. While George Lois had more camera time than anyone else, this sixty-minute documentary of the advertising business included interviews with several other executives, copywriters, and actors. Discussions included the work and philosophies of George Lois, Jerry Della Femina, a casting director, a child actor's father, and a used car dealer in California who sponsored late-night movies on the local television station.

3. In politics, it is still believed that heavy use of advertising can "buy" an election, despite repeated showings of big-spending campaigns failing to win voters. For many years, the U.S. government has broadcast radio programs into Cuba based on a belief that such propaganda can make Fidel Castro's supporters change their minds and start to oppose him.

4. There are various discussions and evaluations of what is meant by the marketing concept, but the basic idea has become synonymous with what is known as "having a customer orientation," meaning the firm starts by knowing (or trying to know) the customers and satisfying those people at a profit. This quote is taken from Franklin S. Houston, "The Marketing Concept: What It Is and What it Is Not," *Journal of Marketing*, vol. 50 (April 1986), pp. 81–87.

5. Some of the extensive research behind these basic truisms of the business are reviewed in Michael Schudson, *Advertising, The Uneasy Persuasion: It's Dubious Impact on American Society* (New York: Basic Books, 1984). He notes in his preface (p. xiii) that "Advertising agencies are stabbing in the dark much more than they are practicing precision microsurgery on the public consciousness."

6. Don Esslemont and Tony Lewis, "Some Empirical Tests of the Marketing Concept," *Marketing Bulletin*, vol. 2 (1991), pp. 1–7.

7. I've never encountered a statement of the marketing concept indicating that it can (or should) be driven by altruism, nor has it been used as the foundation of a book on business ethics. On the contrary, first and foremost, a firm seeks to satisfy its own needs. A business must be profitable and a nonprofit

organization has a mission set by its members. In theory, planning to satisfy consumers increases the probability that plans and activities will help attain these goals. To give these bewildered people the benefit of the doubt, maybe they're intellectually challenged because they think of the marketing concept as a planning tool and, in another context, as an excuse.

8. The most interesting way of putting this impression is the statement that "The Marketing Concept is so ubiquitous in the marketing classroom that the naive student of marketing is generally led to believe that firms who fail to employ this philosophy are business criminals." M. A. Jolson, *Marketing Management* (New York: Macmillan, 1978), p. 81.

9. Colin Jevons, "International Marketing: With Marketing Misplaced, It's Often Not International," *Journal of Consumer Marketing*, vol. 17 (no. 1, 2000), pp. 7–8.

10. This variation on the term was first coined in personal discussions with John Calfee of the American Enterprise Institute during a break at a marketing and public policy conference. Of personal interest to him were those instances in which a social marketing effort might backfire, prompting people to adopt the opposite behavior from the one encouraged by a public interest advertising campaign (e.g., anticigarette advertising that might result in encouraging more young people to start smoking).

11. D. Kirk Davidson, *Selling Sin: The Marketing of Socially Unacceptable Products* (Westport, CT: Quorum, 1996). The book provides an outstanding detailed review of the circumstances and history surrounding the marketing of cigarettes, alcoholic beverages, gambling, pornography, and firearms. By saying that these and other products have a problem of misplaced marketing, critics are seen as applying their own arrogant bias and paranoia toward any sales efforts for products they do not like.

12. Michael Enright, "Marketing Meta-narrative and Its Tenets: At Odds with Marketing Realities," *Asia Pacific Journal of Marketing and Logistics*, vol. 11 (no. 1, 1999), pp. 3–15; Don Esslemont and Tony Lewis, "Some Empirical Tests of the Marketing Concept," *Marketing Bulletin*, vol. 2 (1991), pp. 1–7; Franklin S. Houston, "The Marketing Concept: What It Is and What It Is Not," *Journal of Marketing*, vol. 50 (April 1986), pp. 81–87.

13. Gary Mankelow and Michael Jay Polonsky, "The Future of Marketing Theory, Practice and Academia—Views of U.S. and Australia/New Zealand Academics," *AMS Quarterly*, vol. 2 (December 1998), pp. 1, 5.

SELL, SELL, SELL:
THE "MODERN" PRODUCTION
ORIENTATION OF
MARKETING COMPANIES

"The marketing concept? That's just an abstraction?"

Textbooks provide useful summaries of material, but they can leave misleading impressions that my students hold as immutable as biblical text. As noted in Chapter 1, after a book presents the modern marketing concept, future practitioners believe that all modern successful firms follow a consumer orientation, with the only exceptions found among small or unsuccessful businesses. In reality, many large and successful organizations misplace marketing and, instead, are actually following an inner-directed production or selling orientation in dealing with customers.

However, just because these firms lost the marketing concept's consumer orientation does not mean they are going to be unprofitable. They are just not serving consumer needs. Sometimes products from many firms consistently fail to serve many consumers, so consumers are stuck with what is available. Some people repeatedly go to stores after a bad service experience, especially if alternatives also provide the same bad service. An otherwise bad advertising campaign could seem to generate some desirable consumer reactions by luck or happenstance, with managers unable to see how the dysfunctional messages provide much less than optimal results.

2

Hobson's Choices in the Marketplace

Hobson was a liveryman over 400 years ago who insisted that each client take the horse closest to the door or none. In a similar vein, marketing textbooks often tell the story of the original Model-T car, the first low-priced, mass-produced automobile, about which Henry Ford allegedly said consumers could buy any color they desired as long as it was black. Of course, the textbooks tell of the Model-T in order to point out the limitations of Ford's marketing view, calling it a classic example of a "production orientation." Since they focused on what they wanted to produce and not consumer needs, Hobson or Ford's success depended on them being the only horse trader or low-cost car dealer available.

Supposedly, in the long run, firms that are "consumer-oriented" and produce products based on consumer needs and interests are more successful. As more car dealers entered the market with competing products, they offered cars with new, innovative features as well as a variety of colors, all geared to meeting the interests of more consumers. This marketing competition, in turn, meant that more consumers' basic interests and desires were served. Or so the theory goes.

In the modern view of a marketing orientation, products should be developed based on the consumers' needs and wants in order to de-

liver desired satisfactions to customers. Following this standard definition, a production orientation is always presented with examples of
historic "marketing mistakes" involving product failures. But aside
from these failures, there are less obvious examples of cases when
marketing is misplaced in products currently on the market. More
correctly, there are many instances when marketing is misplaced, not
just by one firm but by many competitors, so the companies all give
consumers the same selection. These customers are also faced with a
Hobson's choice—the illusion of a choice when there aren't any real
alternatives. Consumers can buy the products with this feature or not
buy anything at all.

In the popular comic strip "Dilbert," marketing people are all idiots. Only engineers in the strip think in terms of what is possible instead of demanding production of impossible dreams. Yet even the
engineers are self-absorbed. With their minds shut off from the
worldview of real people who might be different from themselves,
they are unable or unwilling to understand how customers really think.
From a marketing point of view, "can do" does not necessarily mean
"should do."

The better product must do the job in a way that fits consumer interests, uses, and needs; a new feature is an added benefit *only* if it
provides consumers with a reason to buy the product. A production
orientation is when the product or service is made based not on what
a target segment wants or needs, but instead, on what engineers or
others in the firm discover it can produce.

COMPUTERS: FASTER, STRONGER, AND CRASHING MORE OFTEN

Consumers are told that personal computer prices are really coming down, since prices are actually staying the same for computers
with more and more "extras." But an extra feature is not a value if the
consumer neither needs nor wants it. And the extra features could
add complications that increase the need for technical support or just
cause the system to crash. For many people, the old machines did most
jobs with less fuss, yet all the replacements are filled with a pile of
extra distractions. And many people would like a machine that they
could just take out of the box, turn on, and use, instead of spending
hours pouring through setup instructions that even experienced product users now find they must endure with a new machine.

A large number of intelligent people—the average, nontechnical
users—aren't afraid of computers, but are very frustrated by them.
Every October since 1991, Walter S. Mossberg has reported on indus-

try advances in making machines simpler, more reliable, and easier to use. His reports usually find that complications have been mounting and reliability has declined, mostly due to little programs that are constantly running in the background, sucking up memory, conflicting with other programs, and presenting superfluous icons that are both undesirable and unnecessary but never go away.[1]

Anyone who buys a new color television or stereo system spends a few hundred dollars and expects that product to last at least a decade. Every computer buyer expects to spend a couple thousand dollars and have the machine become archaic and unable to use new software within sixteen months. Admittedly, annual product obsolescence is not new or unique to computers. New cars still come out every fall in the United States and fashionable clothing soon becomes unfashionable. However, new car buyers can be assured of a strong market for used vehicles in good condition; buyers of newly in-fashion clothes either are not price sensitive when it comes to their wardrobe or have secondary uses for the old look if the clothes do not wear out by the time they are outdated. Old computers can only be resold if one finds them useful as boat anchors.

Computers that are only few years old still do many jobs; software could be written that would work at a generally acceptable level. Instead, new software always requires the newest machines while those same upgraded machines require increasing amounts of memory and disk space to do the most simple tasks. Many new word processing programs focus more on the look of the finished products—the fonts and formats—instead of ease of input. Each new software innovation requires more and more chip speed to run. It is only in the past year that some old-level products are remaining available after the faster, stronger, more powerful machines have come out, with consumer magazines recommending many uses for old equipment. The latest Pentium chip and laser printers are not needed for the person keeping track of personal expenses, writing letters, and contacting friends via e-mail.

And through it all, computer programs' increasing complexity (and their concurrent complications) serve the worldview of computer makers, not users; even some of the most experienced customers are unable to understand or work with the new machines. While losing the war for setting the industry standard in operating systems, Apple computers remain viable by serving many new users of the product. With unique physical features in style and look, it remains the product of choice for people who want a machine that they can buy, then turn it on and have it run.

For the most part, computer designers of both hardware and software make products to appeal to other designers or people like themselves.

UNNECESSARY AND UNWANTED
PRODUCT FEATURES

Even with the less complicated products in the booming field of consumer electronics, additional features get into the product mix because engineers say they are possible, not because they are desired by buyers. Since every minor feature can't be researched or studied for consumer interest, some guesses must be made. But the guesses often seemed to be based on the judgment of the designers of what can be done, not marketing's assessment of what the product users might want or need.

This engineering mentality drifts down the line into even lower-cost consumer products, such as personal stereo radios used by people during jogging or walking. Most have a belt clip of some kind, but almost all these products have the volume control dials on the back of the unit, above the clip. To the designers, this is where it readily "fits," though it places that dial next to the body when clipped to exercise shorts. It seems logical to the designer, but either loose clothing or a layer of body fat (that comes from weighing more than a *Sports Illustrated* swimsuit model) inadvertently and unavoidably rubs the dial against the skin during the normal bouncing of exercise, so that the volume changes with every energetic step.

Digital station tuning is an increasingly common feature with this same product and quite useful for many people, providing more precise station tuning and easy changes while doing other things. However, try and find a product that has digital tuning and does not have a clock. It is nearly impossible.

The engineers would say that once you have the chips for digital tuning, the clock is a simple addition, providing an added feature at no cost. However, such logic misplaces marketing thinking because it fails to ask if people actually want clocks on their personal stereos. Following the marketing concept, a clock should be an added feature only if consumers will select a product or brand because it has a clock. It should not be included as part of the product if they don't want it.

Do consumers want clocks in their personal stereo radio or tape players? It is doubtful that this question is ever asked by the manufacturers or designers. More likely, a clock on the personal stereo is a pain for many actual users, not a convenience. For most people, the clock is not very functional.

"The time? I'll pull my stereo off my belt and look at it."

There is also a pragmatic limitation. When the battery power drops below a certain level, it can't operate both the clock and the radio, since more power is needed for both than for just one or the other. When this happens, the machine must "choose" which one to run, and the engineers have all apparently decided to program the machines to turn off the radio. This means the consumer will be in the middle of exercise, listening to the clock. Logically, if a jogger cares about the time or timing the workout, a watch is a simple, easy-to-carry, inexpensive item, and better for the job than the one acquired as part of a radio.

As noted, if the clocks were included because people desired that feature, it would be a marketing value, but it is more likely that digital radios all come with clocks because they are a simple added feature to produce. But even if marketing were misplaced, the products might still sell when the engineering-over-marketing mentality (and its resulting decisions) were pervasive for virtually all available brands. Anyone wanting such a radio must get one with a clock because no store carries a different option.

This same consumer problem arises in many different types of products, as if the product designers were talking to each other but not to any of the product users.

In Australia, all toasters in the stores suddenly shifted to "high lift" models, making it easier to get the toast out of the machine. Unfortunately, the machines were not "low toast," since most slices of bread would not line up with the heating elements (and some breads would stick out over the top). Some consumers in the store armed with a piece of paper shaped like a typical piece of bread could not find any toasters that went low enough to heat it.

YOU CAN BUY (ALMOST) ANY TYPE OF MINIVAN YOU WANT

Over the past few years, many friends of mine test drove (and loved) minivans from several major car companies, but they could not find a make or model that was not equipped and styled for a family. For most models, seven-passenger seating was standard. The available minivans seemed to define the product as a station wagon with a gland condition, with seats that adjusted or could be pushed aside when not in use. Even the *Consumer Reports* ratings discussed only models that seated seven passengers.

The dealers said, "The resale value is best with seven-passenger seating" or "The extra seats are easy to remove." But that missed the point. No one wanted to buy a family van, complete with unneeded equipment that went beyond just the seats, when the product they wanted was something else.

The back seat of my minivan sat in a corner of my garage, unused, for over a decade. Like me, my friends do not have children and are primarily concerned about transporting cargo: They have big dogs to transport; they use expensive photographic equipment on their jobs; or they haul bicycle equipment when traveling. In the end, they all bought sport utility vehicles (SUVs), even though the minivans would have handled better and provided better gas mileage. They just could not rationalize buying a product with added features they did not want.

Of course, it is possible that my friends and I are too small of a group to be a viable target market. Maybe we are seeking products that are not available because too few people want it. But we are not alone, and it is possible this is a case of misplaced marketing because we are a missed opportunity the car companies fail to perceive. About half of the cars on U.S. roads today are minivans, SUVs, or light trucks, but that is not because there are a lot of people with large families.

DISCARD INSTEAD OF REPAIR

Annual reader surveys in *Consumer Reports* magazine increasingly find people discarding and replacing microwave ovens, VCRs, radios, and other basic appliances instead of having them repaired. These consumer decisions are not unexpected or necessarily bad. Better products are often available at a lower price than the original, while the old items are technologically archaic by the time problems arise. Yet, even for inexpensive products, potential consumer ire is great when inexpensive or minor components cause grief or early "death" of an otherwise useful product. Marketing questions during product planning and design should anticipate how products are used so that consumers are not forced to trash a product for minor problems that should have been anticipated by the manufacturer.

Yet with thoughtless product design, messy repair systems, or confusing, not-so-hot hotlines, marketing often seems not just misplaced but totally lost. From the firms' perspectives, forced repurchases might be profitable and, therefore, desirable, but that just means that their marketing is intentionally misplaced.

Fine expensive leather briefcases have connecting hooks for shoulder straps that rip free under normal use. Potentially confusing new computer systems charge consumers for calling technical support lines while the new software is expected to have problems the company plans to "work out" as customers call in. Many consumers report a pet peeve with the small light bulbs that would burn out in clock radios long before any other component had the slightest hint of difficulty, with replacements a nearly impossible or unduly expensive repair job.

And yet, not all firms misplace marketing such as the brands that now seem to (finally) anticipate this latter problem, with easy access panels to the light bulbs in General Electric clocks and clock radios—not coincidentally, GE also makes the bulbs—including a replacement bulb in the panel cover. Some new flashlights with especially bright, expensive bulbs come with a replacement bulb stored in the handle.

Anticipating or addressing these problems should be a simple task. They *should* be an opportunity to build customer rapport instead of a source of consumer anger.

My data bank watch is a high-end product from an internationally well-known manufacturer. With a list price of over $250, the myriad of electronic functions were hidden under a stylish flip-top gold face. When my battery died in slightly over a year, it was logical to believe that replacing the battery would be simple for such a ubiquitous brand. Unfortunately, it wasn't. Three jewelry stores were afraid or unable to open the extra-thin battery casing, which also has a unique and specially designed backing connection. The fourth store opened it, but discovered that it used a special type of battery that the store did not carry and, as I later discovered, was not easy to find. I finally located an expert on this brand of watches, and he had a battery that seemed a close enough match. But the watch still didn't work after installation, a situation he did not know how to correct.

At this point, the manufacturer's service phone line was the only option. After an afternoon of busy signals, we finally got through, only to find an automated answering system that provided a long list of new phone numbers, mostly consisting of mail-order sources for parts and batteries for all different types of the company's products. And on the list—though not clearly labeled—were numbers for customer information. This then required another afternoon of busy signals trying to call the watch company's version of tech support, and, once a connection was made, we were waiting on hold for more than twenty minutes. After that experience in waiting, we sought as much information as possible from the service representative.

As with many major brands, the company has a list of authorized service centers. But, as is also often true, there was only one in each state and not many were readily accessible, even if you lived in the state's largest metropolitan area. The repair center for Louisiana was not in New Orleans; for Alabama, it was in Mobile at the southernmost tip of the state, not the centrally located Montgomery or much larger Birmingham in the north. In Illinois, the location was the west Chicago suburbs, and in Georgia, it was an area far from downtown Atlanta in an industrial park. Mail order was a possibility, but it seemed unreasonably costly and trouble-prone for just a battery.

Fortunately, the one in the Chicago suburbs was near where close friends lived, whom we would be visiting the following month. And when we had the service representative on the line, we received detailed instructions on the nature of the reset buttons, two nearly invisible small dots on the face of the internal calculator, both of which (as the hotline informant told us), "must be held down at the same time for a few seconds with the tips of a paper clip" after a new battery is installed. With this information, we found the batteries, a repair shop knew how to open the watch and insert them, and we all knew how to restart the watch.

But what a frustrating mess. Replacing the battery in an electronic watch, especially an expensive one, should be expected and anticipated as part of marketing product planning. Overall, the experience would discourage many people from ever buying the brand again. The battery, access panel, and restart information might have been covered in the owner's manual that was lost after a year, but post-sale support systems should not presume that all customers will act in an optimal fashion. As often happens with these stories, we found the owner's manual a year later, only to find that it did not have any information on battery replacement, nor did it say anything about the hidden reset buttons. Even the jeweler who did the final battery installation called the reset buttons "bizarre." Yet stories like this are becoming more common and they involve a wider range of products.

More people are using electric razors, but these require cutting heads or cover foils that must be replaced every four to six months. The parts alone could be half the price of a new razor, assuming that the parts could be found at all. So many models and brands are in the stores, each with its own unique replacement parts but, without the cutter, the still-working razor acquires the utility of a paper weight. If parts are found on sale, stocking up could backfire, as the razor itself dies with the parts for the now discontinued model in a drawer. Electric toothbrushes need expensive new brush heads, but unexpected model changes could leave a person with an empty handle. Again, the electronic parts could wear out with a drawer full of brushes for a model that went out of production a year before.

Marketing planning should be involved at all stages, from engineering to customer support to replacement parts. It involves anticipating how customers actually use the product or seek minor expected repairs and maintenance. Unfortunately, engineers sometimes seem incapable of understanding that the neat features they find so interesting and clever might eventually result in consumer pain.

SO WHO WOULD BUY THIS PRODUCT?

With new technology, a myriad of new products seem to become available every week. And with each technological innovation, there are also numerous combinations of existing forms that, from the consumer's point of view, create other new and different products and formats. Many ideas sound interesting; it is tempting to just throw everything into the marketplace to see what succeeds. But the basic marketing questions are quite simple and deserve to be asked first.

A few years ago, I bought a new music CD by jazz artist Keiko Matsui, called "Dream Walk." It was only after we got home that we noticed block letters on the side of the case, saying "enhanced CD." We later learned that this term is printed in all promotional literature for the disk and in many mail-order listings. But none of these notices bothers to explain the term; we are expected to know. And my ignorance could not be blamed on my age, since only two of the three hundred undergraduate students in my classes that academic year had ever heard the term.[2]

Only when we opened the package did we learn that "enhanced" means that the music CD also contains a computer program. If your computer is fast enough, has a high enough resolution monitor, uses the right operating systems, and contains enough free memory, the program on the disk enables you to view a music video of the artist playing piano for the second cut. And when you are not listening to the music, the program includes some ugly-font text and pictures, the type of material originally found on old vinyl recordings as liner notes—comments by the artist; pictures of her family—that are included today in printed form in many CD cases.

As we ran the program on a friend's machine, he immediately thought this was a neat idea. One of the few people I know who is more of a "gadget brain" than I am, Frank is an accountant but often thinks like an engineer. It is possible, it is different, so he likes it. He often says I am too negative about all these innovations, but I had to step back and try to ask the marketing questions. And I saw potential problems.

My immediate concern was that many people do not have a computer connected to their main stereo. The computer's speakers are usually small amplified units. It is logical to assume that most people would prefer to listen to their favorite melodies on the best system in the house, and that system is rarely the computer.

However, the marketing question is more simple and basic than that: is this enhancement an added benefit for potential purchasers of the product or an irrelevant detraction that could discourage sales? Would more people buy it because it was enhanced and might other people avoid it?

The video on this enhanced CD was very basic and very simple— "Thriller" or Will Smith's "Wild Wild West" it wasn't—just the artist playing her piano. It would probably not provide consumers with much of an incentive to buy the disk in order to have the video.

For a price that was the same as most other disks in the store, we got forty-five minutes of music and, on a computer, a trite video, a bio in text form, and a picture montage. Since many CDs now deliver almost an hour or more of music, maybe some people would have preferred more music for the money. But there were also some pragmatic problems.

After testing the disk on several friends' stereo systems of varying ages and technical quality, the program caused the machines to read a "phantom" additional ten minutes of music that wasn't there. Every machine would play the full disk of music, but some were unable to be programmed to play only certain tracks. Because of the space taken up by the program, a few were also confused when directed to run the "shuffle-play" command.

Since all copies of the disk are "enhanced," people must buy this type of product, or the audiocassette tape, or pass on hearing the latest album by Keiko Matsui. At the same time, it is intuitively obvious that it is a very rare person who would buy a music product because it also included a video. This also assumes that the purchaser has a passing interest in the style, and has the right equipment and so on. Overall, the new listeners Matsui might attract by producing an enhanced CD are probably negligible.

Of course, this is a cultural artifact and Keiko Matsui is an artist. The enhanced CD could simply be an artistic product she wished to produce, regardless of its value as a marketing tool. On the other hand, if it was meant to benefit purchasers, there should have been a clearer indication of what was meant by the term "enhanced CD." But with the new technology and the daily introduction of new products, it helps to step back and ask the marketing questions about who would buy this product and why.

APPEALING ONLY TO A SHRINKING NUMBER OF PRESENT CUSTOMERS

As a medium, the comic book business is in financial trouble. Circulation has been going down for years. At conventions, in letter columns and on fan Web sites, several industry insiders have been repeatedly asserting a belief that hundreds of titles every month are financially propped up by publishers, while they continue to lose money, in hopes of selling the characters to Hollywood. The largest publisher, Marvel Entertainment Group Inc., creator of the Hulk, X-Men, Spider-Man, and the Fantastic Four, filed for a reorganization under Chapter 11 of the bankruptcy laws, with many people predicting that the company might totally fail.[3]

The obvious culprits are easy to blame: movies, video games, television, and the Internet take away the attention of young people and, since they don't start reading comics when they're young, they never get involved with the medium. However, this explanation is too simple and simplistic.

Competition might provide part of the explanation, but the companies have been selling to a smaller and smaller core of fans, ignoring new markets or new readers as the marketplace evolved. In some ways, the industry is unaltered from the way it started six decades ago with the introduction of Superman. The stories are better written, the art work glossier, and the authors and artists own their work instead of doing work for hire. But the industry is still dependent on monthly or bimonthly magazines, distributed mostly through retail outlets. Subscriptions remain a small segment of the business; advertising revenue, judging by the number of ads per issues, is clearly limited. The major change in distribution has been the relationship of retail outlets to the publishers and distributors, with specialized comic stores replacing general magazine racks as the primary focus for circulation.

These few changes underlie the problem. Comics have become a medium for fans, and new readers are discouraged from even trying to read the most popular titles. Readers must go to specialty stores to be certain they can obtain or even see all available titles, and every publisher has its personal "universe" that requires reading many different titles per month to follow a story. Every story is filled with footnotes that reference past stories or other titles, with both authors and readers carefully watching that everything is consistent with past story lines and characters.

Part of the problem comes from myopia among the business managers of the medium, which is dominated by two major companies. But the writers are also long-time readers and former fans, so sometimes it seems as if they are writing for each other instead of appealing to new readers.

There have been a few attempts in recent years to "revamp" or "restart" popular titles. But the new stories are themselves filled with so many in-jokes and hidden references to how characters were treated in prior story lines that few new readers can enjoy them. Attrition is to be expected with any continuing storyline. Popular television shows like *Dallas* do not creatively burn out as much as they lose old audiences over time (as happens with any story), and new viewers do not wish to bother trying to figure out what is going on now, based on prior years events.

Sometimes the comic book publishers even seem to abuse the fans. Every year, the major publishers run a special event story that has strains crossing into almost every title they own. When this happens, the regular titles become confusing even to long-time readers. It's as if NBC ran a special show on Sunday nights and fans of *Frasier, Homi-*

cide, and *Law and Order* had to watch each show and the Sunday program to understand what was going on. Fans of each show might put up with such a distraction, but new audiences would just tune out.

Also, with an eye toward fans and not new or casual readers, the publishers have lavished limited attention on books and other self-contained formats. When published, they are usually reprints of stories already sold in the usual periodical format, with limited distribution and promotion efforts; even comic shops are often reluctant to carry the titles.

Fans can make a title profitable, or they can give impetus for a movie. But fans can't be counted on forever. They are just the basic core. Unfortunately, the comic producers seem determined to appeal only to the fans and not to new readers. The stories in most comic titles are written for the fans, and sales promotion efforts are aimed at the dwindling number of comic book collectors, while the magazines designed with new readers in mind are on the wane.

A marketing-oriented analysis would start by asking why children start reading printed stories told with pictures, what would keep them reading, and how to tell stories that appeal to youths whose attention is distracted by other electronic media. But instead, these questions are unasked. As a result, the major comic book companies keep trying to repeat formulas that were once the basis of success in an earlier generation. Without asking the marketing questions, they follow a production orientation, printing products that they want to produce instead of what would interest and attract new readers.

BUY OUR CARS, OR ELSE!

A great deal of so-called international marketing by U.S. firms is merely a selling orientation of the unaltered domestic product abroad. It is often pointed out that when it comes to production for an export market, many U.S. firms misplace marketing and replace it with arrogance. If it is good enough for North Americans, the theory goes, everyone should like it.

The literature is filled with advertising failures on the international scene, attempts to literally translate U.S. slogans or names to other languages with humorous results. These are often accidents, not necessarily born of linguistic arrogance. Yet, while we readily recognize that sales efforts must take into account the local cultures and interests, many people overlook the need for variations in the products themselves.

For years, American car companies complained that the Japanese do not buy U.S. cars. The politicians blamed trade barriers, and Presidents Reagan, Bush, and Clinton, plus Commerce Department secretaries and car executives repeatedly went across the Pacific to "encourage" the Japanese to buy more of our cars. Throughout all these efforts at persuasion, one factor remained almost unstated: The Japanese drive on the left side of the road and use cars with the steering wheel on the right. Few Americans would buy a Toyota or Honda with the wheel on the right, yet the Japanese people were expected to ignore this marketing blind spot to appease politicians' and car companies' failure to understand the trade imbalance.

When visiting Japan over three decades ago, I noticed a Japanese driver sliding across the wide front seat of his Buick so he could drop his money in the highway toll gate. The U.S. car sold there did not alter any product features for the Japanese market and my grandfather sagaciously explained that big American cars were a status symbol there. Despite the large size and being forced to drive on the "wrong" side of the car, it was a sign of prestige to have the visible product.

That might have been true then, but not now. Or maybe it wasn't even true then and my grandfather was just expressing more American arrogance than insight into Japanese buying habits. Still, some Japanese did buy U.S. cars despite the grief such ownership entailed, just as some Americans bought expensive, prestigious, imported cars with the steering wheel on the right. But, intuitively, such sales require a prestige product, something that no one now considers a U.S. brand to be. Other sales of U.S. products abroad are the result of luck, not applying marketing to the planning of products for export. And misplaced marketing is not a sound basis for planning international distribution. Yet year after year, U.S. cars continued to be shipped to Japan unaltered from the standard domestic driver's setup.

This might work under conditions of market control, or when there aren't any competitors, or when all competitors offer comparable (nonchoice) alternatives. Sometimes products succeed because the company is lucky, not because its managers planned and studied how to serve consumer needs and wants. And sometimes the "undesirable" or unnecessary features are not so egregious as to turn off significant numbers of potential buyers.

But in the international marketplace, local companies can outmarket the arrogant firms that do not follow marketing concepts outside their own national borders.

When the first set of U.S.–made cars went to Japan with the steering wheels on the right, it was a very minor news item. You might have missed it. But that single change could boost sales in Japan of cars by U.S. manufacturers more than any high-visibility trade envoy.

We readily overlook when marketing gets misplaced by the export market, blaming trade barriers instead of simple (and glaring) adjustments needed to serve foreign customer needs and wants. This is not to say that other markets are as open as those in the United States, nor does it say that many firms don't already practice marketing at all stages of product planning for other countries. Yet knowing the reality about the cries of "unfair trade" surrounding the export of U.S. cars should engender a strong skepticism every time another complaint about trade barriers is heard.

THE MODERN PRODUCTION ORIENTATION

In all these cases, the firms misplaced the marketing concept's consumer focus and, instead, were following a production orientation. That many of them have been successful and avoided glaring "marketing failures" with this orientation can be asserted without any doubt. Moreover, it is uncertain if they would have been more successful with additional attention to particular segments or consumer needs.

In a few cases, the marketing concerns could been intentionally misplaced, in cases where it might be profitable to do so, such as planned product deaths and impossible repairs that impel replacement purchases. At the same time, it is obvious that none could assert that they were satisfying consumers. Some of these might be an unserved segment or other marketing opportunity for a newcomer to the marketplace, but at present it is clear that many consumers are often dissatisfied with the results of their Hobson's choice.

NOTES

1. Walter S. Mossberg, "Using a PC Got Harder," *The Wall Street Journal* (October 28, 1999), interactive edition, available at <http://www.interactive. wsj.com/archive>.

2. Since I am still seeing a small number of music CD cases in the store marked the same way, I asked students in several large undergraduate 2000 classes what they knew about the product. A handful of the students knew what they were. One person liked them.

3. Some successful movies and television programs have been made based on Marvel characters, but the comic book business is still in trouble.

3

Without Bad Service, There Wouldn't Be Any Service at All

In a frequently repeated observation of the modern world, marketing people like to say that major segments of business are turning into a "service economy." However, this phrase usually does not mean "customer service"; instead it refers to the increasing numbers of businesses that are "selling services," a different type of intangible product that, as some textbooks say, can't be dropped on your foot. Still, this attention to the marketing of services as a unique or different type of product has also fed a widespread response to concerns about the declining quality of customer service, with attention toward a so-called "service quality movement."

Both service marketing and the service quality movement have combined to provide endless pages of academic documents and seminar discussions of the intuitively obvious point: better customer service is probably important for all business activities. Yet, somehow, almost mysteriously, marketing perspectives of customer service often remain misplaced—either misdirected or lost—as far as many consumers are concerned.

In her character as Ernestine, the prissy telephone operator, Lily Tomlin would say to irate customers that, "We don't have to be nice, sir. We are the phone company. We are omnipotent." That line was first spoken decades ago, before the breakup of the last great regulated U.S. monopolist utility and the entry of competition into telephone service. The company might not have been literally omnipotent, but customers had a very real Hobson's choice in that they could use "Ma Bell," as many called the old ubiquitous AT&T company, or do without a telephone. AT&T owned almost all local networks, long-distance lines, and even the phones in people's homes, since customers were only allowed to rent the equipment. As the humor in the television sketch implied, the company was generally seen as rude and haughty, seeking to control customers rather than serve them. It possessed all the power inherent in a large, monopolistic public utility that consumers needed.

In theory, with competition, no company could ignore the basic dictates of marketing in planning its service activities. Yet, surprisingly, research has found that some consumers dissatisfied with a customer service experience might still patronize the same firm; in the competition to provide the lowest possible prices, bad service might sometimes seem to be part of the business plan.[1]

Bad service, whether unintentional or not, seems to be both common and counterproductive to what should be standard marketing practice. Some of these examples seem almost basic or simple. In others, there doesn't seem to be an intent on the part of higher management to ignore customers' service needs, since concurrent advertising or promotion materials often make claims of good service, despite the realities to the contrary.

As with the Hobson's choices on product features discussed in Chapter 2, bad service is so pervasive that many customers almost expect it. They do not like it, but the alternative is not to shop.

WHEN INFORMATION BECOMES RULES

Every business needs a few rules for employees to follow in order to keep things orderly. They need policies so everyone knows how to maintain positive relations with customers. And retail stores need to convey some basic information to customers, such as hours of operation and return policies.

It is important to remember that "information" items are not necessarily "rules" for customers to follow. If this distinction is lost, frustrated or angry customers will be a certain result.

Retail businesses post their hours of operation on the doors and in their display advertising so customers know when they are open; few experiences generate greater ire than traveling to a location and finding the doors locked. Retail shops whose owners or managers are erratic in their hours of operation—"I'm tired today, so I'll sleep in and open later"—generally find a drift toward not having any business at all. So posted hours say to consumers, "Come here at 10:15 tomorrow morning and we'll be open." Of course, people don't always remember the hours, so some businesses have their hours set by general "expectations," such as when a collection of stores in neighborhood or a strip mall open and close at common times. When the first grocery stores started staying open for twenty-four-hour periods, their store traffic increased even during daylight hours, a phenomenon attributed in part to customers "knowing" that the place was always open.

Before her death, my grandmother decried the trend toward later and later store hours. Bad for the workers and their families, she would assert, adding "People can be trained to do their grocery shopping during the day." In resort communities, whose populations are heavily made up of weekend visitors from nearby cities, it is puzzling that the local merchants all choose weekends to close up shop and go fishing. Of course, Grandma was not concerned with marketing, a view that does not train consumers but, rather, gives them more options to fit their interests. The store owners want business, but are not interested in basic marketing to get it.

Still, conveying information was important so potential customers knew when they could shop. But, at some point, the retail culture turned the information into a rule and tossed marketing out the window in the process.

Your wristwatch says 10:02, but the door is still locked. At the store, restaurant, or bank, there are people inside ready to work and they are waiting until their master clock says exactly 10 o'clock to allow them to open the doors. The employees are visible through the windows; prospective customers see them and can only think, "What the !@#$% are they doing in there?" At the other end of the day, at ten minutes before closing, the manager begins to stop or dissuade new people from entering, so all business can be completed exactly at closing time. There is no harm in opening a few minutes early or closing late if customers are there, except that it might mess up the manager's sense of decorum or cost a few extra minutes to pay a clerk.

Similarly, at Bob's small restaurant, he doesn't shift from serving breakfast to lunch until 11:00 A.M. A bigger operation might serve breakfast all the time, but with his limited staff and resources, he can only juggle so much. When two people came in for lunch at ten minutes before the hour, the newly hired waiter told them to come back later.[2] Fortunately, Bob overheard, caught the customers before they went away muttering, gave them seats, served drinks and gave them some pretzels, explaining that serving the food might take a few extra minutes since he was shifting the kitchen to the lunch menu. Bob realized the basic needs of marketing, even if his new waiter did not.

If they are ready early, the managers can open early without any harm except to those silly minds that changed the consumer marketing information into a foolish rule.

BOOK STORE CLERKS CAN'T READ
AND CASHIERS CAN'T COUNT

With their discount price schemes for many books, the mega-super-bookstore chains have brought price competition to book retailing. Akin to general discount stores, they have many aisles with books on a variety of topics, more magazines than many newsstands, and some even have a play area where small children can romp while parents browse for books.

I hate them.

It is not because they have driven many smaller bookstores out of businesses or that they also sell many nonbook items, though both of these factors underlie the criticism directed at many of these stores; they even served as part of a subplot in the popular movie, *You've Got Mail*. Nor is my disdain because the children's area gets boisterous or the music most often heard there tends toward loud and popular tunes rather than the jazz played at more of the "literate" stores. The marketing problem is that they have turned books into consumer commodities, and, as such, hire clerks that seem to be literacy impaired.

The sections each say, "alphabetical by author," but they aren't. As I go through the science fiction section, I see authors with names beginning with A, B, and C, then, since one author whose name begins with C also wrote a book related to the television show "Babylon 5," all other books based on that show go next, regardless of the authors' names. Then back to D, E, G, and F, with all books on "Highlander," in keeping with an author in the F group who wrote on that. After that, any resemblance to alphabetical order is an accident.

More than once, I tried to point out the browsing problem to clerks, but they would go to the shelf and say "A, B, C, G, D, F . . . seems okay to me." Then they would go back to what they were doing before I got their attention, stocking magazines by matching either size or cover pictures while also trying to watch the large-screen television that was blasting nearby. In the humor section, the sign says "alphabetical by author," but it seems more in order of similar drawing style of cartoonists or by the name of the main character (with "Dilbert" books under "D," not "A," for Scott Adams).

In his popular book *Dumbth*, entertainer Steve Allen listed many such examples of poor service, from directory assistance telephone operators who never heard of Chicago, hotel desk clerks who can't understand his request for a wake-up call, cab drivers who can't find a location that is virtually around the corner, and bookstore employees who never heard of great authors or their most famous works.[3] Allen's concern was a basic dumbing down of people everywhere, how intellect doesn't seem to matter, and how many parts of society don't seem to care. However, in every example, it is a greater wonder that the managers often leave these people in positions of authority when the employees have been repeatedly shown to be lacking the basic knowledge to do the job and are, therefore, unable to serve customers.

Years ago, a customer at the fish counter of a large retail grocery chain store asked for two-thirds of a pound of seafood. Amazingly, the twenty-something college student counter clerk said, "My machine only reads decimals, not fractions." The discussion then became increasingly surreal, or so it seemed.

Thinking in terms of general volume and not precision, the customer responded with a sigh. "Well, just place them in that middle container and give me six-tenths of a pound."

"No," she said, "I need two decimal points."

"Is there anyone else here. Someone who might have watched 'Sesame Street' last week?"

"Please be nice to me," she explained. "I haven't been working here that long." Placing thirty-two hundredths on the scale, she turned to the customer and asked, "Is this more or less than six-tenths?"

"Do your parents know you're out alone?"

Admittedly, few people would give the customer credit for tact or subtlety, but it is unclear if the clerk was capable of counting the money from coins in her purse. Yet, while the clerk was unable to do necessary primary school arithmetic, it is more inexplicable that, when hearing of the incident, the manager quickly sought out the customer and asked him to leave the store because he was rude to the young, incompetent employee. To the chain's credit, when the senior managers heard of the story from a customer letter, the store manager was removed and the clerk was sent to "retraining," which hopefully required watching "Counting is Fun" videos. Still, one has to wonder about the original training program that produced a store manager who was more concerned with the worker's self-esteem than the fact that she lacked the basic education to do her job. Marketing perspectives were clearly misplaced or totally absent from his management-training program.

Sometimes the senior or regional managers know what is needed but the message is not getting down to the clerks or even the people in charge of the individual stores. A man in Georgia had a problem with product quality on tires purchased from a large warehouse store. He eventually had the problem corrected and received credit for the defect, but he had to repeat the story a few times and work his way up the chain to the district manager before he got cooperation from the store. In Bob's small restaurant, he and his wife try to train and monitor the servers when they greet and deal with customers, but they have trouble keeping track of every possible error.

Admittedly, the level of intellect needed for many basic service jobs is going down. Cash registers do all the counting, bar codes remove the need to even read the numbers, and, in fast food restaurants, the clerk hits a key with the product name instead of noting the price.

Still, it is perplexing when a cash-register attendant, given a $50 bill and a dime for a $16.10 charge, can't figure out how much change to count out if the machine doesn't give that information because he or she had, say, accidentally hit the machine keys for a $20 bill instead of $50.10. What is more amazing is that managers often leave people on these jobs even when their limitations are obvious.

CONFLICTS OF EXPECTATIONS AND EXPERIENCE

A visitor from India found waiters and other people in New York to be a bit on the rude side. Complaining about it to the American relatives she was visiting, she thought racism was behind the rudeness.

Other visitors to that city might consider her lucky that she met people who were only "a bit" rude. Interpersonal impatience is a normal and expected cultural trait for New York City, or so her relatives tried to explain. As made famous in the so-called "Soup Nazi" episode on the popular television program *Seinfeld*, New Yorkers will forgive rudeness for good food. Some restaurants in the city seem to have insulting employees as a proud feature that customers seek out and, to my perpetual amazement, enjoy.[4]

The people the Indian visitor encountered were probably similarly rude to everyone. Coming from the pathologically polite culture that characterized her high-caste Indian neighbors, she did not expect to experience this New York style. (Maybe her views would have been different if she had watched *Seinfeld* on Indian television.) Yet, the unavoidable problem for anyone managing a customer service business is that, especially in the multifaceted and multicultural U.S. society, people walk in the door with a wide variety of prior experiences and expectations. Of course, some customers come in looking for difficulties and are never satisfied, but many problems are avoidable.

Sometimes the problems *are* caused by the employee's sexism, racism, or other bias. There is no other possible explanation for the first saleswoman to meet us at the car dealership repeatedly answering my wife's questions by talking to me.

A strong body of research evidence shows that black customers encounter inequitable treatment and discrimination in some housing, credit, and auto markets, due to their race. There have been many reported instances (and resulting lawsuits) of African-Americans waiting inordinately long times in restaurants, being denied products by car rental agencies, or not getting picked up by taxicab drivers. A field audit of retail customer service counters found that black customers are kept waiting longer than white customers. While males as a whole tended to have longer waits than females, the black male researcher had significantly longer wait times than any other participant in the study.[5]

Of course, not all people working in the same store, restaurant, or bank are equally capable of serving customers. The insensitive employee could be different from the other people working there and the only person who acts like a jerk. No manager can control every employee in the short run.

And some examples of customer frustrations might logically be explained by other means. Some customer experiences are disconcerting, yet caused by relatively innocent motives.

A black man waits in line in the bank and he sees two other people not showing the clerk any identification before cashing a check. However, since he rarely comes into the bank, his being asked for a driver's license to cash his check simply could be because of a policy that requires an picture ID "unless the clerk personally recognizes the customer." He might have been in line behind a few frequent visitors to the tellers windows. On the other hand, the teller's problem also could stem from the difficulty people have in recognizing the faces of members of a race with whom they have had little prior contact or experience.[6] Unfortunately, this recognition difficulty is a weak "excuse" to a frustrated customer, so, at the very least, it raises a need for better employee training on how to recognize and remember the faces of all customers that they meet.[7]

From a marketing management point of view, it is intuitively obvious, but vexing nonetheless, that people from different backgrounds expect different types of service in a store. If management is to correct the problem and not misplace marketing, they need a better understanding of the subjective experiences and expectations of the customers. There exist clear differences in the way people of different races (or other subcultures) interpret identical situations.[8]

The basic problem for marketing is that the manager is rarely the same type of person as his or her customers. At their core, marketing decisions involve an effort to understand different people.

As a confounding variable in service businesses, managers set the policies, but day-to-day customer contacts are carried out by waiters, store clerks, and other people at the bottom end of the business chart. No store can hire clerks from every cultural group that might be customers. And even if it were legal and possible, such matching of personnel and customers would be a logistics nightmare. So management policies and directives need to try and take into account the different possible customer experiences and expectations.

For example, take the intuitively simple situation of asking retail store customers if they want help. Many people consider overly helpful clerks to be intrusive, yet, like everyone else, they will complain when no one is around when assistance is needed. Absent a sales force possessing telepathy, the manager instructs the employees to stand nearby "in case" a customer needs assistance. This seems like a logical solution. However, many African-Americans have dealt with unfounded suspicions by clerks who considered every black face a shoplifting threat. To these customers, the hovering-yet-quiet salesperson is seen as yet another racially biased pain for the honest shopper. Retail store clerks need better training to recognize if assistance is needed and how to then unobtrusively leave the customer alone while being available when help is desired.

Since doing a good job involves even the lowliest employees, it requires more than a manager's simple directive to "go out and be charming." Management rules can only go so far; inflexible rules can backfire with certain groups of customers, and employees need training in how to spot the needs of different types of customers. Unfortunately, even the large organizations report reductions in time or budgets allocated to employee training—usually measured in minutes instead of hours or days. As a result, these customer-contact people do not acquire a marketing perspective aimed at satisfying different types of customers. Instead, they often are able to serve only the smaller group of people just like themselves.

FLY ME, IF YOU DARE

When the airlines were heavily regulated in both routes and rates, the carriers used image advertising with fluffy proclamations of employee pride and friendly customer service. Following deregulation and dropping fares, the advertising campaigns visibly shifted to efforts to stimulate primary demand for various flights and to generate interest in a company's "low, competitive" rates. Today, Internet ticketing allows people to search out the lowest fares. With these options, flight times and price probably would seem to be more important than airline images about service, or so it would intuitively appear. On the other side of the equation, airlines closely assess demand and limit the available bargain seats to try and maximize their income. The amount spent per meal is going down and the meals on many routes have been totally eliminated, while the number and frequency of involuntary passenger bumping due to overbooking of flights have been increasing as the airlines try to guarantee that each trip travels at capacity.

In this competitive environment, it is a bit perplexing that airline advertising has seen a resurgence in service-oriented image advertising. This is not to say that customer service is not desired by air travelers, but it is neither the consumers' most highly valued attribute, nor the one that the airlines can most readily deliver.

In an effort to show how and why they are getting their employees to care about passengers, a United Airlines commercial shows a group of them inexplicably being kept waiting for a meeting to begin. When the man in charge finally arrives, he tells the employees to remember that feeling the next time a ticket holder asks about a flight delay.

Alright, so they say they care. And they tell the employees to care. But the passenger facing a forced bumping, a missed connection, or a canceled flight recalls only the "bad" service that did not match the advertising. Caring about passenger frustrations is all well and good, but the consumer wants frustrations to be minimized—period—not addressed with explanations by caring employees. Airlines can claim how carefully they make the meals, but the passenger: (a) does not choose a flight for the food; (b) can't get different food if the airline meals are not acceptable; and (c) will more likely note that the food is not as good as advertised if the advertising is making service claims that can't be delivered.

This became clearest to me when my wife and I made our first trans-Pacific trip, traveling from the United States to Australia on Qantas Airlines. The seats were spacious, the food above average, and the attendants friendly and helpful throughout the trip. As we transferred to a U.S. carrier for the final part of the trip from Los Angeles to Atlanta, we needed to call for some assistance just before takeoff. "Wadda ya want?" we were gruffly asked by a woman whose bloodshot eyes said she was badly in need of some rest. As she went away, my wife could only turn to me and say, "We're obviously not on Qantas anymore."

With hub-and-spoke systems giving some major carriers near monopoly power over some routes and airports, it intuitively appears that most passengers have little choice about what airline they fly in order to get travel times or prices they desire. Concurrently, the cost pressures on all levels of the business limit the ability of the airlines to actually deliver the kind of old-time service that was standard in the days of the image-oriented (and sometimes sexist) campaigns that had the personnel saying, "Fly me to Miami," or cheerfully singing "We really move our tail for you." And yet, the airlines *say* service is important in the advertising even though they are unable to deliver it.

LIKE, I CARE?

Recognizing that retail customers want good service, many stores are acting like the airlines, using upbeat slogans and advertising about the good service they claim to provide. And yet, while asserting a devotion to service, some employees at those same stores and the stores' basic policies take a different direction. Retailers are spending reduced amounts of time on training salespeople and general shopper satisfaction with customer service is declining. When employees can't or don't want to deliver the service, the advertising is a waste of money, or, worse, it can trigger an even stronger negative reaction.

Zachery told me that he was no longer going to be shopping at a large warehouse-style electronics outlet. The chain had established a reputation for low-priced electronic equipment, computer supplies, and music CDs and tapes—and for the limited abilities of its salespeople. A corporate motto of "I care," printed on lapel pins worn by everyone in the store, was trying to counter this image of weak service, but Zachery found that the slogan lost something when disseminated down the ranks. Actually, he found that it was totally ignored.

He had purchased a sound board from the store, only to have his office computer person return it, unopened, saying it was the wrong one. Unfortunately, it was not returned to him with the receipt. No problem, or so my friend thought, for a store that cares.

He was just asking for store credit, not a refund, but the clerk was not empowered to accept any return without the receipt. The manager, visible in his loft but not willing to come down and talk to the customer, sent the message, "Tell him he is out of luck," even though the package was unopened. A little put off by this "Like, I care?" variation on the motto, Zachery informed the clerk that he would take his business elsewhere. The clerk shuffled back upstairs and returned to report, "The manager said, 'Too bad.'"

Granted, Zachery has been credited by his friends with possessing the patience of a toddler. But his reaction was understandable. He cut his store credit card in two, informed the clerk he was going home to repackage everything purchased from the store in the last thirty days, and said that, in the interim, the manager should access his account record to see how much he has spent at the store in recent months. Zachery told me, "I thought if he saw the activity on just my card, he might think it worth his effort to get off his *tuchus* and do some customer service."

In short order, Zachery returned with receipts and over $500 worth of computer goods purchased over the previous few weeks. He tried to get the attention of the clerk from before, but that man actually turned and ran away when he saw the irate customer coming in the door. The manager ignored him. After making the returns and going down the street to another store, Zachery found higher prices but helpful salespeople and a willingness to match the prices of the nearby competitor. They even gave him credit on his unusable sound board, knowing that it was purchased from another store and not from theirs.

Zachery spends a lot on electronics for himself and his business. But the size of his monthly orders should not be why the store would want to avoid losing him as a customer. Every customer has friends. Every supportive act of good service brings customers back as well as the people they know.

Of course, the first store might have been using a policy of limited service and strict rules for all returns as a shortsighted strategy to hold down costs. And maybe the rules are inflexible because they consider all their employees idiots. When Zachery complained to the national office, he received a form letter that just repeated the clerks' whine: "By requiring receipts we are able to hold down prices." It was as if the details of what Zachery had written were never read; the reply letter was so sloppy it looked as if it had been written with a blunt crayon. Actually, it came off an inkjet printer in need of service; the letter was apparently folded and slapped into an envelope unviewed and unread immediately after it was printed, adding additional smearing to the not-yet-dry ink.

Again, minimizing attention to customers was probably just a way to cut costs. Likewise, the chain might have been trimming costs by hiring clueless clerks who, when asked if something was in stock or how something worked, would walk to the exact spot where the customer was looking and stare at the shelves or read the package as if they, too, were just another lost customer. This company is not unique in having store managers or clerks who don't want to be bothered.

In the large chain store specializing in computer equipment, I found seven clerks standing in the back of the store staring at a computer screen that seemed to be displaying an inventory list. Meanwhile, the checkout lines were snaking around tables into the store. When another man and I tried to get someone from the gathering to answer product questions, we were told we wanted customer service and "That's not our job." Unfortunately, it did not seem to be anyone's job.

In a chain store specializing in office supplies, a cheerful young person at the door says "Hello," and hands out sales brochures to people entering the store. Meanwhile, a few feet away, seven people are lined up behind a single clerk for questions or desiring to check out, while two other clerks are having a debate about the proper way to register a customer's product return. A third clerk walks over and joins the return discussion, since none of them know what to do (the customer later says that his return ended up taking fifty minutes), but no one thinks to open another checkout line. Meanwhile, the single open line gets longer and the woman assigned to greet people at the front door gives an empty smile to the frustrated customers, since no one has entered the store during this entire time.

Still, what made the bad service at the first store all the more galling to Zachery was that they were running an advertising campaign and having clerks wear lapel pins with the slogan proclaiming that they cared about customers. Apparently, someone in the home office felt the attention to customer service was needed. Unfortunately, no one made certain that clerks and managers carried out what the slogan claimed they were doing, nor was such "caring" evident from the office people who responded to customer complaints. When it comes to the marketing role of customer relations, what matters is actions, not slogans.

LOST PRIORITIES

The restaurant was almost empty, since it was early for the usual dinner crowd. Yet it was surprising that there were three groups lining up behind us before anyone came to the doorway to seat us. Then the woman who had been talking to the bartender all along, in a fashion that made us think she was a customer, looked up, came over to the door, and took us to a table.

And getting seated was the nicest part of the experience.

Waitresses walked past us while we waited and waited to give our orders. "Not my table, sir. I'll try and get someone." When a server finally did stop by, we were told that she had just come in, having been called to work special because two others had not shown up for their appointed shifts. When the meal finally was delivered, it had several important errors, including a nearly raw piece of meat, so it had to be sent back for corrections. The appetizer did not appear until after we had finished the meal. This situation, we were told, was caused by a cook with personal problems that had him messing up several orders.

When I asked to speak to the manager, I was directed to go to the bar. (No, he wouldn't come to the table!) There he was, giving the bartender directions about not overfilling drinks. The manager could have been helping wait on tables, or he should have been managing the distraught and dysfunctional cook, instead of worrying about bar customers who could come in later that night and, heaven forbid, get too much alcohol to drink. A common consumer problem of bar service, right?

"Bartender, there's something wrong with this drink. I prefer my drinks with a lot of extra water to thin it out. I think I'll take my business elsewhere."

Years ago, Chicago columnist Mike Royko wrote about declining restaurant service.[9] As his nonmarketing mind put it, a restaurant manager with the right priorities would have been doing some of the personnel-short jobs and would have gone into the kitchen with a meat cleaver, saying to the cook, "You will do your job or I will kill you." Instead, in a place where the cook was messing up orders and the waitress was overworked because another person did not show up, he found the young manager sitting in a front booth reading computer printouts. The customers were not being served and the twenty-something Hotel Restaurant Management graduate was aloof and removed, supposedly fretting about the business by reading data on costs and cash flow. Mr. Royko tried to tell him about the problem, but, like the manager at the CD and electronics store, he seemed to react with a "Like, I care?" attitude, concerned more about his stack of printouts.

The manager probably got a bonus based on profits, and profits come from restricting controllable costs. And yet, the marketing issues help reveal what could bring in more income, or, at the very least, stop a loss of business, as people experience it once and don't return. The basic dictates of marketing make the focus on controlling costs, while relevant, a secondary issue.

OPPORTUNITIES LOST

In public presentations and writing, University of Texas–Austin Professor of Advertising Jef I. Richards has described the Internet as a melding of mass and personal communications with great potential for improving consumer contact with companies, making all marketing efforts more efficient and effective.[10] In theory, with great potential for long-term returns, firms could use technology to maintain and improve customer service.

But, so far, the more common situation is that the customer focus is lost. The new technology is being misused in ways that mimic the failures to use old phone or personal systems. Service phone lines are usually just a promise of an afternoon of busy signals, usually only to yield an automated answering system that provides a *long* list of new phone numbers. Customers who try calling those numbers sometimes only find another series of busy signals or long waits. Consumer hotlines are mostly anything but hot. When humans are finally contacted, the supposed customer assistant most likely will be clueless, helpless, rushed, untrained, or just plain rude.

While I was traveling abroad, my wife received notice back home that the corporate credit card that I had through Auburn University had been canceled. She called me and I called the toll-free number for the heavily advertised internationally-known company. I thought I could get assistance, but, instead, I was told that the card had been canceled because "Your company had terminated your employment." I tried to tell her that, as a tenured full professor, such terminations could not be done without my knowledge, but the woman was clueless as to what might have actually occurred.

"Who told you I was no longer employed there?" I asked.

"We did not keep a record of that. We don't know," she replied.

"So was the information anonymous? Could anyone call in?"

"I don't know," she said. "We just know that you are no longer working there."

"But if you don't know who told you this, then the information could be in error. If the information is in error, I am traveling far from home without a card from your company. Don't you watch your own advertising? Don't you verify information before acting?"

"You are no longer employed by Auburn University," she repeated.

"But your source of information is as reliable as the Psychic Friends network," I tried to explain, but it got me nowhere.

I wanted to correct the problem with the canceled card, but the woman was now yelling at me that I had to get my "supervisor" to write a letter correcting their information. I finally got her supervisor on the phone, but he, too, kept saying that I was apparently fired and he did not have a source for the information, giving me a bigger source of angst besides not having a credit card in a strange country. As was later discovered, they had terminated my card midway through the annual renewal period because I had not used it often enough during the prior months, *not* because my employment had ended.

Increasing numbers of companies have toll-free telephone numbers and Web sites, both of which are promoted as ways for consumers to keep in contact with the companies. But use of technology should mean more than just putting technology into the system. A "mystery shopper" study of 200 companies found more than half of them were poor or, at best, "only fair."[11]

With international businesses, plus the Internet, a "lifetime" guarantee should have special meaning for a foreign traveler. But that depends on being able to contact the company that sold the product.

Getting to the hotel, it was discovered that a new suitcase had sustained a major hit on the frame. It held together for the trip, but now it could not be closed. Sales literature for the bag, as well as decades of advertising for the well-known brand from an international company, proclaimed a lifetime guarantee, but where or how this could be enforced when the owner was not home was not known. Carrying the ever-present laptop of today's business traveler, I turned to the Internet, which seemed to be a logical place to find the nearest service centers, or, at least, instructions on how to get the suitcase repaired. The company does have a Web site, but the Web address was not on any of the materials. When some searches finally turned up the Web address, there wasn't any e-mail address for direct contact and no service information was to be found. All that could be seen were announcements of new products and other advertising materials.

This instance was not atypical. While the Internet is touted as a major resource for consumer contact, many of the Web locations for major firms are mostly filled with advertising and slogans. By computer or phone, technology holds great promise for major improvements in customer contact and service, but it should be intuitively obvious that failure to follow through can result in customers souring on a business even more than if nothing were done at all.

NOT EVERY STORY IS BAD

Consumer Reports magazine periodically reports instances of manufacturers going way beyond the needs of customer service. When a man lost a single shoe, he sent the other one to Reebok in hopes that the company could find it a mate. The company sent a new pair and paid for the shipping and handling. A woman seeking repair information on her Oster bread machine was faxed a letter authorizing replacement from the local store. After losing a top snap on her faded and aging Bugle Boy pants, a student of mine called to find out where she could get a replacement button, only to be told by the company to go to the nearby outlet store and get a new pair as a replacement for the pants under the company's lifetime guarantee.

In each positive example, the firm could just as easily have given the reverse and negative response. The higher management of these businesses each realized that the long-term value of customer relations would far outweigh any short-run profit gain from holding the line against potential abuses of customer return policies.

A reporter from a consumer protection news program once went to a collection of department stores with a tough problem. The show's representative was asking them to take a post-Christmas return of a dress shirt without a sales receipt, with the label denoting a house brand for a competing store. While most places gave excuses, one store estimated an approximate price and cheerfully gave a cash refund. While the entire transaction was handled by a clerk, a manager was sought to explain the logic. He told the interviewers that "You now have cash in a purse pocket while still in *my* store, plus a potential willingness to spend it here if not now, then at some future time." The mere fact that the return was requested at that store indicates a past customer that the manager would want to keep coming back.

In a similar vein, the term "relationship marketing" has been in vogue. At its core, managers use an understanding of consumers to build long-term relationships and more meaningful connections with their customers. The concept has received a lot of rhetoric from many managers and academics, but in reality it is seldom practiced.[12] A *Business Week* cover story noted that, instead of using their data about consumers to improve service, some companies tier the customer groups by past spending patterns and decide to give bad service to some and preferential treatment to others. This might be logical from a short-run financial point of view, but, as the author noted, "What someone spends today is not always a good indicator of what they'll spend tomorrow. Life situations and spending habits can change. In some cases, low activity may be a direct result of the consumer's dissatisfaction with current offerings."[13]

In customer service, the marketing questions are really quite straightforward and simple. The marketing opportunities for service are great, especially with modern technologies, and old-style service needs go to the core of many businesses. Therefore, it is all the more perplexing when marketing gets doubly misplaced: lost with a failure to ask marketing questions and misdirected when the firms substitute substance-free advertising or vapid slogans for real actions, communications that customers easily see as contradicting what is actually done.

NOTES

1. Richard Feinberg, Richard Widdows, Marlaya Hirsch-Wyncott, and Charles Trappey, "Myth and Reality in Customer Service: Good and Bad Service Sometimes Leads to Repurchase," *Journal of Consumer Satisfaction, Dissatisfaction and Complaining Behavior*, vol. 3 (1990), pp. 112–114.

2. In the 1993 movie, *Falling Down*, when the rule-rigid clerk won't serve the desired meal because it is a minute too late, frazzled customer Michael Douglas responds by blowing the place to smithereens with a machine gun. Of course, few customers are both this touchy and well-armed, but everyone in the theater seemed to thoroughly enjoy the fictional character's reaction to a too-common experience.

3. Steve Allen, *Dumbth: And 81 Ways to Make Americans Smarter* (Buffalo, NY: Prometheus Books, 1989).

4. I have often wondered about this overlooked marketing "benefit": consumer masochism as a patronage motivation.

5. Thomas L. Ainscough and Carol M. Motley, "Will You Help Me Please? The Effects of Race, Gender and Manner of Dress in Retail Service," *Marketing Letters*, vol. 11 (no. 2, 2000), pp. 129–136.

6. Geraldine R. Henderson, unpublished comments and presentation, Marketing and Public Policy Conference, Washington, DC, June 1–3, 2000.

7. Kathleen Seiders and Leonard L. Berry, "Service Fairness: What It Is and Why It Matters," *Academy of Management Executive*, vol. 12 (May 1998), pp. 8–20.

8. Jacqueline A. Williams, Sonya A. Grier, and David Crocket, "Experience Matters: Consumers' Perceptions of Discriminatory Shopping Experiences," unpublished paper presented at Marketing and Public Policy conference, Washington, DC, June 1–3, 2000. Their data dealt with race-based differences, but the conclusions could readily be extended to many other subcultures and their members' differences in experiences and expectations as customers.

9. Mike Royko, "Shortage of Short Greeks Ruining Us," reprinted in *Dr. Kookie, You're Right!* (New York: Plume, 1990), pp. 42–45.

10. Jef I. Richards, "Legal Potholes on the Information Superhighway," *Journal of Public Policy and Marketing*, vol. 16 (Fall 1997), pp. 319–326. In the conclusion of that paper, he wrote, "As an interactive medium that reaches around the world, [the Internet] promises an interpersonalization of advertising. As mass communication becomes mass interpersonal communication, marketing efforts become more efficient, effective, and extensive."

11. Tom Duncan, "By Phone or Online, Customer Contact Bungles Hurt Brands," *Advertising Age*, vol. 70 (May 24, 1999), p. 24.

12. For example, see Susan Fournier, Susan Dobscha, and David Glen Mick, "Preventing the Premature Death of Relationship Marketing," *Harvard Business Review* (January–February 1998), pp. 42–51.

13. Diane Brady, "Why Service Stinks," *Business Week* (October 23, 2000), pp. 118–128.

4

Advertising Only a Copywriter Would Love

A few years ago in Wellington, New Zealand, during the question and answer session of a public lecture about advertising, a woman who had just returned from her vacation in San Francisco asked, "Why are New Zealand commercials so bad?" The simple and obvious answer was that most of them aren't bad at all, not really.

The real "problem" behind her question is that New Zealand's total national population is smaller than the number of people in the metropolitan areas of U.S. cities, such as New York, Chicago, San Francisco, Philadelphia, and Los Angeles. Companies spend a small proportion of the total budget on production—this is not a formal rule that anyone is forced to follow, but a general practice stemming from various pragmatic constraints—and since the size of the potential media audiences sets the budget, most of the smaller-scale, tinier-audience, New Zealand commercials probably have weaker production values than the national (or even some local) commercials that she and her husband saw in the United States. But a cheaper-quality video style or acting at the level of an Ed Wood movie doesn't necessarily make New Zealand advertising bad.

The source of most bad advertising is not a lack of creativity, entertainment value, or money for production. Actually, a lot of really bad print ads and commercials are creative, entertaining, and well produced because misplaced marketing can readily be found in some of the most expensively produced campaigns from the largest advertisers and agencies.

It is easy to forget a basic dictate found in any undergraduate's textbook (and, as a practical matter, it is often ignored by too many people in business): a good idea badly presented is still better than a bad idea that is well presented. And with the misplaced marketing behind some advertising efforts, the men and women involved in making many print advertising or broadcast commercials failed to consider the audience interests that a marketing perspective would require.

THE DILEMMA AND BANE OF BUSINESS TERMS

The business term for advertising writing and writers contributes to many misdirected views of message quality. The people involved with the day-to-day decisions of advertising message planning and writing are called "creatives"; they work in the "creative department"; and their job description involves "creative strategy and tactics." For many years, Coca-Cola's advertising was produced by Creative Artists, a group that, like many big names in the business, was known only for their work in producing interesting and unique advertising messages.

By placing so much emphasis on this being a creative job, business assessments often allow entertainment interest, artistic value, or simple originality to outweigh concerns for the advertising as a message that has a pragmatic job to inform or persuade a target audience. And some of this emphasis loses track of a focus on *management* of the message or planning how and why the message might play a role in the marketing plan.

Many advertising agencies allocate large sums of money to decorate the work areas (or floors) where copywriters are housed. They believe that clients who see the decorations will therefore know that very creative people are working on their advertising (as if decorating a room or a hallway translates into business communications). In an agency with a conservative dress code for account executives or media planners, people involved with message strategy and tactics have more freedom to look different and convey their personal, creative style in the clothes they wear. Similarly, good copywriters might be criticized if their sartorial tastes run toward conservative suits. Years ago, the undergraduates in the advertising program in which I taught were angry that Fred was teaching the course titled "Creative Strategy and Tactics." They could not believe a person who always wore an expensive business suit, a white shirt, and an in-style (but conservative) tie could know anything about good advertising writing, despite Fred's very solid credentials as a successful businessman prior to his getting a doctorate.

To a certain extent, this is easy to explain: so little is known about how or why advertising works (or if it works at all). As the dean of the University of Illinois College of Communications, Kim Rotzoll, has often noted, the uncertainty of the advertising process explains more about all advertising thought and practice than any other variable. To people in the business, this becomes the "creative dilemma." Since they are uncertain about just which advertising ideas would work or why, assessments of the advertising itself turn on creativity, values, and aesthetics. And since there is typically no closure for most mass-media forms of advertising, the people who write and produce those messages often seek feedback from the praise of peers or awards.

Unfortunately, few awards make any reference to assessments of success in doing the marketing job and, of those that do, the actual assessment is usually intuitive, ad hoc, and only weakly related to any pragmatic accomplishments.[1] In one direct comparison of this issue, a sample of viewers were found to respond positively to commercials if the message touched on their personal concerns, regardless of whether it was a past award winner, while creative department employees responded best to commercials that won awards.[2]

EYE-CATCHING AND ENTERTAINING BUT NOT COMMUNICATING

Years ago, Mike was assigned to prepare the commercials for a new type of car battery. Possessing one-and-a-half times the cold cranking power of what was then a commonly perceived standard for a powerful battery, the Sears Die Hard, the new battery would offer a major benefit to people starting their cars during the bitter cold winter mornings in places such as Minnesota or North Dakota. The selected approach for strategy was a demonstration that started with a question: "How do you get the power of 1½ Sears Die Hard batteries?" In the preliminary television commercial, Mike's script gave two answers. First, you could saw a Die Hard in half and strap it to another battery, as the "demonstrator" did on camera with a chain saw and booster cables. Or, using the product as a solution via the second answer, you could get the new brand of battery.

Time was tight and secrecy was important, so they could only pre-test the rough commercials with a few small focus groups. But the results were consistent.

"Where did the battery acid go when he used the chain saw?" several people asked. "Does sawing a battery in half give you half the battery's power or just a mess?"

"Why would anyone want to cut a battery in half?" some people wondered.

"I can't see how cutting the battery and strapping it to another with cables gives you more power [or 1½ batteries]."

In other words, the demonstration was eye-catching, but distracting from the message. Most respondents did not even notice that the first battery was the then-famous Sears product and no one seemed to remember the advertised brand's name or what it could do. The commercial had to be scrapped. And Mike was livid with rage.

"I could have won a Clio award," Mike angrily snapped at all who passed by for the next few days. He would name all the members of the creative team who thought his original storyboards were a real "breakout" effort—they say that a lot in the business, "breakout," meaning different—and he insisted that their creative assessments should outweigh the "dumb research." How can anyone get an award, he asked, if you depend on research? Prior to the research, his fellow creatives all thought it was a good idea and that should have carried more weight than a copytest, or so he thought.[3] No one seemed able to make him understand that he was missing the basic point: The idea was so different and unusual that the attention-getting idea was the only thing that left an impression on the audience, while they did not remember anything about the client's product.

At least in this case, the agency and client realized the problem and scrapped the original commercials that were unable to do the job. In many other cases, millions of dollars are spent on commercials that never had the consumer in focus.

In fall 1988, the then-new CBS News program *48 Hours* spent the two days "on Madison Avenue."[4] Among the various activities covered in the program was the filming of commercials for a new Reeboks advertising campaign, including interviews with the people who created the effort for what was then the top-selling brand of athletic shoes. The commercials featured a collection of vignettes of people doing all sorts of possibly strange and certainly different things—a group of people running up a hill with bicycles on their shoulders; a man walking back and forth with a false third leg; a woman coming out of the subway wearing a fairy-tale wedding gown and running shoes; a camera shot that focused on the distended stomachs of fat people wearing brightly colored lycra tights while doing exercises. The advertising theme proclaimed that "Reeboks let U.B.U.," with "U.B.U." typed on screen, lest viewers not catch the cute label.

On camera in an interview for the program, one of the commercial's creators working on the account said that the ads should evoke a longing for the milieu of innocence and other aspects of an inner drive in the psyche of the populace, speaking in a syntax and style than might get a spark of attention at a doctoral seminar in psycholinguistics or semiotics or even in a popular culture seminar presented in an English professor's deconstructionist dialectic. The CBS interviewer cut away from the audio of this rambling statement by the advertising manager about what he "hoped" to evoke in consumers, stating in a voiceover of the still-viewed interview his personal impression about this clearly creative speaker: "He's hip. He's articulate. I have no idea what he is saying."

And, apparently, the commercial audience was equally lost. The campaign lasted less than two years and the formerly top-selling brand lost market share during that period. But, then, one wonders why the commercials were even produced. Even if consumers understood the commercial message, it could have been a good campaign idea *only* if people would buy athletic shoes as an expression of personal style and individuality. If people did not seek these types of shoes to be different, if the primary motives for buying them were performance, current styles, or emulating a favored athlete, then the ads were a simple case of misplaced marketing.

That same CBS program also included several interviews with noted advertising creator and agency owner George Lois, filming him as he had meetings, planned, or produced campaigns for a variety of clients: Lifestyles condoms; Jiffy Lube; the *New York Post*; Mug root beer; and a new, yet-to-be-introduced coffee substitute. As he often does in such interviews, George talked about his 1972 autobiography, since it had what he thought was an appropriate title for describing why he has been a success in the business, *George, Be Careful*.[5] The title was selected because everyone always told him to be careful, but, as he said, you have to take risks in this business. And he's right, since there is so much uncertainty about what works and no one can research every detail or potential misstep.

As commercial clutter increases, consumers seem to be more able to physically avoid advertising or mentally tune it out. Every advertiser has a pragmatic need to stand out. As they focus on developing messages that stand out, too many of them forget that their focus should be on the subject of the message, not the message itself.

A basic marketing question starts from consumer perspectives and asks what consumers consider important.[6] Beyond wanting the advertising to get attention, it also has a communications job, and if the marketing perspectives are misplaced, the advertising effort will probably not do that job, regardless of how creative or original it might appear.

ATTENTION AND DISTRACTION

A lot of advertising seems to get attention but do little to sell a product. Many people think that if they have the audience's attention they have done the job. However, an attention-getting device that is unrelated to the message will not attract readership or viewers interested in what the advertiser has to say. At best, the audience will remember the device and not the message.[7] This loss of focus on the audience and message makes for a lot of misdirected advertising.

In one of his advertising reviews for *Advertising Age*, Bob Garfield once noted that there are two things that could be done by a fool with a lot of money: (1) run for president promoting some crackpot idea, even though you have no charisma or intellectual appeal; or (2) mount an elaborate advertising campaign, featuring expensive celebrities with no connection to your product whatsoever. His point was that no one (except Steve Forbes) would ever be so foolish as to undertake the expensive and humiliating effort of the first but, amazingly, many business owners will quickly go after the latter. "As we have said repeatedly, celebrities are seldom used in support of an advertising idea; they're used in place of an advertising idea."[8]

This is not to say that celebrities should never be used in advertising. Many decades ago, George Lois's ads for Maypo cereal had to fight the product's image as something just for small children. Since people saw it as something children would "outgrow," he used Mickey Mantle and other rugged sports heroes, crying "I want my Maypo." The star presenters' images were tied to the message. Maureen O'Hara, whose movie star image included her beautiful hair, appeared in advertising for Lustre-Creme Shampoo. A more contemporary good use of a celebrity in marketing is when Olympic winners are on the Wheaties box, because the cereal is "the breakfast of champions." A movie or television actor whose media-generated image is of a demanding person who is trusted might be a useful consumer-trusted presenter for an investment firm.

Unfortunately, many celebrities are used in advertising in a way that can only be a waste of money. In addition to the costs of hiring a good actor to take a part, the star celebrity also costs a high-priced premium for his or her appearance. But if the image of that star does not fit the advertising message, the audience will only recall the celebrity, not the product. In these cases, the advertising message costs more to make but does not improve its communications to the audience.

Bill Cosby's talent with children probably helped communicate the fun message of various Jell-O products. However, featuring William Bendix in advertising for the American Meat Institute four decades ago probably did more to promote his television program, "The Life of Riley," than it did to encourage people to eat more meat. Michael Jordan's championship image is a good fit for selling Gatorade or Nike shoes, but it is questionable as to whether his personal charm enhanced the images of MCI's long-distance service or McDonald's restaurants. Charles Barkley probably did not sell many Hyundais, though he certainly increased the cost of the advertising, and Chevy Chase did not enhance the appeal of Dollar Rent-a-Car.

Similarly, advertising that makes direct comparisons with competing brands also needs to take the consumers' mind set into account. Just because the other brand is a better seller or more famous does not mean that there is a value in making comparisons. A comparison advertisement is a good idea only if the compared brand is the target audience's standard for a quality product and the advertising message would show a consumer-desired benefit for which your brand is better. Lots of comparison advertising forgets this, using the better-selling brand for just the attention getting value, and having an audience that remembers only the competitor.

Entertainment values or outright humor *can* help a selling message. Federal Express' jokingly made strong illustrations of how deliveries "absolutely, positively have to be there overnight," turning the company into an icon of the reliable overnight delivery business. More commonly, irrelevant humor gets large numbers of people to watch the commercials or read the ads, but fails to encourage those people to buy the products or go to the stores. Audiences remember the joke, or the entertaining ad, but all too often they don't remember the sponsor or the advertised reasons given for them to become customers. As was repeatedly observed on numerous business news programs, the sometimes-entertaining Internet company commercials on the 2000 Super Bowl, which cost millions of dollars per spot, did not generate an upswing in visitors to the sponsors' Web sites.[9]

And then there's sex.

An advertisement for a pizza place near a college campus ran an advertisement in the school paper that said, "Put a hot piece between your lips. We're hot and easy, fast and cheesy." In another city, a Mexican restaurant showed a woman dressed in lycra and posed with her hands on her hips over the headline, "Tickle my taco." Running for years in various sporting magazines is a bold-type proclamation, "Better than five-gallon jugs," over a picture of a bikini-clad woman with most of her large breasts visible as she bends over to fill the boat gas tank with gas from the product—"gas dock"—an extra large gas tank built on a wheeled cart. As the movie *Eyes Wide Shut* filled the news, newspaper advertisements for a gardening supply store in New Zealand ran the headline "Eyes Wide Open for Spring," with a picture in the center of the page of the rear view of a person's thigh to mid-back, covered only by bikini briefs.

In each case, the advertiser probably thought it was good advertising, not realizing that the irrelevant use of sex distracts the target audience, hinders communication, and fails to persuade. It is intuitively obvious that a product is sexually relevant for marketing communications only if people buy it for a sexual reason. While breath mints, clothes, or exercise equipment may be purchased to enhance sex appeal, it is doubtful that anyone buys pizza or tacos in anticipation of an orgasmic experience, even on a college campus. The garden shop advertisement draws so much attention to the sexy body part that it would only be read by people in search of the latest bun-tightening video or maybe an exercise gym.

The issue, though, is more than just simple misdirection and distraction. The people who wrote or produced these ads lost track of what they were trying to say to the target audience. A California pager company ran newspaper advertisements asserting that its product is the brand preferred by pimps and hookers to "keep in touch," thinking perhaps that these "working people" are a consumer-perceived standard of working men and women who need to keep in touch. In the print advertising for a shower gel brand, the body copy is in the middle of two pictures: The product sits on a shower stand to the left; on the right is a naked man from the thighs upward (discreetly sideways), with a headline "The one on the right can also stimulate your mind." This could be considered an effective message in a woman's magazine only if the audience would perceive a shower gel as a sexual and mental turn-on.

After years of talking to advertisers and watching them produce these less-than-optimal efforts, one comes to the ineluctable but reluctant realization that some of the advertising creators are so myopic that they believe that publicity prompted by offending people is always beneficial. They do not see it as being a distraction from saying positive things about the restaurant or store. Instead of communications, attention of any kind—to anything, at any cost—is their goal. The man who wrote the "Tickle my taco" advertising thought it was the greatest campaign he had ever written because the numerous complaints generated publicity.[10]

However, advertising is a very limited and limiting form of communication, costly to undertake and difficult to carry out successfully. The marketing question of how to best communicate is a conservative one, but it is also an effort to maximize the likelihood of a favorable consumer response. Because, in the end, there is a communications job to be done.

In the newspaper advertisement from Los Angeles, the woman wearing only jewelry with her hands covering her breasts and exclaiming, "What do you mean they're not real?" might convey an association and image that helps sell imitation and fake jewelry. The message to either a male or female audience is definitely not about sex. And yet it must be noted that the message's various innuendos and associations also would carry the negative connotations about breast implants while gratuitously offending many people, both of which would get in the way of communicating anything to anyone about fake jewelry.

SEX AND THE TRUCK CALENDARS

Some marketing textbooks give "specialty advertising" its own section and definition as an advertising medium that uses imprinted, useful, or decorative products. Numerous companies make all sorts of products available for this special printing of advertising messages with company names, logos, slogans, addresses, and phone numbers. Many of the men and women selling the products are top-notch marketing planners, helping the clients use this unique medium to solve advertising communications problems. Unfortunately, people buying the products sometimes let their interest in the communications tactic override their marketing strategy.

Many years ago, Lou's company serviced the various trucking companies in Chicago, repairing seats and canvas tarpaulins as well as providing various products used in cargo hauling. An undifferentiated service with non-unique products, his success depended on his customer contact abilities and his willingness to be available for customers who needed him. In an area of work where business cards are thrown in drawers and lost (I guess, just as in many other businesses), there was a unique opportunity for advertising specialties to keep Lou's business and phone number in front of every customer if they needed his services between his regular sales calls.

And therein arose a puzzling problem. All his colorful wall calendars were grabbed up by everyone as fast as he could print them, with some people asking for three or four (or more). Illustrated with a set of explicit sexual pictures in a style often found in many of the men's lockers—I don't have to spell it out, do I?—most truck drivers loved that calendar! Yet when he would call on the small trucking companies that made up the bulk of his business, they couldn't remember Lou's company name or his phone number.

Of course, the unasked first question was this: "Who calls Lou when they need him: the truck driver, the company owner, or a secretary?" The answer was the office secretary, who set up the purchase order or other paperwork.

"Were these secretaries former truck drivers?" No. While the dispatchers or company owners were former drivers—usually men—the secretaries at these mostly small businesses were often wives or daughters or other women hired to do a clerical job. Even if men were doing the work, rarely were they former drivers.

Knowing that Lou's wife often came into his office, the next obvious question was what Margie said when she saw the calendar in his office. Of course, I knew the answer: He didn't have any of his own calendars in his office because he knew she wouldn't like them.

The solution was easy. Knowing that many of the blue-collar men and women working in these offices were weekend campers and (sometimes) hunters, Lou commissioned some specially designed outdoor and wildlife scenes that they would be happy to look at day after day on the office wall.

In these litigious times, when all sorts of charges are raised against pictures in an office that might create a "hostile environment" for the women who work there, Lou's attorney would have stopped him from even thinking about making his first type of calendars. But, then, recently visiting the back areas of a small shipping and storage company, the "bare bodied" calendars for various service firms were still in evidence on inside doors of the men's lockers. But beyond any potential for offending employees, the marketing question still involves first assessing who makes decisions for a purchase, who needs the information on service suppliers, and what type of specialty advertising product the purchaser would find useful.

Marketing gets misplaced in a lot of specialty advertising when the advertiser forgets the basic definition of the medium: The usually short advertising message is placed on *useful* products. The "useful" part of the definition of specialty advertising is what often gets lost, since they must be useful for the target market. As happened in Lou's case, sometimes even questions of who might be the target are forgotten.

In all areas of marketing work, there is the "danger" that tactical decisions sometimes lose track of the initial marketing plan and its strategy. With the buying of specialty products, the problem is compounded, since advertisers are buying a product that is to be given to the audience and also carry the message. So it is easy to forget that a useful pen is one the target audience will use to write notes, not a pen that is so cheap the customers will quickly toss it aside. Marketing planners want the target audience members to hang the calendar over the desk and not to give it to a friend. A name on a coffee mug is supposed to be a reminder and aid that would encourage customers to make a purchase, though the mugs selected (or maybe all mugs because the target receives so many) might get tossed onto a collection shelf along with those from all competitors.

The reality is that various advertising specialties, such as pocket knives, radios, coffee mugs, and a host of other products, are often bought by advertisers for all types of reasons unrelated to marketing strategy or tactics. Sometimes the marketing manager just spotted a new toy he or she would like to own or give away, and the manager is seldom a typical consumer. Yet important questions of marketing strategy still need to be asked about the target audience and what it considers useful. If these are forgotten, the specialty itself becomes useless from a marketing point of view.

NOT-SO-SUPER COMMERCIALS
AT THE "SUPER BOWL"

The annual National Football League championship game, the Super Bowl, has become a major advertising event. Arguably, the Super Bowl draws the largest single mass-media audience in any given year, with Americans throwing parties tied to television viewing of the game. So advertisers repeatedly pay record high prices for the time for the commercial spots run during the game. Each year they pay more than advertisers did the year before. And, many times, the advertisers do not make good use of their money.

Understanding why marketing views get misplaced while spending millions of dollars first requires a brief background on how TV advertising time is bought or sold.

For any consumer-goods advertiser, the bulk of the budget goes to the purchase of media time and space. As the audiences for any given vehicle are increasingly fragmented, the number of options available and the process for deciding what to buy has become more complicated. Media buyers and planners have access to a huge array of data on media audiences; computer programs provide increasingly detailed ways to mix, match, and compare options. Yet the final decisions are still regarded by many as "more art than science."

The reasons for this are easy to understand. The data are not provided free of charge, so the data any one firm may use are limited in their potential detail, since more precise data cost more money that few are willing to pay. In addition, the information is not pruned and collated through a central source, so making comparisons, even with the best information, can be very confusing. Most important, computer programs can weigh quantitative concerns, but not all variables relevant for media decision making lend themselves to numerical assessments, such as how closely an audience reads a magazine or how much a media vehicle lends itself to communicating a particular type of message. It can all get very confusing; hence, the "art" aspect of the work.

In addition, media space or time rates are not offered at a set price; the final sale is more like an agreement for purchase of a farm commodity. The major broadcast networks do not even have printed rate cards with prices, letting "marketplace" discussions with buyers determine price, so the price paid depends on the negotiating skills of the advertiser's representative.

In the end, the final decisions about how much to pay and what to buy basically comes down to the media planner or buyer's specialized expertise. Unfortunately, while the specialized expertise involves a marketing perspective, this is sometimes misplaced or flat-out ignored to meet all sorts of irrelevant concerns of managers.

A former student told me that his computer-manufacturer client had a fixed rule against advertising in *Playboy* magazine. Even though the magazine's readership was very heavy in the types of people who were interested in the advertised product, management felt that the publication denigrated women. This same firm also required that advertising space be bought in the political, gay-oriented publications *Out* and *Advocate*, primarily because a large number of gay men and lesbian woman worked for the organization. At the time, this meant that a struggling company's computer products appeared next to ads for padded underwear, which claimed to help readers "Get Shapelier Buns Instantly."[11]

There exists a degree of prestige from airing a commercial during the Super Bowl, and almost every Super Bowl advertiser has their brand name repeated in a few news stories. But they also need something to say and something that would be targeted toward that audience. Everyone is still talking about the Apple Computer ad, titled "1984." The commercial ran just once, but has been repeated many times in a wide range of news stories. A well-placed and interesting advertising effort can generate a huge amount of positive publicity, well beyond the initial exposure.[12] However, publicity and value do not come from placement alone. Most of the Super Bowl commercials are forgotten by the next morning, which is a quick way to blow more than $2 million without gaining anything except bragging rights for having a commercial on the program.[13]

For the January 2000 event, the so called "dot-com" firms went crazy. For some strange reason, a large number of them felt they had to be on the program to make a mark. These are firms that are repeatedly noted as having overvalued stocks for firms that have yet to show a profit. Just to be on a high-profile sports program, they were paying grossly overpriced rates for the privilege. They bought out the time and, with heightened demand for the limited time, increased the price.

Many long-time advertisers opted out of the program in 2001, deciding that the audience might be large and attentive, but not *that* large. In fact, the ratings have been stagnant to declining for many U.S. sporting events in recent years. For the limited and inane value of being a part of the show, the advertisers are overspending and probably accomplishing little of pragmatic value.

THE REAL PROBLEM OF "BAD" ADVERTISING

I find myself repeatedly telling my students that just because the slickly produced commercials they see are part of an expensive campaign by a large firm, it does not mean that the campaign is based on a good marketing strategy, or, for that matter, that it had *any* strategy behind it. The commercials can be successful or not. Reviewing the advertising from out in the audience, we have no data on results, and "accidents" do happen. So, for our discussion, I ask them under what conditions could this be a good advertising idea. It is amazing how often we can't even conceive of a situation in which the advertising would do a worthwhile communications job, even when the eighteen- to twenty-five-year-old consumers in my class are the apparent primary audience for the advertising effort. Instead, they conclude that it is misplaced marketing and, therefore, bad advertising.

My students' conclusions fit with an experience that is repeated many times when I sit in on advertising agency presentations to clients. After giving detailed data on the present and potential consumers, followed by a specific goal statement of what the campaign is to accomplish, the advertising planners then describe their recommended advertising strategies and tactics that have, at best, a tenuous relationship to the first part of the presentation. Tactics are done without strategy and the "strategy" (if it exists at all) is presented without reference to consumer views.

I sometimes ask why they even bothered to collect data and set goals if they were going to ignore their own preliminary work. Producing a "breakout" advertisement or an "attention getting" campaign does not do any good if they get the attention of the wrong people for the wrong reasons. An instructor who has a loud case of gas in the front of the class will certainly get attention, but I doubt if the students would hear or recall anything that instructor said for the fifteen minutes after the event.

It misplaces marketing when decision makers set out to be creative only for the sake of winning creative awards. Instead, they should be designing original and entertaining messages that appeal to the purchase interests and values of their customers. If consumers strongly think the shoes are ugly, a good-looking celebrity will not change their minds. If sex is irrelevant to the purchase decisions, then a sex appeal will only have the audience remembering the sexy pictures. A funny joke unrelated to the product's benefits could have many people talking about the commercials but not making a purchase.

Some very bad advertising will succeed due to either outstanding products (for which any advertising is superfluous) or simple inertia from prior profits. But with a lost marketing focus, there is a disservice to many potential customers and many firms are spending money on messages that appeal to no one.

NOTES

1. Sandra E. Moriarty, "Effectiveness, Objectives, and the EFFIE Awards," *Journal of Advertising Research*, vol. 36 (July–August 1996), pp. 54–63.

2. Arthur J. Kover, William L. James, and Brenda S. Sonner, "To Whom Do Advertising Creatives Write? An Inferential Answer," *Journal of Advertising Research*, vol. 37 (January–February 1997), pp. 41–53.

3. If anyone intended the creative team's intuition to carry so much weight, the advertising would not have been subjected to testing in the first place. Admittedly, many copytests are done to support decisions that have already been made, or to plan a defense if things go wrong—"I don't understand what happened! It tested well"—but such problems are just examples of how office politics and paranoia can generate bad business decisions and wasted money.

4. This was *48 Hours* title for that day's program, even though show personnel did not spend very much time in offices actually located on that street.

5. George Lois with Bill Pitts, *George, Be Careful* (New York: Saturday Review Press, 1972).

6. Howard Luck Gossage, *Is There Any Hope for Advertising?* K. Rotzoll, J. Graham, and B. Mussey, eds. (Urbana: University of Illinois Press, 1987). David Ogilvy, *Confessions of an Advertising Man* (New York: Ballantine Books, 1963).

7. Ogilvy, *Confessions of an Advertising Man.*

8. Bob Garfield, "TD Waterhouse Makes Trade With Celebs," *Advertising Age*, vol. 70 (November 29, 1999), p. 79. While the first four paragraphs of this column repeated his prior observations about misuse of celebrities in advertising, he then pointed out how and why he (reluctantly) felt that the new TD Waterhouse on-line brokerage campaign was using them effectively.

9. Jennifer Gilbert, "Top 10 Ads Score Raves, Not Hits Post-Super Bowl," *Advertising Age*, vol. 71 (February 7, 2000), p. 63; Phillips Graham, "Not-So-Super Ad Bowl Says Y&R's Phillips," letter to editor, *Advertising Age*, vol. 71 (February 14, 2000), p. 30. At that time, many business analysts on television news programs reviewed these commercials and not one was able to state what the spots were supposed to accomplish for the companies.

10. The owner of the restaurant could easily have won a "stupidity in community relations" award. He angrily called the university's Woman's Resource Center, which he felt was the source of most complaints, telling the students that it's "too bad you broads ain't got a sense of humor." He was out of business within a year.

11. In order to attract more "quality" advertisers, the *Advocate* has since eliminated most of its sex-product advertising. The magazine's improved image, as both an advertising vehicle and a source for political commentary, can be attributed (at least in part) to that change of policy.

12. The classic discussion of this is found in Miller Harris and Howard Gossage's *Dear Miss Afflerbach, or The Postman Hardly Ever Rings 11,342 Times* (New York: Macmillan, 1962).

13. Bonnie Tsui, "Bowl Poll: Ads Don't Mean Sales," *Advertising Age*, vol. 72 (February 5, 2001), p. 33.

PART II

OPPORTUNITIES LOST: PITFALLS OF ARROGANT IGNORANCE

"We know what we're doing. Trust us."

Our class had a lot of material to cover during the term, so I didn't feel we could waste a day. But an assistant to the dean scheduled a guest speaker for us without asking me in advance. When I objected, he told me the visitor could talk expertly on any topic I planned to cover. "After all," he said, "your course is only marketing. How difficult can that be?" As demonstrated by the examples in the last section, it can be very difficult.

The basic directives for public health organizations, trade associations, and even many government agencies in this section are to "serve public (or members') interests or needs." Logically, this means that their decisions should apply a marketing perspective, though, in most cases, the group's decision makers don't understand what marketing means. Well, maybe the people in charge don't misunderstand it, but, unfortunately, they tend to act as if it is irrelevant. Losing the view of the marketing concept, they follow a production orientation.

The misplaced marketing perspectives of the next chapters are most vexing because these groups do not need to maximize profits. Their main agenda is not necessarily political. Whatever the reason, the misplaced marketing in this section results in an organization's failure to serve anyone except for, perhaps, the organization's leaders, who feel they are accomplishing something by the sake of the activity.

5

"Hey Gang, Let's Put on a Show!"

For many years, the U.S. government broadcast anticommunist propaganda toward Cuba, while Fidel Castro's government transmitted interfering signals on the same frequencies so Cubans could not hear the programs. The Cuban transmitters also caused reception problems for audiences of some U.S. commercial radio stations. Both sides in this expensive transmitter war believed that if the American broadcasts got through, Castro's supporters would turn on him, forcing the island nation to become a capitalistic and democratic society.

When I was a faculty member at Penn State, John, a colleague of mine, wrote an article pointing out that this radio–TV battle was wasting money. Even if everyone in Cuba heard the messages, no one would be "converted." Radio programs would not turn communists into capitalists any more readily than Tokyo Rose demoralized allied soldiers in World War II and convinced them to surrender. John's article applied basic communications theory; his conclusions were intuitively obvious to anyone who had studied how advertising and marketing worked. But he still got a phone call from someone in the federal government who insisted that the article was wrong. To the caller, it was equally "obvious" that if the U.S. broadcasts got through the Cubans' jamming, the programs would cause a public insurrection in the island nation.

After some lengthy and intense discussion, John called out to the faculty talking in the hallway, asking us to step into his office. With his hand over the mouthpiece, he quickly told us of his frustration and handed the phone to Vince. Our senior colleague was initially polite, but he reached his tolerance level more quickly than John.

"Young man," Vince asked, with the probing intensity I had seen him exhibit with a less-than-sharp student, "how much advertising would convince you to wear a dress to work?"

I imagined the caller's reaction as he gave a puzzled shrug of his of shoulders, "A lot, I guess."

"So if you see a lot of advertising with men modeling dresses, you'd wear one?"

"I guess."

"Calf-high or floor length? Strapless? Maybe with a pair of spike-heeled shoes?"

"Hey, what kind of guy do you think I am?"

"I have no idea," Vince calmly replied. "But whatever type of man you think wears that outfit, you're the person who said you'd become one with exposure to enough advertising."

In effect, most public service advertising campaigns try to convince traditional conservative men to wear women's clothes.

Many people believe advertising has magical powers that it does not possess, and advertising practitioners feed these mistaken beliefs by spouting all sorts of nonsense.

Just as advertising people like to claim the power to move products, they also claim an equally great ability to move the public mind in "selling" various social goals. But such claims depend on a logical non sequitur, conclusions that do not follow from the initial premise. Just because advertising sometimes can help generate consumer interest in specific brand names does not also mean that every advertised effort will get people to make significant changes in their behavior. There are numerous pragmatic differences between selling brand-name products or services and convincing people to change the way they live their lives.

An advertising campaign that aims to serve a social goal faces many pragmatic obstacles. The obstacles are so great and the problems so numerous that money spent on advertising would often be better used on other activities, such as law enforcement or personal counseling with the people who are most at risk.

But the greatest problem is that the decision makers who control and direct the public interest campaigns do not understand the most basic of marketing perspectives. They have no expertise on using marketing tools. They do not misplace marketing by losing it, since they never bothered to learn it in the first place. They are medical doctors or rape counselors or political workers who nonetheless see themselves as marketing or advertising "experts." Since these public-spirited men and women think they "know" what the people in the at-risk groups need, marketing questions are not even asked.

And they *believe* in the power of advertising.

NEVER MIND THE QUESTION, ADVERTISING IS THE ANSWER

A huge color picture of a new billboard in town filled a newspaper's front page. The main story's headline proclaimed, "Rape problem now being addressed," and the article told readers that the outdoor display was a major element in a solution to the problem of date rape. Apparently aimed at men who might become rapists, it said that a woman's statement of *no* means no.

The local rape counseling group that sponsored the advertisement was confident that billboards like this would help raise public awareness and, in turn, reduce the number of rape incidents in the local college community. And, apparently, the newspaper reporter agreed.[1]

Rape is one of many social problems whose solution is seen as an advertising campaign. Government and public service agencies concerned about drunk driving, road rage, unsafe sexual practices, underage cigarette smoking, illegal drug use, and even littering all expect advertising to reduce the incidence of these not-infrequent, socially undesirable activities.

The rape awareness billboard violated every textbook rule on how to write, illustrate and display effective outdoor advertising. It had too many words (four complete sentences), weak and confused graphics (a pair of intertwined hands, explained by the sentences saying, "He's not holding her hand. He's holding her down"), and multiple messages. But despite these technical problems, the display was important for reducing rape, or so the counseling group believed. In part, the news story revealed that the sponsors possessed a certain arrogance, and they should have gotten some help from advertising professionals. Or maybe they had professional help that was less than competent.

In any event, badly done advertising was the focus of Chapter 4, not here. Some public service advertising campaigns are well produced. The best of them win awards from advertising business leaders and trade groups. But even if the rape counselors had produced a technically good billboard for their message, there would still exist a valid question of whether *any* advertising effort could have an impact on rapists or their friends.

Rape is a violent criminal act. Advertising does not turn criminals into law-abiding people any more than speed limit signs get motorists to slow down. Date rape involves an act of force by a man whose mind is incapable of overruling his hormones. It is doubtful that any form of mass communications can inculcate the sensitivity needed to make any change in a rapist's behavior, any more than rapists could be persuaded by advertising to wear the victim's evening gown the next day.

The real problem with this campaign and many others like it is that even with well-written advertising and an "award-winning" production, the same basic marketing question is overlooked, as it was here. No one asks whether mass media advertising can persuade anyone to change their "problem" behaviors. Usually, it can't. Success for an advertised brand merely involves convincing a small, already predisposed percentage of the population to try or use it, while social campaigns need to persuade larger numbers of people who are fully aware of what they are doing and have decided to ignore the risks. Business people know that not every product needs or uses advertising to be sold; some products can't be sold no matter how much they are advertised.

For most public service advertising campaigns, not only is this basic question not asked, but it is not even considered. The power of advertising is presumed, and the people behind most public service campaigns see the advertising itself as a solution.

Of course, such a misconception and misuse of advertising is not reserved for people supporting a social cause. Business trade associations or political action groups also see advertising as the solution to all sorts of problems.

Many farmers pay an annual fee to national or regional associations to fund advertising campaigns to encourage generic demand for items such as beef, milk, orange juice, or prunes. Like many other towns, Niles, Illinois, launched an advertising campaign to encourage residents to shop at local stores instead of using the Internet. Political or opinion advertising campaigns are an expected aspect of the diversity of public dialog: Unions fund advertising to support boycotts of opponent manufacturers; groups such as Citizens Concerned for Human Life broadcast television and radio commercials to discourage abortions.

In each instance, the dues-paying or donation-making backers of these organizations feel good when they see or hear advertising that fits with their views. So while nothing pragmatic is accomplished from a marketing point of view, the messages serve the emotional needs of the advertisers. Money is wasted, or, at the very least, spent in a less-than-optimal fashion, but no one really cares.

Arguably, this ineffectual advertising sometimes yields an intellectual "benefit," even if no one's attitude is changed, when it engenders public debate on an important issue. For example, a hard-hitting, pro-euthanasia television commercial in Australia generated numerous news stories about the woman it featured. Many people prefer to avoid dealing with that topic, but the advertising forced public debate. And the television commercial stimulus would appear to be a more desirable and less destructive way to get discussion going than Dr. Jack Kervorkian's law-violating assisted suicides in the United States that are followed by his daring the various states' prosecutors to bring him to trial.

In San Francisco, billboards and bus shelter ads showed seductive-looking models, photographed in the style of Victoria's Secret advertising, their uncovered chests revealing scars where their breasts used to be. One billboard company pulled down the ads as "offensive to community standards"; a second firm agreed to run them for free. But the controversy over whether the ads should stay or go from the public space caused publicity that was the core of the Breast Cancer Fund's goal. The advertising's existence (if not the messages) generated national news attention and greater awareness of breast cancer among young women.[2]

But these are not the usual cases. More commonly, the goal is not "discussion" but changing actual public behaviors by which people place themselves or others at risk.

Optimally, public interest advertising campaigns need to consider in advance what the advertising would or could accomplish. Most often they don't. The Breast Cancer Fund had a detailed advertising plan, with a clear perspective: Forcing women to see breast cancer as a real and personal threat would impel them to more readily conduct self-exams and have regular check-ups. The style of the display and the blizzard of publicity met those goals. But that organization's approach is the exception. It is more common that advertising is employed for the indefinite and less-than-pragmatic aim of "doing something."

BUT CAN ADVERTISING DO ANYTHING?

Advertising is seen as the solution for schools needing funds or students. Because New Zealand parents have full school choice—children are no longer required to attend neighborhood schools—the schools must attract students to get attendance-based government reimbursements. Almost all of the local schools are now advertising, facing public criticism for spending money in this fashion and not knowing how or why it might attract students. The administration of the University of Canterbury in Christchurch, New Zealand, facing budget problems and a slight enrollment decline, decided to start advertising even before it was fully understood just why more students would wish to attend there. Similarly, back home, faced with tight funding from the state legislature, Auburn University launched an image advertising campaign, though the target was uncertain, the goals were amorphous (tell them we are a wonderful school?), and the resulting advertising appeared to many students, faculty and alumni to be poorly conceived and executed.

Teenaged drivers throughout the United States joke about how many "points" they get for hitting various types of pedestrians, but San Francisco pedestrians must feel like they really are targets in a game. They are injured and killed at an epidemic rate at intersections and in crosswalks. As various possible solutions are discussed, some groups want to put an emphasis on advertising, telling local drivers to look out for pedestrians at intersections. While the news reports are filled with increasingly common reports of pedestrians hit by cars, one wonders what advertising could tell motorists that they don't already know. The potential creator of the campaign told reporters that he wanted people approaching intersections to think and slow down, not mentioning that the drivers who cause the accidents are speeding, running through red lights, and ignoring crosswalk signs. In Auburn, a nineteen-year-old drove around a stopped school bus, killing a small child. Advertising would not have had any impact on this young man who was too rushed to be concerned with obeying the law.[3]

Aggressive driving, now commonly known as "road rage," has become another major traffic problem in the United States. And like other such problems, advertising messages have appeared to address the problem. Of course, there is more to solving the problem than telling people, "Excuse me, but I think you're acting like a jerk." The basic question is whether aggressive or angry drivers would recognize or admit that they are a hazard to themselves and others on the road.

Two television commercials a couple years ago tried to point out the stupidity of the aggressive driver without ever showing the car. In one, to the sounds of revving engines, two male pedestrians take the measure of each other and then aggressively "race" across the street. (They are in the crosswalk and obeying the traffic light, which is more law obedience than is shown by some aggressive drivers.) In the other, two people with baby strollers start an increasingly fast and reckless race, ending with a crash into a innocent bystander. The message is clear and the statement is creative, but the commercials probably will not change anyone's behavior. People who recognize other drivers in the message will slap the table, laugh, and point it out to friends. And the jerks who are aggressive drivers will watch it, slap the table, laugh, and point it out to friends, too, because, . . . well, they're jerks.

It is a classic scene in movies and television. "Excuse me," says the hero, "I think the woman said she wanted to be left alone." Whether the hero is John Wayne, Gary Cooper, or Chuck Norris, the obnoxious guy does not walk away, but instead, draws a gun or swings a fist. If the "hero" is Jerry Seinfeld or Tim Allen, we expect the jerk to still start a fight, but the star will escape the brawl by hiding under a table. To most people in the audience, the man causing the problem is very realistic, so knowing we can't fight or depend on luck, most of us pray we're never trapped in that position.

In real life, as a jaywalker finishes crossing the street, the impatient motorist honks the horn. The pedestrian thinks the driver is a childish jerk and the driver is thinking the same thing about the pedestrian.

The Outdoor Advertising Association of American (OAAA) has unveiled its new effort to combat road rage. The copy says "Give your fellow drivers the finger," with a picture of an enlarged head and arm sticking out of a car with a thumbs up gesture. Next to the thumb is a balloon saying "Drive nice." I guess this makes the OAAA people proud that they are doing something to address the problem. With the advertising space donated by the organization's members, they are not drawing any public money from law enforcement or other driver education activities. But as tactics without strategy and advertising that lacks a meaningful target audience that can be persuaded, it is doubtful that anything will be accomplished by the billboards.

THE LIMITS OF BUSINESSES' PUBLIC SERVICE

During World War II, American advertising practitioners volunteered their efforts, and media vehicles gave free time and space, to help stir up patriotic fervor and to sell war bonds. After the war ended, the War Advertising Council organization renamed itself the Advertising Council, "dedicated to using the great resources of the advertising industry" to serve the public interest. It is now the largest producer of public service mass communications campaigns in the United States. Donations of work time by advertising agencies, plus the donations of time and space by the media vehicles for the messages, have been estimated to be worth around a billion dollars per year.

Free public service work from anyone is admirable, and the Advertising Council's dedication to public service is a wonderful credit to business groups supporting it. But advertising agencies that provide this professional "help" are also trying to build their own portfolio of award-winning advertising; the campaigns have a value for agencies as a showcase for a company's creative work. The problem is that copywriters and art directors, eager to produce new "breakout advertising," will concentrate on the creative advertising and not the public interest they are trying to serve.

So while the creative people involved with these campaigns face the usual distractions described in Chapter 4, the pro bono nature of the work means their *only* incentive is to produce a creative showcase. Without a requirement for them to show actual impact or success, there do not have a strong incentive to think in terms of consumer perspectives or values. As a result, the advertising might be interesting and attention getting while still misplacing the basic marketing questions.

Not all Advertising Council campaigns have been unsuccessful. Some have helped change the public's perceptual agenda, or so we are told. The council's famous campaign featuring Smokey the Bear saying, "Only *you* can prevent forest fires" is credited with reducing the incidence of human-caused conflagrations. At the very least, people today are more conscious of things that cause fires than they were when the campaign began. An award-winning television commercial featuring a Native American with a tear on his cheek as he views trash on the landscape is commonly believed to have played a major role in changing people's views about littering, which, in turn, reduced the number of motorists who toss garbage out the car windows while driving down the road.

Yet these well-known claims of success are noteworthy as exceptions as well as being exceptional. An extensive body of literature concludes that most public information campaigns fail to alter the behaviors of people who are the source of the problem. Even when the campaigns emphasize issues of the audience's personal health or safety, and even though there might exist some evidence that people are aware of the PSA's message content, the target group's "dangerous" behaviors usually remain unaltered.[4] And some claims of advertising success could just as readily be attributed to other factors that occurred at the same time.

If nothing changes, no one asserts that the advertising might have been a wasted effort. And if there is a change in public behaviors, the advertising is given credit. For example, the television spots of the "crying Indian"[5] were shown during a period of increased enforcement of antilittering laws (with larger fines for violators and roadside notices of the law), while stores distributed free litter bags for cars and more roadside rest areas had garbage bins. While littering might have gone down during this time, it is uncertain whether it was the advertising that caused the drop. Similarly, safe driving advertising campaigns usually begin while police concurrently intensify their enforcement of traffic laws.

Beyond the strategic myopia of some public service campaigns, there are some barriers to success. The problems are outside the control of any marketing people involved with the effort, and the reliance on media owner's largess is an intrinsic problem of misplaced marketing.

Many U.S. ad campaigns run their course with few people ever knowing they existed, running their entire span with few target consumers ever seeing the commercials. Since the Advertising Council and other groups depend on time or space donated by the media for Public Service Announcements (PSAs), they take the placements they can get for free without question. No one is in a position to make certain the free media placements reach the intended audience.

While the advertising associations claim that donated time and space are worth millions of dollars each year, their estimates are a tad bogus. For almost every vehicle, and especially with radio and television spots, PSAs tend to be used as time or space "fillers" for slots that would otherwise go unsold. As something no one wants to buy, the real market value is zero. And the times when the commercials run reflect this.

Some broadcasters claim to run a large number of commercials in support of specific campaigns, but the spots tend to appear in late night or other fringe periods. Under even the best PSA schedules with the greatest number of spots, a review found the commercials reaching a small percentage of total households, and even this small audience might not have been the people desired for the campaigns.[6] And if no one sees the message, there are serious doubts as to whether most of these campaigns possess hope of accomplishing anything, meaning that their only "value" is to the people producing them.

In an old joke, a minister's funeral prayer is repeatedly interrupted by an old Jewish woman who repeatedly yells, "Give him some chicken soup! Give him some chicken soup." The minister finally responds in measured tones, saying, "Madam, it's too late. It wouldn't help." "Well," she says with some thought, "it wouldn't hurt."

It could be argued that with PSAs, the time or space is donated, so there is no harm. It wouldn't hurt. Advertising agencies, producers, and media groups use these donated commercial productions as examples of their high-quality work; they meet high production standards, often win creative awards and are proudly included as part of an agency's work resumé. The public can't tell the difference between these donated commercials and those that are produced or placed as part of a purchased effort.

On the other hand, even with donated media time and space, there are still costs involved. And not all public interest advertising campaigns are PSAs. In other countries that lack the traditions of the U.S. Advertising Council, the advertising-based campaigns draw on government tax funds or limited resources of a public group. Even in the United States, many new campaigns purchase media time and space, hiring salaried advertising professionals to write, produce, or buy the time and space for the ads. These funded efforts might have better executed tactics, but the budgets are still limited. It is difficult to place the messages where they can be seen or heard by the targeted audiences often enough to have any persuasive power.

And even when spending millions of dollars of government funds or donated money from public interest groups, the efforts to change public behaviors often have a misplaced overreliance on advertising.

So they do "hurt." Sick people become dead people when they rely on alternative medicines instead of seeing a doctor. Similarly, public service advertising makes people feel good by giving the impression that something is being done, but other options are ignored while no one does the work that would better reach and persuade people who are at risk. And since total funds to deal with the problem are finite, ineffective advertising draws money from other activities.

THE BLOODY IDIOTS BEHIND THE WHEEL

Starting in 1989, Australia's Traffic Accident Commission in Victoria undertook an intensive paid advertising campaign to encourage safe driving practices; the New Zealand Land Transport Safety Authority started a similar advertising effort in 1995. However, while the Australian campaign claimed success with a concurrent reduction in the number of highway accidents and fatalities, the New Zealand effort was unable to make comparable claims, with at least one academic study noting that any link between the campaign and changes in the New Zealand road toll to be tenuous at best.[7]

The probable reasons for the difference provide a strong example of misplaced faith in the power of advertising to change behaviors. The Australian advertising was probably not as successful as they claimed, and definitely not for the reasons the Victorian government wanted to believe.

In both countries, the publicly funded ads used intense images to appeal to the drivers' fears, showing both gory outcomes from not getting enough rest, driving at excessive speeds, driving drunk or failing to wear seat belts. Death and disabling injuries were shown in graphic detail with a slogan, "If you [don't wear a seat belt; drink and then drive; drive too fast; etc.], you're a bloody idiot."

A young woman who loosened her seat belt to whisper to her boyfriend goes flying through the windshield and then, weeks later, is crying as her maimed and disfigured body fights through physical therapy. The speeding and boisterous crew of youngsters zooms through a stop sign and gets hit by a truck, ending with scenes of survivors screaming and crying over their friends' bodies. The sleepy driver flies off the road and wraps his car around a tree. The drunk teen is goofing off while driving, has a terrible smash-up with a truck, and, later, on his back in the hospital with his head and body in a brace, he cries, "I killed my brother!" who was the passenger. A group of drunken young people roll the car off the road, laughing all the way, but as the still-laughing driver crawls free of the wreckage that trapped his friends, the car bursts into flames as viewers watch and hear (along with the driver) the death screams of the passengers. A New Zealand print ad shows a young and generally fit-looking man in near-fetal position in a wheelchair, while the copy at the side only says, "If you drink then drive, you're a bloody idiot," indicating that drunk driving is what put him in such a sorry position.

Comparable advertising efforts have been undertaken in the United States, though they have tended to avoid portrayals of such extreme and intensely graphic accident outcomes.[8] Still, while the U.S. non-government sponsors are proud of the advertising work, the actual impact on driving practices is questionable and uncertain.

In all instances, government or public interest groups presume they have done the job if their supporters believe that more people are generally "thinking" about safety. But since money for improving traffic conditions and reducing road fatalities is finite, advertising spending logically reduces funding for other activities, such as enforcement of traffic laws.

And therein lies the basic difference between the campaigns in New Zealand and Australia, and why any U.S. campaign would have limited impact.

In Australia, the advertising campaign coincided with increased enforcement of relevant laws. Hidden speed cameras photographed and ticketed the fast-moving drivers. Traffic would be stopped at almost any time or location where police-owned trailers, called "booze buses," would test all motorists and all drivers who were drunk faced immediate arrest and loss of their license. Laws requiring seat belts are strictly enforced, with unbuckled passengers and drivers getting tickets for violations.[9] It should be intuitively obvious that once young drivers see tickets, fines and other penalties as a very likely outcome for their unsafe driving, they will change their behavior.

This logically explains the difference between the Australian experience and that in New Zealand and the United States. In New Zealand, the traffic stops by booze buses are restricted to certain areas or times of the week and, apparently, they are easy to avoid. New Zealand speed cameras are tied to warning signs, saying the driver is entering a "speed camera area." I even saw signs saying, "You are leaving the speed camera area." And being caught by a speed camera in New Zealand only means a fine without any points against a driver's record. In the United States, radar detectors are legal in all except two states and police often must chase and catch individual speeders one at a time, making traffic violations a cat-and-mouse game for motorists. Australian limits for blood alcohol are lower than those in the United States, and U.S. police spot checks for drunk drivers are rare; license revocations or suspensions are even rarer.

By the Traffic Accident Council's own data, road deaths and injuries in Victoria, Australia, were generally declining from a high in 1970 even before the "successful" advertising campaign started. With the newly increased enforcement efforts undertaken at the same time as the advertising, there was a major immediate drop, but that had leveled off by 1992. In 1999, a discussion of new measures to encourage further drops listed many efforts or programs—lower speed limits on residential streets; alcohol ignition interlock devices; safety programs to improve roads or car features—but conspicuous by its absence was any mention of new advertising.

APPEALS TO FEAR

If some people can be persuaded by mass media messages, then decision makers should first ask who these people are and why they would change their behaviors before deciding what or how to advertise. If these questions aren't asked, useless advertising results. And the same intrinsic misplaced marketing problem of section I also applies to public service advertising campaigns: what the target audience considers important may be vastly different from what the people making the messages consider important.

Good advertising requires a recognition that the audience's motives are rarely the same as what the decision makers presume, but public health officials are very reluctant to admit this. Not having the time, money, or inclination to conduct research, mistaken of impressions of how people think make for misdirected messages.

There might exist a group of drivers in every country that could be persuaded by advertising to drive safely. And if this is true, they might change their behavior out of a fear of what could happen if they do something unsafe. But, first and foremost, ads need to appeal to something that the drivers consider important.

Logically, people would not do things that are self-destructive. No sane person wants to die. Yet showing threats of death and injury from reckless driving do not seem to have much impact on young motorists. Either they do not fear death or they do not see the accident as something that could happen to them. Unfortunately, even when business professionals design public health campaigns, mythology about how an audience thinks has come to outweigh insight. Sometimes the advertising people are not much better "experts" on this than the public health officials.

Many years ago, in the hallway outside a government agency's hearing on advertising regulation issues, a staff member repeated to me a statement found in many marketing textbooks, that there is "an optimum level of fear" for audience persuasion. In reference to the above road safety cases, this would mean that the New Zealand advertising messages were too strong and gory, not hitting on the audience's "optimal level of fear" for persuasion. Of course, the agency staffer was not talking about public safety campaigns. Instead, he was making what he thought was a valid point, based on his belief that audience-manipulating marketing people know exactly where that optimal point is located.

He was trying to tell me why he personally disliked any use of fear to sell products, calling it "consumer manipulation," but his stated belief triggered several skeptical reactions on my part. While I had also read the textbook assertions of this optimal persuasion point, I doubted that the marketing professionals were so sagacious as to intuitively divine where it might be located. If he were correct, advertising copywriters could always tell what types of campaigns worked best for any audience, something I knew to be false. Curious, I started my own review of the extensive literature on mass communications appeals to audience fears.

The academic literature mostly traces its origins to two psychological studies almost five decades ago. Groups of subjects were presented with different versions of an illustrated lecture on dental hygiene and each version stated a different degree of harm that could be an outcome of dental neglect. In the studies, what the researchers designated as the weaker "fear appeals"—though (as I will explain shortly) it should be more appropriately called "weaker threats" or "appeals to audience fears"—were more effective in getting high school students to adopt the recommended tooth-care procedures.[10]

In an almost offhand comment attempting to explain the results, the authors speculated that there might exist "an optimal level of fear" for audience persuasion. This comment has formed at least a partial basis for most marketing research in the following decades and, to this date, most new academic studies published in marketing journals start by stating either that there is some (unknown) "optimal level of fear" to maximize persuasion power, or, after citing two or three journal articles from the many hundreds published since 1952, simply state that past research data are "mixed" in support of the existence of a moderate amount of fear being optimal for consumer persuasion.

One would think that if the data are repeatedly "mixed" after decades of data collection, the theory would be discarded as unsupported. Instead, marketing researchers elevated the concept of an "optimal level fear" to that of dogma.[11] In any event, the advertising managers are not as all-knowing as their clients would like to think. As a result of advertisers' arrogance and their clients' trust, they both end up almost clueless as to what the audience really fears or why. Instead, they base the advertising on their own fears.

In addition, they fail to make a basic distinction between threats and fear. And this problem gets even worse with various public health advertising efforts to encourage safe driving, discourage cigarette smoking, or promote safe sexual activities.

Threats illustrate undesirable consequences from certain behaviors, such as damage to a car, bodily injury, or death from unsafe driving, or bad breath, breathing problems, or cancer from cigarette smoking. However, fear is an emotional response to threats, and different people fear different things. No threat evokes the same response from all people. A threat is an appeal to fear, a message that attempts to evoke a fear response by showing some type of outcome that the members of the audience might want to avoid. Fear is an actual emotional response that might prompt changes in a person's attitude or behaviors.

Research has consistently found that the strongest persuasive power comes from telling the audience how to avoid the outcome it fears the most. Many literature reviews and meta-analysis of past research data have shown that the greater the actual fear engendered by a communication, the greater the persuasion.[12] But strong threats do not necessarily evoke strong fear responses with all possible audiences because different people fear different things. The strongest, goriest, or most deadly outcomes might not be readily feared.

MINOR SIDETRACK: AUDIENCE SEGMENTATION

The distinction between threats and audience fears also shows how a basic tool for marketing planning, namely, audience segmentation, is misplaced and otherwise lost in public health advertising campaigns.

The term "market segmentation" has been mentioned enough in the popular press or television news that it has entered the general consciousness: marketing efforts target specific groups by offering certain product features or advertised benefits that the group is expected to prefer. What is often misunderstood, however, is that no segment's response is a certainty. A defined market or audience segment is, at best, a probability. The people fitting the definition are more likely to respond in an expected or desired fashion than people who do not belong to that group. Some people inside the segment might not respond as expected; some people outside the group will respond favorably to things not "aimed" at them. In others words, there only exists an increased likelihood that members of market segments will respond in the expected fashion.

The segment itself is not something intrinsic in a person. A segment is a collection of data that describes commonalities found in groups of people.

Broadly speaking, there are two types of data used to define segments: (1) demographic data, such as age, gender, race, or income, which comprise a physical description of a person or group; and (2) various forms of psychological or "mental" data, such as lifestyles, attitudes or beliefs, that give more detailed descriptions of how people think. Logically, mental data are better predictors of how people think or act than a physical description of who they are. There are many demographic similarities between President Reagan's daughter Maureen and Jane Fonda, for example, or between Al Gore and George W. Bush, but no one would dare assert that these pairs are psychologically the same person. And yet, when discussing audiences of public interest campaigns, the physical data are presented as determinant and other inputs often ignored.

The advertiser's primary use of demographic data is in buying media time or space, since that is how the mass media define their audiences. Mostly because of the prohibitive expense and difficulty involved in gathering more information, the makeup of audiences of a television program, radio station, cable network, or newspaper are provided to advertisers with little insight beyond broad demographic characteristics. However, since an advertising campaign is trying to inform and persuade a target audience, the crucial data indicate how people think. The psychological data tell this story, not the demographic.

And therein lies the real problem with public health campaigns for traffic safety, AIDS prevention, or antismoking efforts that appeal to audience fears. The ads are written from what the advertising writers fear, or they simply presume that death and destruction is a most-feared outcome. They show young people in the ads, but they do not really think in terms of threats that the targeted young people could or would actually fear the most. Failing to understand the values and concerns of the groups most at risk, they fail to alter the behaviors of those people engaged in unsafe behaviors.[13]

For example, efforts to get children to brush their teeth tend to focus on the dangers and harm from tooth decay, but the very young tend to see dental visits and fillings as almost minor distractions. It surprises me when I hear dentists tell children to brush their teeth by phrasing the concerns in terms of health or hygiene. Some small children actually enjoy getting fillings, since it confers a certain degree of bragging rights on the playground; small boys might compete for who has the worst breath. Deep down, the dentists know this. Every dentist I have ever asked about what gets children to realize the importance of dental care gives me the same answer: "Puberty!" When children are old enough to care about social interactions, they brush their teeth to help themselves look and smell better.

The "America Responds to AIDS" advertising campaign was an ongoing effort to encourage young "at risk" populations to refrain from unsafe sexual behaviors or drug use. And when I show the commercials to my undergraduate students (who, I might add, are the primary target for the television spots), they laugh. As the marketing director of a condom manufacturer explained to us when visiting the class, today's college students have lived with AIDS their entire lives and consider the most current appeals to "safe sex" humorous, not presenting anything to really fear. Messages that advertisers presume would engender intense audience fear reactions are, instead, easily ignored. Since most at-risk youths are already aware of the dangers, the advertising is only preaching to the converted.

It is intuitively obvious that the optimal type of threat to persuade many teens to stop smoking would be to show that smokers have trouble getting dates. The students are told that it will cause lung cancer, but high school students with the arrogant confidence of youth would not see that as personally probable. Young people think they can smoke without getting cancer and they are right, at least in the short run. Damage to their health is far in the future. Studies of various types of warning labels would imply that under a "forbidden fruit" theory, antismoking advertising that obviously comes from a parental or adult world view might backfire and encourage more young people to take up smoking.[14]

This is not just an issue of how to encourage young people not to smoke, since antismoking messages have been singularly ineffective in changing adult behavior, too. The cancer threat is known to smokers, but they apparently fail to see it as relevant or realistic. Logically, even educated and intelligent adults are moved more by sex or dating issues than concerns for their health. I know several people my age who kept smoking after a close friend or relative died from cancer, only to quit when they started dating a nonsmoker. Despite smoking bans, publicity on numerous lawsuits, and many antismoking advertising efforts, the smoking rate among U.S. adults was unaltered during the 1990s. Tobacco critics blame this lack of success on the addictive power of nicotine, and no one seems to say that maybe the public service advertising doesn't give anyone a reason for not smoking that they would accept.

Talking with college students in Australia and New Zealand, I would quickly hear that they saw the traffic safety commercials' portrayals of death, destruction, and severe injury as threatened outcomes that would be feared *by people other than themselves*. Almost none of them perceived the strong threats as something that could happen to them; the imagery was personally relevant only to people who had experienced such an event or knew someone close to them who had been injured in a major accident. What they would fear would be the loss of their license, or even paying a high price for speeding tickets.

Their comments, plus logical intuition, indicates that law enforcement and the threat of fines or a lost license is realistic and relevant for all drivers. But they didn't fear the death and destruction shown in the ads. In Australia, some of the commercials focused on law enforcement practices that were initiated or increased during the same period and the other ads spotlighted gory outcomes. It might have been only those law enforcement messages and practices that changed public behaviors.

Laws can only do so much. They must be enforced or the public, knowing they are irrelevant, will ignore them. Various laws all over the United States now require car passengers to wear seat belts, but these laws are not strictly enforced and are among the most readily disregarded of all safe driving requirements.[15] Similarly, areas where drunk driving or speed laws are not enforced would probably find the motorists most likely to engage in unsafe behaviors.

At best, advertising can only engender very small and moderate changes in weakly held attitudes. Since it works best when it provides information that fits with attitudes people already hold, the effectiveness of any advertising effort depends on either encouraging the audience's current beliefs or giving them sound logical rationales that are not strongly contrary to those beliefs.

A traffic law is written not to change how people think but to make them behave in the proper fashion. Drivers don't care if those around them are thinking about safety, but they would like to presume that those on the road with them are awake and sober. Finite funds might be better spent with the first priority on law enforcement. By airing commercials showing death and destruction instead of raising the threat of law enforcement, governments' misdirected efforts become an example of misplaced social marketing.

DON'T SING OR DANCE
WITHOUT MARKETING SENSE

In the movie *The Mask*, the main character is trapped by police and gets away by singing and dancing, creating a magical compulsion for all of the officers to join in. In the old *Andy Hardy* movies with Mickey Rooney and Judy Garland, the characters often solved problems by putting on some type of show. The characters would need to quickly raise money for some cause or they would try to save the day by being just so darn cute. Of course, audiences knew it was just a script device, an excuse for the stars to sing and dance. As a movie, pragmatic logic was not a concern, but it is amazing how many real-world problems also turn to entertaining advertising as a solution.

There do exist examples of successful communications efforts that are locally targeted, carefully planned and appeal to the values of a closely defined audience. Over the long term, some campaigns can change the public agenda, increasing public awareness and changing general perceptions of issues previously ignored. In Australia, where the Antarctic ozone hole has boosted the incidence of skin cancer, a long-running, mostly positive advertising campaign has generated greater public awareness of the need for people to wear hats and sunscreen outdoors. However, many people still prefer not to wear hats for style concerns and don't want to mess with lotions.

But, in most cases, advertising can't do anything to help solve the problem and the often-lost initial analysis from a marketing point of view would reveal this. Instead, for a variety of reasons, the people involved with public health issues acquire a misplaced trust in the power of advertising to change the world.

The world is not a movie. Advertising is not magic. Maybe, sometimes, in some ways, it can encourage some good changes in some people, but that weak collection of "maybes" is not a valid basis for all the faith placed in it by people wanting to serve social goals. Whether in business or to serve social goals, a marketing decision maker should use advertising only if it is more efficient than other means of doing a particular job. And for the deep-seated problems behind many social ills, mass media advertising is a very weak or near-useless tool.

NOTES

1. Jacqueline Kochak, "Rape Problem Now Being Addressed," *Opelika-Auburn News* (February 17, 2000), pp. 1A, 2A.

2. The organization's Web page, available at www.breastcancerfund.org, which was established to help generate donations, also includes a link to the "Obsessed With Breasts" ad campaign. These associated pages provide detailed background and a businesslike statement of the goals of the campaign, reviews of how the publicity fit those goals, links to the news articles that the controversy generated, and copies of the billboards and bus shelter ads that were the focus of attention.

3. In this unfortunate case, children should be told not to blindly run in front of the bus and presume that everyone obeys the law. Laws requiring all traffic to stop for school buses are designed to limit problems for children who carelessly rush to or from the vehicles, not so lazy adults can avoid helping small children who have yet to learn road safety. Advertising to motorists would not alter the need for the bus drivers to watch the children as they cross.

4. For example, see Robert S. Adler and R. David Pittle, "Cajolery or Command: Are Education Campaigns an Adequate Substitute for Regulation?" *Yale Journal of Regulation*, vol. 1 (no. 2, 1984), pp. 159–193; Hae-Kyong Bang, "Misplacing the Media Role in Social Marketing Public Health," *Journal of Consumer Marketing*, vol. 17 (no. 6, 2000), pp. 279–280; Brian R. Flay and Thomas D. Cook, "Evaluation of Mass Media Prevention Campaigns," in R. E. Rice and C. K. Atkin, eds., *Public Communications Campaigns* (Beverly Hills,

CA: Sage, 1981), pp. 239–264; Walter Gantz, Michael Fitzmaurice, and E. Yoo, "Seat Belt Campaigns and Buckling Up: Do the Media Make A Difference?" *Health Communication*, vol. 2 (1990), pp. 1–12; William J. McGuire, "Public Communications as a Strategy of Inducing Health Promoting Behavior Change," *Preventive Medicine*, vol. 13 (1984), pp. 299–319; David G. Schmeling and C. Edward Wotring, "Agenda-Setting Effects of Drug Abuse Public Service Ads," *Journalism Quarterly*, vol. 53 (no. 4, 1976), pp. 743–747.

5. While modern, politically correct sensibilities would denigrate "crying Indian" as a negative term, this has always been the name of the commercial, it is used as a label or description when the spot won awards, it is the name that is still used in textbooks to describe the spot. I didn't create the name; I'm just using it.

6. Alyse R. Gotthoffer and Kent M. Lancaster, "Estimating the Audience Coverage of PSAs: The Ad Council's Drunk Driving Prevention Campaign," *Journal of Advertising Research*, vol. 41 (May–June 2001).

7. Terry Macpherson and Tony Lewis, "New Zealand Drink-Driving Statistics: The Effectiveness of Road Safety Television Advertising," *Marketing Bulletin*, vol. 9 (1998): pp. 40–51. Another study questioned whether Macpherson and Lewis were correct, but also concluded that the money might have been better spent on enforcement of other noncommunications activities. Richard Tay, "Effectiveness of the Anti-Drink Driving Advertising Campaign in New Zealand," *Road and Transport Research*, vol. 18 (December 1999), pp. 3–15.

8. One of the people involved with the U.S. campaign expressed her belief during a radio news interview that Americans would not respond to the kind of images used on the other side of the world. That may be true, though even more graphic videos are often shown to U.S. high school students and are used in some driver education programs. As will be explained in Chapter 8, a more logical explanation for the greater "restraint" from gore in the U.S. campaign is that most television stations and networks would not broadcast the more graphic commercials.

9. Australians are also barred from talking on the phone while driving. Despite strong evidence that this distraction increases the probability of accidents, the U.S. state and local governments have been reluctant to pass a similar restriction. A Congressman called a radio talk show on his car phone to argue against such a new law and was in an accident during the conversation.

10. Irving L. Janis and S. Feshbach, "Effects of Fear-Arousing Communications," *Journal of Abnormal and Social Psychology*, vol. 48 (January 1953), pp. 78–92; Irving L. Janis and S. Feshbach, "Personality Differences Associated with Responsiveness to Fear-Arousing Communications," *Journal of Personality*, vol. 23 (December 1954), pp. 154–166.

11. It could be argued that the theory has such staying power in spite of a lack of support because it has been adopted by the textbooks. Herbert Jack Rotfeld, "The Textbook Effect: Conventional Wisdom, Myth, and Error in Marketing," *Journal of Marketing*, vol. 64 (April 2000), pp. 122–126.

12. Franklin J. Boster and Paul Mongeau, "Fear-Arousing Persuasive Messages," *Communications Yearbook 8*, Robert N. Bostrom, ed. (Beverly Hills, CA: Sage, 1984), pp. 330–375; Herbert J. Rotfeld, "Fear Appeals and Persuasion: Assumptions and Errors in Advertising Research," *Current Issues and Research*

in Advertising, vol. 11 (1988), pp. 21–40; Stephen R. Sutton, "Fear-Arousing Communications: A Critical Examination of Theory and Research," in *Social Psychology and Behavioral Medicine*, J. Richard Eiser, ed. (New York: John Wiley & Sons, 1982), pp. 303–337; Stephen R. Sutton, "Shock Tactics and the Myth of the Inverted U," *British Journal of Addiction*, vol. 87 (April 1992), pp. 517–519.

13. Robert P. Bush, David J. Ortinau, and Alan J. Bush, "Personal Value Structures and AIDS Prevention: Are Safe-Sex Messages Reaching High Risk Groups or Merely Preaching to the Converted?" *Journal of Health Care Marketing*, vol. 14 (Spring 1994), pp. 12–20.

14. Many people have asserted that the "don't smoke" ads run by cigarette companies might have the opposite effect on the targeted youth, resulting in increased smoking behaviors. The intent of such criticisms are cynical attacks on the tobacco industry, but such an outcome is logical in that it has been shown with alcohol warnings, television viewer advisories (as are discussed in Chapter 8), and warning information on full-fat foods. L. B. Snyder and D. J. Blood, "Caution: Alcohol Advertising and the Surgeon General's Warnings May Have Adverse Effects on Young Adults," *Journal of Applied Communication Research*, vol. 20 (1992), pp. 37–53; B. J. Bushman and A. D. Stack, "Forbidden Fruit Versus Tainted Fruit: Effects of Warning Labels on Attraction to Television Violence," *Journal of Experimental Psychology: Applied*, vol. 2 (1996), pp. 207–226; Brad J. Bushman, "Effects of Warning and Information Labels on Consumption of Full-Fat, Reduced-Fat and No-Fat Products," *Journal of Applied Psychology*, vol. 83 (no. 1, 1988), pp. 97–101.

15. Some state laws have an exemption for drivers of pickup trucks so they don't have to wear the belts. In Georgia and Indiana, adult passengers can ride in the open rear gate area of the truck, which makes a belt irrelevant and makes a mockery of the law itself.

6

A Trade Association Serving Itself

I find myself frequently repeating a line from the sword and sorcery novels of Robert E. Howard, in which his most famous creation, Conan the Barbarian, says that "Being a king is easy as long as you remember what it was like at the other end of the scepter." A marketing perspective is often lost by managers who fail to consider the needs or values of people unlike themselves, but the elected leaders of professional associations should readily apply marketing perspectives. After all, the leaders of even the largest trade associations, labor unions, or advocacy groups were once general members themselves. A member-as-consumer focus should be intuitively obvious for them.

And yet, by the time these men or women become organization leaders, they are so far removed from their time as members that they forget their prior lives. Some seem to become more enamored of being leaders than of serving the members; as a result, the association loses track of those it is supposed to serve. Or maybe it is just a story of the giant who gets too big to see its own shoes.

When trade-association marketing becomes misplaced, some organizations retain members by virtue of sheer market power. The oldest or largest groups retain members who feel they are not served but still feel "forced" to pay dues.

This is especially true when these groups try to serve both educators and practitioners, such as professional or business associations. The educators might even be involved in the leadership and be elected to the top management positions, but, regardless of their roots, a leader loses a marketing focus by forgetting the interests of the people who are members.

ARROGANCE IN PRICING DECISIONS

One spring not too long ago, a large trade association for business educators and professionals announced that it would be raising annual membership dues by 25 percent. Dues increases are not uncommon; organizations raise membership fees all the time. What bothered some members of this group were the reasons given for the change. The members were told in the newsletter that the organization needed the increase to keep up with inflation since the last increase. Instead of explaining that the money was needed to provide services to members, an article in the members' magazine explained that the final dues level was based on a market comparison to dues charged by several other trade associations.

At a basic level, the stated reasons for the increase itself show an old production orientation on the organization's part, starting all planning based on what leaders want to do. They did not follow a marketing perspective, neglecting to start planning with consumer (in this case, member) concerns. Judging from the comments on electronic, member-oriented bulletin boards after the announced dues increase, many members, especially among the educators, felt that the association's leadership had lost touch with them. Still, the commenting people noted that they wouldn't quit because they still saw membership in this large group as necessary for their jobs.

A marketing orientation for a nonprofit trade association should be based on some assessment of how much money is needed to provide services to members. With this in mind, keeping up with inflation or assessments of competitor charges may possibly be relevant, but they should not be the determining factors.

A pricing approach based primarily on elasticity of demand, instead of the organization's financial needs, also could be seen in the prices this same group set for various member conferences. Some conferences, especially those for educators, charged registration fees of $250 to $500, but a list published in 1999 of upcoming conferences included a one-day event for practitioners with a registration price of more than $1,500 for members. They probably found that employers would be willing to pay the high price for an educational program for practitioners on an important subject.

At some level the association's employees and leaders realize that the needs or concerns of educators are at least slightly different from those of practitioners, since the registration fees for the semiannual educators' conferences are much lower than any practitioner event they run. On the other hand, staff members have frequently indicated to insiders a desire to price the academic conferences even higher.

The association's leadership tried to give an additional explanation of the dues increase to the educators in an article in a magazine that was printed and distributed as part of the dues to all the group's education-based members. Written and bylined by the elected chairman of the board, the article admitted that, prior to the dues increase, a member survey had indicated that educators already felt that the dues were too high, while the marketing practitioners had indicated a willingness to pay dues as much as three times higher.

These distinct reactions to dues should not have seemed unusual to the elected leaders. In fact, they had some research data that told them both why the difference existed and what they could do about it.

Several years previously, a survey of members included a question about who pays the member's dues. About 95 percent of practitioners reported that all dues and expenses were paid by the employer and roughly the same percentage of educators reported paying it themselves. The Board of Directors meeting where this survey data were discussed illustrated their limited mind set and preconceived notions about member values. According to a person who was there, the conversation reportedly went something like this:

"There must have been some error in the coding of the data," one person observed.

"Why an error?"

"We have the same numbers but they are reversed. Ninety-five percent of practitioners are supported by the firm and 95 percent of educators pay themselves. The person coding the data must have accidentally reversed this item."

"Like hell they did," a few educators on the board reportedly said. "In fact, we want to know who is that 5 percent of educators who managed to get these things paid by the school."

As it later was revealed, the 5 percent of educators who did not pay their own way held endowed chairs or were senior administrators at colleges or universities. As every educator knows, even when general faculty get support for travel to conferences, the dollar amounts tend to be very restricted. Only educators with the top salaries have their own support funds to pay for membership dues or other association charges.

So it should have surprised no one that there were two distinct groups of members—one viewing the dues as too high, and the other saying they were lower than expected. The obvious marketing reaction should have been differential pricing, charging the two groups—educators and practitioners—different prices to match their personal needs or interests.

This would not be unusual at other associations. Government or business-oriented groups often invite educators to join with fees greatly reduced from those charged to the business-supported members. Most academic associations charge lower dues for student members, or for graduate students who had yet to take their first salaried position.

However, the leaders of this large trade association did not seem to even consider differential prices for two groups of regular members. Rather, they simply announced the different views, saying that such a "vote" via the member surveys could be seen as support for the increase, thereby showing the limited marketing mind set of the people in charge.

Maybe the leaders forgot what it was like at the other end of the scepter. Around the time that the dues increase was announced, another member publication for this group included a photo feature, supposedly presented to give the members a positive view of the association and its leaders. In it, the chairman was attending a special function and, in the picture, he was shown in conversation with Jane Fonda and her then-husband, Ted Turner.

"OUR LAWYERS SAY . . . "

Any large professional organization needs to consult with attorneys now and then, especially if it runs conferences or publishes journals, books, and magazines that involve issues of copyright. Yet, for some groups, like the store managers in Chapter 3 who treated customers as nuisances, lawyers can encourage an adversarial or power mentality when dealing with members. Instead of serving members' needs, the lawyers could become an enforcement tool of that power.

The editor of an association's newsletterlike magazine visited the group's Web pages and was surprised when he found the full content of his last issue posted there. He did not have a generic concern that the material was posted, especially since some of it was general news or information for members. However, article writers were never told that their work would be posted, nor were they asked for permission. Some of the pictures were sent to the main offices with copyright statements on the back; one article had previously been published in a copyrighted book and was reprinted in the magazine after the author's permission for the printed version of the magazine was obtained.

The editor's concern was courtesy to the authors, and he saw the solution as simple: Ask them.

"I would like to publish your paper in our small-circulation magazine. And once the printed copies are distributed, we would also like to reprint it by posting the issue on the association's Web page. Is that okay with you?"

"Sure. Why not. Go ahead."

Instead, in consultation with attorneys, the association leaders decided that all contributors to the magazine would be required to sign away full copyright to the association prior to publication, giving the trade group reprint rights, as well as the power to sell the article to others. The association opted for power over members instead of working with them. In a similar vein, when planning to acquire an Internet e-mail discussion list, leaders and lawyers initially wanted to include a notice that all statements on the free-wheeling discussion line would become the association's copyright property.

Some aspect of legal actions are understandable, but others are plainly petty, serving merely to enhance the association's power instead of responding to member needs.

Another interesting example of legal overkill arose several years ago when a number of university faculty were sharing a suite of rooms at a conference center for their professional association meeting. Only some of them were attending the conference or presenting research papers, but all of them were involved in interviewing potential new faculty members from the soon-to-graduate doctoral students who were in the city for the event. As circumstances had it, one of the men who was not registered for the conference needed to find a person who was at a meeting session downstairs. It was personal. Apparently he was spotted by an officer of the association or some other employee. Even though he did not attend any sessions or meals, shortly after he returned home he received a letter from an attorney demanding payment for full conference registration.

No one would argue that people should not sneak into conferences without registering, and every academic association has a right to protect the copyright to its journals. But there are so many examples where a large association's first response is to call in lawyers.

Lawyers are, by the very nature of the job, adversarial. But being adversarial runs contrary to the marketing concerns of a trade or professional association, which should be to serve member interests.

A STRANGE CASE

You would think that a professional association would be the least likely to lose a consumer orientation for members. After all, unlike almost any other business or organization described in this book, the managers who make decisions for these organizations have a great deal in common with the members. Yet, for some of these groups, especially the largest, there are two basic forces that may be operating against it.

First, the leaders tend to be senior professionals in their employing organizations, many years removed from their days as typical rank-and-file members. They are senior business managers or owners, partners in the firm. If the association also has educators in these top posts, they tend to be senior administrators at their universities or holders of endowed chairs. And second, many of the large and established trade groups are run from central offices with a large infrastructure of non-member employees, including a salaried set of executive officers and other staff who carry out the day-to-day operations. These employees have never been members.

Ever time I hear a story of another trade or professional group that misplaces marketing in the treatment of members, I try to see if the problem is not its leadership, but, rather, the disconnected mentality of employees who refuse to think. When a man joined one international group, he indicated that he would join the Montreal chapter, since that was where he lived. From that point onward, all his correspondence from the group was in French, prompting a comment that if you were not fluent in French, you should either join a different chapter, buy a dictionary, or find a French spouse. Apparently, no one asked what language he spoke and no one noticed that all his prior correspondence had been in English.

Sometimes the arrogance that drives the misplaced marketing comes from the top. These groups are run by people, and all the flaws of business are also found in trade groups. Just because it is a nonprofit, member-based organization does not make it immune from losing a marketing perspective. When that happens, power or profits become a larger priority for leaders than the consumer-oriented marketing of services for members.

7

Government "Serving" the Consumers' Interest

In my version of a very old joke, a physicist, an engineer, an economist, a lawyer, and a marketing manager are shipwrecked on a deserted island, having salvaged only a box of canned food from their sunken ship. The physicist says, "If we put a can on the fire, molecules would speed up and expand in the can, forcing it to open from the built-up pressure." The engineer says, "I think I can design a containment tray so we can catch and hold any of the food that might come out of the can as it opens." The economist then says, "Assume we have a can opener. . . ." Using the economist's assumptions, the lawyer writes rules for allocating the food based on each person's expected nutritional and emotional needs, complete with detailed procedures for appeals by people who feel they need an extra share.

Meanwhile, the marketing manager walks away from the theoretical debate and wanders down the beach in search of wood or stones that could work like a can opener. Faced with starvation, everyone except the marketing manager seems to say, "Reality? That's an interesting concept."

Obviously, a person's education and vocation influence how problems and potential solutions are perceived. Even as castaways, the physicist and the engineer had some complicated and less-than-useful ideas on how to get to the canned food. The economist and lawyer just presumed that the cans would be opened and worried about what to do next. The marketing person went looking for some makeshift tools that would open the cans to serve everyone's needs.

The misplaced marketing problem is that economists, engineers, and lawyers write many laws and enforce government regulations based on their worldview and presumptions of how they believe people should think or act. Marketing's consumer-oriented perspective gives additional insight into how consumers actually respond to proposed regulatory actions, asking key questions about what government organizations hope to accomplish and how those goals fit with consumer needs or wants. While marketing people can't dictate laws and regulations, they should be able to provide evidence when legal decisions are made.

This is not to say that marketing views are always lost or ignored. The Federal Trade Commission (FTC) regularly hires marketing consultants, but their views are never central to the decisions being made. And other agencies write marketing regulations without any reference to market research. Too often, even when laws and regulations are based on presumptions of how segments of consumers will respond to various marketplace situations, lawyers use a combination of their own intuition plus evidence from economists and (sometimes) engineers to decide on how marketing "works."

As on the island, when marketing is misplaced, the resulting regulations might have little, if anything, to do with reality.

MISSING THE MARKETING ANALYSIS

There is a historic logic here. Regulatory agencies are law enforcement organizations. And the legislation setting up the agencies are often aimed at theoretical economic concerns, not the marketing view.

And sometimes the lawyers or economists fear a power marketing is presumed to possess.

As noted in Chapter 1, a significant number of people see "marketing" as synonymous with "manipulation," an inherently evil distortion of consumers' freedom of choice. To the lawyers, economists, and other regulatory agency staff members who accept this worldview, economic analysis gives a better view of consumers' rational choices, or so they think, while marketing manipulates consumers' desires. They apparently believe that engineers reveal how technology would serve people under a "pure" system that is free of marketing's "distortions."

Of course, some regulatory decisions make full use of a marketing perspective or expertise. Not all lawyers or economists have such negative or paranoid views of marketing. But Congress writes laws based on economic presumptions. And lawyers write regulations based on their presumptions about how people think. For insight into the marketplace, lawyers turn to economists, practitioners of the academic discipline with a lengthy tradition as the predominant basis for legal-regulatory analysis of markets and marketing.

By both law and tradition, regulatory commissioners are presumed to have expertise in how consumers respond to marketing tools. The law presumes that Federal Trade commissioners possess expertise about advertising theory and practice because it is the predominant government body involved with the regulation of advertising veracity.

If this sounds like the logic is getting a bit circular, it is. It's also a bit arrogant. The law says they can be marketing experts, so many of them believe that they are.

Regulatory commissioners' legally bestowed "expertise" on marketing is really just non-expert intuition. The well-educated public health doctors and specialists described in Chapter 5 retain their faith in advertising as a tool to influence the public, despite repeated evidence of public service campaigns that do not work. Similarly, just because lawyers are involved with government regulation of marketing issues, they are not privy to special insight. Instead, the government lawyers, economists, engineers, or doctors believe some distorted things about marketing, using data as valid as a supermarket tabloid's "proof" of the latest extraterrestrial landing on the White House lawn.

For example, a former Federal Trade commissioner once expressed his own view of marketing practice, showing his distorted perceptions of reality despite the "expertise" his office theoretically bestowed. He told reporters of his fear that if regulations required strict definitions of honesty, the advertisers would avoid regulatory scrutiny by "resorting to greater use of subliminal messages." The topic of subliminal advertising might be a focus of the public's popular paranoia, but all marketing professionals and educators know that it has never been (and never can be) a useful advertising tool.[1]

Similarly, when the Bureau of Alcohol, Tobacco and Firearms (ATF) updated rules for distilled product advertising, they included a ban on subliminal advertising that they feared might otherwise exist. Without any evidence that it was a real or potential problem, ATF apparently felt it was important enough to make it part of the rules and thereby state that they were against it.[2]

In those same ATF rules, beer advertisers also were directed for many years not to use "active" sports figures in commercials, though former players could endorse the products as long as they did not refer to the drink as a performance enhancer. The distinction is strange. I can't explain the difference between an image a consumer might hold of a person who has star power because of current prowess or because of past accomplishments. And it is doubtful that any modern advertiser would make such outlandish claims, as the regulators feared. Even after his retirement from basketball, Michael Jordan remains quite visible in advertising and could endorse a beer if he so chooses. But in the pragmatic realm of consumer decisions, the most gullible of childlike young men probably would not believe a statement that his talent came from a brewery.

"Michael Beer, the breakfast of champions!"

Well, this might become a commercial satire on *Saturday Night Live*.

For almost three decades, I have read articles in law, economics and medical journals that attempted to address marketing issues. And I have always been amazed at how often the authors did not appear to know or understand the most basic material in any undergraduate marketing or communications course. If an article or case report was written by a lawyer involved with marketing regulation, the author would assert his or her authority while still exhibiting a limited understanding of marketing terms or perspectives.[3]

This is not to assert that the lawyers are stupid. But marketing analysis is not part of legal education; lawyers' intuitive views of marketing are often in error. Their worldview and basic priorities deal with legal history and precedent, not communications theory and research. Under a legal worldview, a jurist's intuition decides a case based on consumer perspectives that he or she thinks exist, and those views of how people think are later repeated as having been "decided" in prior cases.

That is how the law works.

Legal precedents are the context for laws and regulations. And predominant views of any agency involved with regulation of marketing concerns are provided by lawyers, using evidence and expertise supplied by economists, scientists, and sometimes marketing people when determining how to best understand and apply laws. Doctors and lawyers at the Food and Drug Administration (FDA) are experts on drugs, and they properly use medical research to assess the nature and value of drugs or medical devices. But they also use this research to decide on legally acceptable methods for the products to be marketed. The Federal Communications Commission (FCC) uses engineers to help set technical standards for broadcasters, but these technical decisions also depend on assumptions about how audiences are expected to view or listen to the electronic media. FCC technical decisions deal with marketing problems while ignoring marketing perspectives.

To repeat, it is not that marketing expertise is never part of the regulatory evidence, but it is seldom accorded the value or centrality that might improve decisions specifically aimed at impacting the market.

IN ENGLISH, PLEASE

A few years ago, I entered a faculty office in the Auburn Department of Finance, finding three of my friends studying a newspaper ad with the help of note pads and calculators. An Atlanta car dealer was offering two different special sale options on new cars, so Charlie, Carl, and John were trying to figure out which was a better deal. The two options had different sets of purchase terms stated in combinations of down payments, annual percentage rates and other payment alternatives, and these three senior professors with doctorates in economics or finance from MIT and other respected universities were unable to discern which option would be more desirable.

None of them were intending to buy a new car. They were just curious. They could not understand why anyone would advertise using such recondite and abstruse language.

It is possible that the advertiser's goal was obfuscation. Perhaps the dealership was trying to deceive potential customers, and neither option was a real bargain. However, an equally likely explanation is that the advertisement simply contained the terms used for loan or payment disclosures. When cars are sold, these are the terms they are legally required to include on the forms, and no one provided plain English translations. The car dealer's advertising agency might have preferred some clearer language, but any advertising claims with financial terms usually must be screened and approved by the business' legal department. And even if the ad wording was clearer, purchasers still have to deal with these same confusing terms on the "disclosure" forms.

It is ironic and not uncommon. Few people are able to understand information that is legally required by government regulations aimed at helping purchasers make informed decisions.

Years ago, an economist gave me his view of a proper regulation goal: Even if only 2 percent of buyers select a product based on rational data, those data should be readily available and provided by the company. To some extent, laws and regulations attempt to meet this standard. They use standard terms in an effort to limit potential consumer deception and to force advertisers to provide easily understandable consumer information. While the car dealer's ad is an extreme example, the basic problem is that a consumer's "plain language" is not the same as a lawyer's.

Government regulations on advertising terms or product labels are drafted by lawyers whose world involves legally set standards for the interpretations of specific words. As a result, for a variety of products or services, specific words or terms are mandated, based on a legal presumption of what these words or terms mean.

This is how lawyers think: A word has a meaning because the law says that is what it means, and definitions are established by law and precedent.[4] Every first-year law student takes contact law, a course that focuses endless hours on how to interpret the terms of an agreement. A law dictionary provides a statement of how the law has agreed that certain words are to be defined.

But the legal view of language conflicts with reality when applied to consumers' actual use of words and their meanings in everyday life.

People do not read ads or labels as a legal contract. Businesses employ lawyers to write and interpret sales contracts, but people don't go to the store with a lawyer in tow. To an attorney, a legally accepted definition is exactly what a word means. Consumers, however, do not carry around a dictionary of "generally accepted terms" under their arms.

The discussion of market segmentation in Chapter 5 also shows another limitation of efforts by the law to "create" consumer information by mandating that certain words be used. Regulations can create standardized terms, but consumers won't necessarily understand them in a standardized fashion. Basic perspectives of marketing indicate that, at best, only *some* consumers possess an intuitive understanding of the terms in the manner the lawyers intended. While a large group of people are most likely to respond to literal content in the desired ways, lawyers presume that consumer responses are nearly universal. In reality, the lawyers are wrong.

Despite these marketing facts, lawyers at regulatory agencies often specify what literal terms can be used, believing they always will convey the information they want consumers to have.

With many household products making claims of the product's potential environmental impact, the FTC has specific guidelines for terms that can be used, though some states have their own legal definitions that contradict those of the FTC.[5] The FDA has specific terms for grades and quality of certain foods that, in theory, should provide information to consumers. Yet, in repeated surveys of highly educated shoppers, consumers are less than clear on what the terms mean. There are different legally accepted definitions for "alcohol-free" beer and beer that claims to have "no alcohol," but I doubt if many people know which allows the product to retain trace amounts.

Beyond interpretations of mandated terms, other laws presume how people respond to certain literal words.

Decades ago, University of Wisconsin–Madison mass communications scholar (and nonlawyer) Ivan Preston heard the confident legal statement that advertising puffery is considered incapable of deceiving consumers because no one would believe it. A law dictionary published thirty years ago described the logic for puffery law by first noting that "a superlative was a stronger statement than a comparative in standard English, but in commercial advertising, a superlative was a weaker statement because no one would believe it."[6] Curious about the consumer research that formulated such a strong and certain rule of law, Professor Preston studied the legal records to trace its origins. But instead of any consumer research or marketing analysis, he found a series of judicial assertions, legal precedents, and cases under British common law going back to 1602. Puffery is deemed to deceive no one because "judicial expertise" pronounced that such was the case centuries ago in the British common law.

In other words, the law concludes that no one believes puffery because a British court decision before the voyages of Columbus had ruled that it doesn't. Contrary to the legal assumptions and court precedent, when marketing researchers assess how consumers respond to puffery, they consistently find that people do believe that puffery statements are facts.[7]

There are some modern cases in which a court will not deem something as puffery unless marketing research establishes that no one actually believes it. So marketing research can have an impact. Still, the defense lawyer's refrain is often heard to charges of advertising deception, "Oh, that's just puffery."

Regulatory agencies are expected to be more flexible. The goal of regulatory agency requirements is to prevent consumers from being deceived. Yet, when specific phrases are mandated, consumer understanding is still just a hope. And sometimes the consumer is confused instead of informed.

BETTER TELEVISION, BUT FOR WHOM

North Americans often make two discoveries if they watch television in other parts of the world. First, U.S. programs are ubiquitous, filling out major parts of program schedules in Britain, New Zealand, Australia, and even countries where English is not the predominant language. Action and adventure series and situation comedies show up in some of the most unexpected places; segments of the U.S. broadcast news magazines are borrowed or inserted into local adaptations of CBS's *60 Minutes* or ABC's *20/20*. And, second, the traveler can't help but notice that the picture is clearer and sharper when these familiar faces and programs appear on foreign television sets.

The reason is simple technology and history.

The U.S. government set basic broadcast standards earlier than most other countries—and never changed them—putting in place a basic screen with only 525 lines. Other countries either started broadcasting later, when the technology had improved, or updated the local standard before the old hardware became too entrenched. As a result, most of the world outside North America uses a television standard with more lines and better resolution.

Technology, once adopted, creates systems, from the most basic QWERTY keyboards on typewriters (and now, on computer keyboards) to home entertainment centers. Systems are tied to both hardware and public acceptance; once these investments are established and widespread, systems resist change. Since large numbers of people have bought television sets, the government is discouraged from changing standards that would make not-so-old (and expensive) equipment worthless.

When adopting standards for color television broadcasts, the U.S. government required that the new standard be compatible with the one that was used in black and white sets to minimize problems for both broadcasters and consumers. A few countries used the advent of color as a time to improve their original broadcast resolution standards. The United States did not.

For most of the final decade of the twentieth century, the FCC delved into possible standards that would be used for a newer High Definition Television (HDTV) system. When HDTV standards first came under review, the FCC insisted that any new high-definition broadcast system be compatible with old technology. They threw out that concern with their eventual rule-making decisions as they focused on introduction of a possible digital HDTV broadcast system whose use would make current analog broadcast equipment and home receivers obsolete. They also misplaced marketing, forcing expensive changes in something that is important in every American home, creating problems for both people making and receiving home entertainment.

With new technology, new standards are not trivial.

Up to a point, new technologies for distributing recorded music or taping television could entrust the "battle" to the marketplace. Owners of "orphaned" equipment still were able to play their old eight-track tapes or vinyl record albums; owners of defunct Sony Betamax videocassette recorders still could use the machines to record programs until they wore out.

Over the long haul, many consumers choose to upgrade collections of old recordings to the newer systems, though many still may regret the wasted expense involved in purchasing a system with a limited lifespan. But with broadcasting, new equipment is forced in the short run while the broadcaster must make very expensive alterations to transmitters and studios. When programs on the old system are no longer being distributed, consumers' home equipment instantly acquires the utility of a hairbrush for a bald man unless they purchase "converters."

Regulations can also give consumers direction and confidence in what they purchase. In broadcasting, FCC standards assure people that the equipment sold in stores will receive programs. This was the basic concern underlying the creation of the FCC; when FCC commissioners forgot this in the rush for deregulation, the FCC contributed to the market failure of AM-stereo radio.

My students chalk it up to the ramblings of an aging professor when I tell them that in the same year that the first *Star Wars* movie was released, most people were still listening to monaural AM radio. In that not-so-distant past, FM was just starting to break out from the margins of the broadcast landscape. For consumers at that time, FM often was not even a purchase option, except in more expensive car radios or new stereo systems. And with small audiences, it accounted for a minuscule part of radio advertising revenue.

As the better stereo sound of FM finally made it the music medium of choice by the 1980s, the introduction of new technology that allowed the broadcast of stereo-AM was touted as the way holders of old broadcast licenses might retain the value of their radio stations. But, unfortunately for the broadcasters, it was the Ronald Reagan era of deregulation. The FCC decided to let the marketplace decide the standard for AM-stereo radio, so broadcasters and consumers had to predict which of these different incompatible systems they should buy.

When no single system quickly "won," most people opted not to buy AM-stereo receivers, since they were not worth the extra price for uncertain reception. Those systems that were purchased tended to be a nonchoice, when consumers purchased whatever system was included in the FM-stereo they selected. For any market, few consumers would even be able to receive the stereo signal for any specific AM station, so the AM-stereo broadcasts were unable to serve as a significant audience draw. And a limited audience meant no advertising revenue. AM radio's sole market strength now appears as the home for talk radio, such as news, sports, or call-in discussion programs.

In the 1980s, the FCC left AM-stereo radio's future to the market, while not understanding marketing. Without standards or guidance, no one wanted to buy the product. In the 1990s, with HDTV, marketing was usurped. Instead of just setting a standard and letting cable or satellite systems convert (or not) to serve customers, all broadcasters are required to convert to digital distribution of programming over the next few years.

With a new system for digital HDTV, not only were new standards needed, but a program for implementation also required an assessment of how the system would be phased in. But that required at least some idea of who would be served by the changes. In a policy that appeared to have been written by engineers and lawyers, the FCC not only set the standards for receivers and signals, but apparently directed that conversions be forced on everyone.

When all TV distribution options are required to use a system that is incompatible with the old one, everyone wanting to watch television by any means must either purchase an expensive new television, or purchase a special conversion box for the old receivers, estimated to cost $100. With the large number of multiset homes, everyone would be buying more than one box, even people who decide to buy a new HDTV set. In addition, the broadcasters were given new frequencies and more bandwidth, but they needed to purchase expensive equipment to convert program productions and broadcasts to actually send digital signals.

The FCC's desire for broadcast conversions was the target of immediate criticism, focusing on what many called "the big giveaway." This meant that current station license holders were given (and not sold) the rights to additional spectrum space to facilitate the transition. But the FCC also misplaced marketing, failing to consider which consumers (if any) need or want the new and improved products. At a very basic level, it might have been unnecessary to require local, over-the-air broadcasters to start sending digital signals. The marketing question asks if the audience for digital TV will also be people depending on broadcasting. While television itself has become a basic public utility, seen as serving an important role in virtually every home, many consumers receive their programs via systems other than broadcasting, such as cable, satellite, or purchased and rented programs.

Since the technology is still new, the digital television sets that are available are extremely expensive, and even anticipated long-run cost reductions would still keep the basic HDTV sets costing as much as the largest analog receivers now available. With the least expensive HDTV sets still priced over $2,000 (more than four times the cost of a high-quality large-screen analog set), early users of digital HDTV will be either very affluent people or techno-geeks whose personal priorities direct all available disposable income toward their television. For these people, how signals are "broadcast" is almost irrelevant, since they are already connected to satellite or cable delivery systems (or both).

The costs of the sets probably will come down over the long term. But while broadcast network programs still command the largest audiences of any single advertising vehicle, most homes receive their TV programs by means other than over-the-air. With over two-thirds of homes receiving their television programming from cable or satellites systems, it will be a very long time before the HDTV sets become common for the other people who are dependent on broadcast signals.

And it is not that clear if people are clamoring for better television pictures. While not directly relevant to the FCC decisions, greater spending on technology would not necessarily make for better programs.

Seinfeld or *Rosanne* would not have been any more popular if they had been broadcast in a digital format. No amount of improved pictures would make a show with poor writing worth watching. *Babylon 5* and other science-fiction or fantasy programs use extensive and expensive special effects, but they gain popularity from the writing and acting. As in movies, any high-tech special-effects production that is poorly written or directed results in an expensive, box office bomb.

And even if the FCC could mandate better writing for new digital programs, improvement of broadcast signals would not alter the production quality of the overwhelming majority of programs that the people receive. For many years, most of the available programs still will be produced as analog. Cable networks, satellite systems, and independent broadcast stations are dependent for most of their schedule on libraries of past television shows. Upgraded or improved production standards may not readily translate into increased payments for broadcast rights, so costs alone may discourage many new made-for-television productions from being produced any differently than those currently under production.

At least in the short run, digital television will be of greatest value to lovers of home theaters, spectator sports, and pornography. Except for the Olympics, baseball's World Series, and football's Super Bowl, these audiences are all quite limited.

Even without the expense of conversion, the typical consumer's problems with digital HDTV are not limited to the new television itself. In the music business, the compact disk replaced the vinyl album, with the new improved recording technology virtually replacing the old by consumer choice. Many people eventually bought their favorite old albums when they were re-released on CDs. But several other technological innovations in digital music did not crack the marketplace, in part because they were too different or did not offer any new benefits beyond CDs. And while CD players fit into the existing physical home audio system equipment, digital television requires ripping apart what people now own.

Most homes have more than one TV set, and the main unit is also furniture, part of a system often involving a VCR, maybe a video disk, and a video library of old favorites and family keepsakes. Many people own expensive entertainment centers with a space in which the current square-shaped, smaller-sized sets fit perfectly. People who use VCRs for time-shifting new programs would also have to buy a new recorder so they could watch a digital program on their new and expensive television. Yet it can't replace the old VCR, since consumers would want to retain their libraries of old movies or favorite programs. Home videotapes and old video cameras would need to be converted to be played on the new set and the various video disk systems would also need special connections to both old and new systems.

The people choosing to buy a digital television are the same people most likely to own more than one set, but even these people would not purchase more than one digital television right away. It should be obvious to anyone who looks at how people buy or use television sets that it will be a very long time before any consumers buy multiple sets with digital capability. And consider the consumers who own the thousands of small, portable "watchman" sets that would become not-so-portable once consumers needed to attach a converter box to receive any signals.

On the program delivery side, there are high conversion costs for broadcasters and networks (even with the free bandwidth from the FCC) that must install new equipment. Local cable systems also have to upgrade. Program producers must start using better stages and sets for programs, and there will also be a need to improve the technical quality of taped or filmed regular programs—all at a higher cost per show.

The broadcasters would need to recoup these expenses through increased advertising revenue. However, I doubt that advertisers would be willing to pay a big jump in rates to cover these costs for the mere benefit of a clearer picture of the commercial. Digital television's improvement in terms of commercial impact would be minimal, if it had any impact at all. Obnoxious commercials would still make audiences zip or flip or zap. The ineffective commercials described in Chapter 4 would still be ineffective if produced in HDTV formats.

But then, these were all the marketing questions never asked. The frequencies were handed out to the stations and conversion is now underway. While some broadcasters have expressed a reluctance to convert to a digital broadcast system, preferring to use the extra frequencies for other consumer services, major networks are now starting to send out programs in digital format.

Unfortunately, for many consumers the changes will only mean a cost without benefit, as they purchase boxes to enable them to watch the digital signals on old analog sets. Generally unmentioned is that these marketplace "losers" would be the poorest members of the public. The overwhelming majority of those who watch television via broadcast signals are poor people, plus others who probably don't care if their picture quality is that much sharper and clearer. So the requirements for conversion to digital broadcasting would be either irrelevant or undesirable for a major proportion of the public.

All this as the result of a rule from a regulatory agency whose mission is to regulate broadcasters so that they best serve "the public interest, convenience, and necessity."

REGULATING MARKETING AND
MARKETING REGULATIONS

A major government fight over the past two decades involved whether the FDA had the power to regulate cigarettes as a "drug delivery device" for nicotine. Regardless of rulings by the appellate courts and the Supreme Court, the FDA's activism in this area duplicates a common effort by city, state, and federal government agencies to discourage and prevent underaged children from smoking. These efforts included the antismoking marketing discussed in Chapter 5. They also encompassed the general "fear of marketing" itself that will be discussed in Chapter 10. And other aspects of the FDA's program were marketing efforts by the agency to convince Congress and the public that their proposed cigarette regulations were in the best interests of society.

It is difficult to think of regulatory agencies as needing or using marketing to promote their policies. And many don't. But as Michael Pertschuk discovered in the 1970s, as chair of the FTC, basic marketing principles should not be ignored (though he never used that word).[8] He noted that, as a former staff director of the Senate Commerce Committee, he should have known to promote the FTC's programs to Congress and the public. Instead, because of his marketing failure, the FTC became a major target, assailed as the "Tyrannosaurus Rex" of regulatory agencies and the "national nanny."

Similarly, the FDA rules to "save children from tobacco" are an example of misplaced marketing. The original rules were scattershot, attempting everything imaginable that they thought might reduce smoking activity, possibly in an effort to please a wide array of anticigarette forces. However, a marketing analysis of the overall plan reveals that the breadth of the effort itself weakened the program and detracted from the FDA's ability to do the job.

From a marketing point of view, there were four basic public policy activities that the FDA initially said would discourage smoking by young people:

1. Strict enforcement of bans on sales to children and other restrictions that make it difficult for them to acquire the product.
2. Raising cigarette taxes, which reduces demand for the product by raising its price.[9]
3. Public education efforts, including antismoking campaigns.
4. Bans or restrictions on advertising and other media images.

According to published marketing research, the above are listed in order from most to least effective.[10] Despite that research, antismoking advocates strongly believe that brand advertising is a major impetus for young people to start smoking. Supposedly, without brand advertising, young smokers would never realize how enjoyable addiction to a carcinogenic substance could be and children wouldn't want to light up if billboards never told them about it. In reality, as noted in Chapter 5, new antismoking advertising campaigns *might* have a weak influence on how *some* children think about smoking. As will be discussed in more detail in Chapter 10, a cutback in brand advertising exposure *might*, under very narrow circumstances, effect a minuscule drop in smoking activity by the young.

Not only are advertising restrictions the weakest potential force on influencing generic demand for cigarettes, but Supreme Court cases involving the First Amendment, which were decided before the FDA plan was even considered, indicated that such restrictions would be found unconstitutional. At the very least, the existing law encouraged companies to oppose an advertising ban in court. It still is uncertain how far the courts would go to accept restrictions on information for adults in the name of protecting children.

Another problem was that the FDA's restrictions were so pedantically detailed and otherwise petty as to be almost laughable. Based on a presumption that mere contact with color cigarette advertising or the brand names themselves encourages children to smoke, use of these advertising tools was to be restricted in places where children might see them. At the same time, by trying to cover every single potential area of advertising influence, gaping holes were left. As one political cartoon noted, the rules would have permitted a black-and-white, text-only billboard saying "Hey kids, smoking's cool!" They also had detailed restrictions on ads in publications with a precise, numerically defined, "significant" youth readership, but such a rule would have been difficult to enforce and implement, since it required precise data on vehicle audiences in terms of specific and precise age groups—data that did not exist then.

A marketing analysis of the FDA's overall program should have been based on a fundamental maxim of advertising practice: "Keep it simple." The more you try to say in ads, the less you communicate. In marketing, trying to do too many disparate things weakens the ability to attain the primary goal.

Few oppose a program to prevent or discourage young people from smoking. Even the cigarette companies now publicly state that they do not wish children to be their customers. But the advertising restrictions—the weakest means of accomplishing this laudable public policy goal—in turn weakened the other programs by drawing energy and resources away from them.

Seeing the FDA rules as an attack on advertising rights in general, an array of trade and media associations jumped (sometimes reluctantly) to the defense of the cigarette companies. If advertising had been left out of the rules—that is, if the FDA had just focused on restricting sales and distribution of the product—these same groups would probably have rushed to assist the FDA, possibly volunteering to help design and execute the public education campaigns. The advertising rules gave all the groups a basis to attack the FDA in court, distracting from implementation of sales restrictions and other efforts.

As noted previously, the inclusion of advertising bans might itself be the result of political marketing. Despite what marketing researchers know, the public often believes that advertising possesses great powers of mind control. The extensive advertising restrictions might have been part of the rules because of their intuitive appeal and political marketing value. Yet, the FDA attack on parts or forms of advertising became a distraction from more direct and effective efforts to restrict actual sales to children.

"REGULATION" WITH A HIDDEN AGENDA

In November 1998, the major cigarette companies signed a joint consent agreement with attorneys general of forty-six states, following closely on the heels of comparable agreements individually signed with the law enforcement officers of the four others. These agreements ended legal actions whose purported basis was to compensate states for medical costs treating citizens' illnesses caused by smoking. Like the FDA efforts, the agreements also included restrictions on the companies' marketing practices. In announcing the agreements, many attorneys general claimed that they had taken a *major* step in stopping children from taking up the smoking habit.

However, cigarettes are a legal product, with laws restricting purchase to adults old enough to know what they are doing. Instead of a misplaced focus on marketing practices to stop many young smokers, the FDA or the law enforcement agencies should make it harder for them to get a steady supply of the product. The real problem is that sale of cigarettes to young people is restricted by a collection of state laws with weak penalties that often are ignored or unenforced. Joe Camel was a successful ad campaign because he appealed to people who are able to buy cigarettes, regardless of the age of the target.

If the attorneys general were serious about decreasing teen smoking, they would have forged a different agreement.

To have a meaningful impact on youth smoking activities, each state should have promised to enact strict laws on sales or transfer of the product to those underage, with strong financial penalties on retailers or adults who sell or give the product to young people. These laws should also have included mandatory enrollment in smoking-cessation programs for anyone under eighteen who is caught with the product in his or her possession. The cigarette companies would then have had to pay the costs of both enforcing these laws and running the programs for children going through nicotine withdrawal. Law enforcement aimed at product sales or possession would have had a clear, strong, and direct impact on people's behavior.

As noted in Chapter 5, few seem willing to admit that money is finite. Dollars spent on regulation of marketing or on antismoking advertising is money that is not available for law enforcement or medically treating young smokers to help them quit.

Regardless of how high school students start their habit, they have to acquire the product to use it. Maybe some steal from their parents, but the large number of high school students who report smoking a pack or two per day must be able to buy them. Under terms of the recent settlement, the tobacco companies pay money to the states and alter their marketing practices; the states claim victory while doing little.

Though none would publicly admit it, many states probably signed the agreement only because they wanted the cash.

Legislating an increase in cigarette taxes is politically unpopular. Yet as the companies raise their prices to cover costs of the settlement, it will have the same effect. Any increased law enforcement on use of these popular "legal" drugs is also unpopular. When children can easily buy cigarettes at any store, the amount or nature of advertising or other marketing activities for brand-name products is irrelevant. If state governments were really serious about stopping young people from smoking there are other better things they could do instead of putting a misplaced focus on marketing.

MISPLACING MARKETING VIEWS

While the original proponents of the 1914 FTC Act envisioned it as composed of experienced business people and communications experts as well as economists and lawyers, to this day a marketing or communications expert has never been appointed as a member.[11] By naming economists as his first two commissioners, President Reagan appointed the first nonlawyers to ever hold that position.

Marketing people have not been totally absent from FTC decisions. There have been many consumer research experts hired as consultants or case witnesses during the past three decades, but their main policy direction comes from the people staffing the in-house Bureau of Economics, even when a case involves interpretation of claims conveyed to consumers.

Professor Ivan L. Preston has advocated that expertise in understanding consumer behavior be incorporated to a greater degree into a Bureau of Consumer Behavior Research to complement the existing Bureau of Economics.[12] However, like most regulatory agencies, the FTC has been facing a shrinking or stagnant budget, so its salaried in-house marketing expertise is skimpy and creation of a new bureau is unlikely. Other agencies, such as the FCC and the FDA, apparently have never seen marketing perspectives as adding much to their decision-making procedures.

Views of marketing of government agencies will remain dominated by nonmarketing people, so reality often will be just a concept.

NOTES

1. Timothy Moore, "Subliminal Advertising: What You See Is What You Get," *Journal of Marketing*, vol. 46 (Spring 1982), pp. 38–47; Herbert Rotfeld, "Subliminal Foolishness," *Los Angeles Times* (April 1, 1986), pp. II-5; Eric J. Zanot, David Pincus, and E. Joseph Lamp, "Public Perceptions of Subliminal Advertising," *Journal of Advertising*, vol. 12 (no. 1, 1983), pp. 39–45. As will be discussed in Chapter 10, anyone using subliminal advertising is wasting money and risking a negative public reaction from discovery of an effort that will not accomplish anything of substance. But even if there are some such idiots out there, there is no reason for anyone to care.

2. Code of Federal Regulations, T.D. ATF-180, 49 FR 31674, section 5.65, "Prohibited Practices," part (h) at p. 74, adopted August 8, 1984. The bureau's full statement of regulations can be found on-line at <http://www.atf.treas. gov/alcohol/regulations/index.html>.

3. Admittedly, this cuts both ways. Many legal articles in marketing journals are written by people who did not bother to learn the most basic aspects of legal analysis.

4. In 1998, President Clinton announced plans for implementing a system of plain language in the writing of government regulations. While a laudable goal, even the plan's supporters noted that a massive rewriting of the Code of Federal Regulations in plain language would change the legal meanings of established terms and cause many problems for businesses. For example, see Vern McKinley, "Keeping it Simple: Making Regulators Write in Plain Language," *Regulation*, vol. 21 (no. 4, 1998), pp. 30–35.

5. Thomas J. Maronick and J. Craig Andrews, "The Role of Qualifying Language on Consumer Perceptions of Environmental Claims," *Journal of Consumer Affairs*, vol. 33 (Winter 1999), pp. 297–320.

6. For many years, under German law, advertisers have not been permitted to say that their product was better than a competitor's because that con-

stituted trade disparagement, but they could assert they were "the best," since that statement in the superlative was considered an expected puffery and, as such, it was legally presumed that no one would think it was true.

7. To this day, these laws (and some others) remain unchanged, providing some very large "loopholes" for legally acceptable, yet fraudulent, advertising. See Ivan L. Preston, *The Great American Blow-Up: Puffery in Advertising and Selling* (Madison: University of Wisconsin Press, 1975, rev. 1996); Herbert J. Rotfeld and Ivan L. Preston, "The Potential Impact of Research on Advertising Law," *Journal of Advertising Research*, vol. 21 (April 1981), pp. 9–17; Jef I. Richards, *Deceptive Advertising: Behavioral Study of a Legal Concept* (Hillsdale, NJ: Lawrence Erlbaum Associates, 1990); Ivan L. Preston, "Puffery and Other 'Loophole' Claims: How the Law's 'Don't Ask, Don't Tell' Policy Condones Fraudulent Falsity in Advertising," *The Journal of Law and Commerce*, vol. 18 (Fall 1998), pp. 49–114. Other marketing efforts that stretch and abuse the bounds of truth are discussed in Chapter 9.

8. Michael Pertschuk, *Revolt Against Regulation: The Rise and Pause of the Consumer Movement* (Berkeley and Los Angeles: University of California Press, 1982). Pertschuk discussed his experiences at the FTC, writing his book during the early years of the Reagan administration when he was no longer the chairman but still serving the remainder of his term as commissioner. While President Reagan could not remove Pertschuk from the commission prior to the end of his term of office, the president could appoint a different member to serve as chair, which he did.

9. The FDA rules did not involve taxes and prices, since these tools are outside the agency's regulatory power.

10. Karen H. Smith and Mary Ann Stutts, "Factors That Influence Adolescents to Smoke," *Journal of Consumer Affairs*, vol. 33 (Winter 1999), pp. 321–357.

11. Paul H. LaRue, "FTC Expertise: A Legend Examined," *Antitrust Bulletin*, vol. 16 (Spring 1971), pp. 1–21.

12. Ivan L. Preston, "Dissension at the FTC in Identifying Consumer Response to Advertisements," paper presented at the Annual Marketing and Public Policy Conference, Atlanta, Georgia, May 19–21, 1995.

──────────

PART III

PROBLEMS OF JUST
SATISFYING
CONSUMER NEEDS

"We're providing a service people want, just like Al Capone."

In the *Star Trek* television programs and movies, each alien culture personifies a human archetype. Ferengi are the marketing-spouting, graft-riddled, avarice-driven creatures who travel the universe searching for profit by any means necessary. Many of the examples in this section involve decisions by people with the worldview of graduates of the Ferengi School of Business Ethics.

The businesses and organizations of Parts I and II misplaced marketing because they were not following a marketing perspective in basic decisions. At best, their consumer orientation was lost, and they followed a production orientation in decision making. The organizations in this part could be doing a good job of applying marketing perspectives, but marketing is either abused or results in outcomes that are not in the best interests of either the customers or society.

Businesses satisfy customer needs to help maximize profits. Non-profit organizations find marketing useful to work toward their self-interested concerns. Yet a firm's self-interest might not serve the best interest of the customers and, even if those people were well served, good service to consumer segments is not a societal goal. Giving people benefits they think they need instead of what they should be getting distorts important social values and priorities. And marketing sometimes is attacked for helping a firm maximize profits from products that groups of noncustomers would like to make illegal (if they could).

8

Self-Regulation as a Marketing Tool

Many advocates of government deregulation have voiced a consistent mantra for decades: "All government regulations are bad and undesirable." But they don't always say this when the topic is marketing. Instead, the strongest and most ideology-driven antiregulation voices from the Reagan administration and onward have implicitly stated that some marketing regulations are desirable, but that organizations other than those in government could be depended on to do the job.

Before serving as President Reagan's first chair to his Council of Economic Advisors, Murray Weidenbaum wrote a book on the future of government regulation of business, giving his opinion that self-regulation would make virtually all government activity unnecessary.[1] Interviewed on television's *MacNeil–Lehrer Report* in 1982, Federal Trade Commission Chairman James Miller III defended his proposed cuts in Commission activities by stating that "The FTC is not the only body with a program of protecting consumers from false and deceptive advertising. The Better Business Bureau has an excellent program. The media, and especially the broadcast networks have ongoing programs to screen commercials [for honesty]."[2]

Many firms have implemented noteworthy internal codes of ethics.[3] While companies might try to "set an example" for others in an industry, a business' ethical code can only hope to regulate its own employees and does not have any power over other companies. As a broad concept, "self-regulation" refers to organizations that are independent from (or "outside") a given firm, such as trade associations that can try to influence the business practices of their members.

Business leaders assert that self-regulation serves as a major constraint on their activities; business critics, by contrast, observe that self-regulation appears to possess a limited ability to stop undesirable practices. And both are correct. Many firms choose to follow a voluntary self-regulation code, while many others ignore it.

Self-regulation may influence the decisions of many firms; when an undesirable activity stops by self-regulation, government involvement is not needed. But for some firms, self-regulation might not be a strong enough force to police the marketplace abuses. Uncertain whether a majority of individual businesses would comply with trade-generated guidelines, Charlayne Hunter-Gault asked FTC Chairman Miller on the same *McNeil–Lehrer Report* program, "Can we honestly expect business to regulate itself without government looking over its shoulder?"

Government can't be replaced by self-regulation because self-regulation addresses business goals that are different from the consumer protection focus of a government agency. While government bodies misplace marketing perspectives that would help them optimally serve the interests of the greater society (as shown in Chapter 7), self-regulatory organizations misuse marketing when the outcome serves only their narrow, short-term interests.

DOING, NOT DOING, AND PRETENDING

During most of the 1970s, it seemed as if the United States was consumed by a fear of television's impact on children. Well, at least the people in government were concerned. The FTC, Congress, and the FCC all held their own hearings on the content of child-oriented programs, and each of them considered possible restrictions on advertising that sold products to children. Clearly, as a reaction to this public activity, the leading toy and cereal manufacturers provided the funding for a new Children's Advertising Review Unit (CARU) through the Council of Better Business Bureaus. CARU was charged with reviewing and "controlling" self-regulation of advertising directed at children. But the initial enthusiasm waned and its funding levels dropped in 1980, when all the government groups ended their hearings without issuing new laws or regulations.

More recently, airline passenger complaints were reaching a fever pitch in 1999 and early 2000. Luggage was often lost, and when flights were cancelled or delayed, no one at the so-called service desk would provide information to help travelers make other arrangements. Congress was about to institute public hearings, and new regulations were considered, but both options were temporarily suspended when the major airlines promised to improve the situation through self-regulation. But as the 2000 summer travel season began, members of Congress were heard to say (in an election year), "not good enough." The airlines were not solving the problems and few of the companies had made any effort to implement the promised reforms. Some airlines got better. Others got worse.

Some countries legislate support for self-regulation, and some U.S. professions, such as lawyers or doctors, have their professional codes enforced by laws and licenses for members. But when this happens, the business groups become an arm of government. And if it is an arm of government, it can't be considered self-regulation.

A group of competitors that attempted to control how all companies in the same business sell their products or services would be violating antitrust laws in the United States. In a truly free market, a trade association, on its own, can't force any of its members to adhere to the code; they can only suggest desirable practices. When businesses are left on their own to truly regulate themselves, a business group or trade association's only "enforcement" powers are limited to member cooperation. And this limitation means that self-regulation, by itself, is a very weak force in business decisions.

A few businesses may cooperate because it is the "right" thing to do, but other companies will do what is expedient or profitable. Government regulations that are active or threatened "encourage" firms to cooperate, though some firms will not cooperate until the law knocks on the door.

As it had done many times before, the CBS program *60 Minutes* investigated a company that was not delivering on its promises. After showing viewers the complaints from some of the ripped-off consumers, the segment played the interview with the business owner. Correspondent Ed Bradley logically asked if he could see the data proving that the marketing claims were true. Without missing a step, the owner looked at the camera and said, "You're not the FTC. We don't have to show you anything."[4] And he was right. They don't.

Many trade associations have written codes or guidelines for members, and every association presents its code as a strong force for consumer protection. But the codes are usually weak to meaningless when it comes to regulating actual business activities. In reality, these requirements for "good practices" are often ignored. Many trade groups do not even possess a mechanism for enforcing their code on their members. Even if a code is followed by some "leading" firms in a business, many other competitors consider it irrelevant for their daily operations.[5]

Faced with many threatened laws and regulations, the Direct Selling Association wrote a code of ethical practices for its members. However, only a fraction of the membership decided to publicly say that they subscribed to the code, and many of their competitors did not even belong to the association. As an effort to impose an enforcement mechanism as part of this self-regulation, the association's leadership decided that membership would also require a promise to follow the code. As an immediate result, membership dropped.

In the mid-1950s, public concern about the potential harm to children caused by horror comic books engendered threats of possible government censorship. In response, the comic book companies agreed to abide by a code of good practice that covered all aspects of their publications: storylines, illustrations, dialog, and advertising. Before distribution, each magazine was submitted to the Comics Code Authority and, if approved, would be permitted to carry the Seal of Good Practice on the cover. As an enforcement arm, the local magazine distributors all agreed that they would not carry any issues that did not have the seal.

This situation was unique among self-regulation codes. Since competitors decided whose products were distributed, this arrangement was per se a violation of antitrust laws. But no one objected at that time, even though it forced some companies out of business. Hearings in both the U.S. Congress and the New York State Legislature had openly discussed bans or limitations on comic book publication and distribution. Under the banner of "protecting children," business and government officials probably saw the Comic Code Authority's activities as acceptable. No publisher sought legal redress against the authority under the antitrust laws, nor did the Justice Department attempt to end its activities.[6]

In 1971, three panels of the story in an issue of *The Amazing Spider-Man* failed to meet the authority's requirements. It mentioned drugs. It was not a positive portrayal of drug use; in fact, it could readily be labeled an antidrug message, but any mention of illegal drug use violated the code. It was the best-selling title issued by the company that published the majority of the most popular comic magazines at that time. Despite the absence of the seal, that Spider-Man comic book was still carried by distributors who probably feared repercussions on other moneymaking titles. Besides, public attention by then had drifted away from comics and toward more ubiquitous television content. By then, government involvement in comic book regulation was no longer a realistic threat.

The seal has since become irrelevant for distribution; many comic books currently found on store racks are not even submitted to the authority, though some publishers still proudly point to the code as evidence of strong and effective consumer protection. While adult comic book fans still criticize the code's restrictions, they feel the presence of the code defuses the threat of any possible new government intrusions.

Absent a threat of government activity, there does not exist much incentive for widespread self-regulation by business. In fact, the strange marketing goal of self-regulation is to establish an image that government activity is not needed. Contrary to Miller and Weidenbaum's assertions, if the threat of government does not exist, the incentive for self-regulation dies.

DOING ALL IT CAN DO

Today, U.S. self-regulation of advertising has become synonymous with the activities of the Better Business Bureau's National Advertising Division (NAD) and its appeals body, the National Advertising Review Board (NARB). This two-level system of self-regulation represents the advertising industry's most ambitious effort at self-regulation of deceptive advertising. Complaints from consumers, competitors, and the local Better Business Bureaus first go to the Council of Better Business Bureaus' National Advertising Division (NAD) and the advertiser is asked to withdraw the advertising, modify it, or attempt to show the NAD that the claims are substantiated. If the NAD feels that the data do not support the claims, the advertiser may then withdraw the advertising, modify it, or appeal to a five-member National Advertising Review Board (NARB) panel.

Since they started operations in 1970–1971, the NAD and the NARB were clearly a reaction to the increasingly strong regulatory programs of the FTC, which itself became a major force in regulating advertising practices at that time. From its inception, consumer advocates have sought to have the organization exert more muscle and be more forceful, but they do not understand that the NAD and the NARB were never intended as a clearinghouse for consumers' advertising complaints. Possessing a limited staff and a small budget, they are industry directed, not consumer directed. They avoid controversy, and most consumers aren't even aware of their existence.

From the advertiser's point of view, the NAD/NARB is a very efficient and active body. Only one firm has ever failed to go along with a final decision of the NAD/NARB (and that was in 1997, after many thousands of cases). Of course, no company is required to participate in the process, but very few have ever refused. In fact, cooperation is so high that almost all firms follow the initial NAD recommendations and only 109 NARB panels met to handle appeals of NAD decisions from 1971 through July 2000.

This business cooperation is important. The NAD/NARB is power-less to force its will on other firms and it would probably prefer to deal with advertisers that are most likely to go along with the pro-gram. It does not attempt to set codes or go beyond the basic require-ments set by government case law because such muscle-flexing would cause all cooperation to evaporate. The only real "power" it might possess, such as it is, is the advertising community's fear of the FTC or other regulations by government.

In other words, the implicit statement from the NAD/NARB to all firms facing an adverse decision is this: "We are your fellow members of the business community, people who understand how you operate and how advertising works. We are on 'your side,' yet we still found potential for your advertising to mislead people. Just think what a government agency would say in your case!" An FTC complaint would be more lengthy to resolve, more costly and would probably entail a burden on all future claims made by both the firm and its advertising agency.

The NAD is concerned only with questions of deception. Since issues of advertising style, offensiveness, or ethnic stereotyping are outside the scope of the FTC, the NAD does not touch them, either. Almost all NAD cases come from the organization's own monitoring or from challenges by competitors, helping it to quietly settle disputes among its own before the public or the FTC becomes aware of a possible problem.

As shown in Chapter 7, government agencies seek to serve the greater society. A marketing perspective would help government agen-cies define and understand how regulations would assist consumers in the marketplace. On the other hand, self-regulation serves the nar-rower self-interest of trade associations or businesses, with consumer protection as an occasional outcome but not the primary goal.

THEY COULDN'T AND DIDN'T
BUT CLAIM THEY DID

Regardless of actual powers or activities, trade associations market an image to both government and the public that the association's self-regulation code makes members responsible corporate citizens. And as part of this public relations effort, an association will often claim credit for causing a widespread desirable business practice, even if such claims are not valid.

Industrywide practices sometimes result from happenstance or co-incidence, and it may be useful (but misplaced) marketing for a trade association to claim to have had a hand in the outcome.

The code of the Distilled Spirits Council of the United States is gen-erally given credit for keeping gin, scotch, vodka, and other products off television by their decades-long, self-imposed ban on such advertising. When Seagrams started a new campaign in 1996 using television commercials, many business writers called it a "breakdown in self-regulation." That was understandable, since the association would like to claim credit for having had this power, but such claims are more image than substance.

Many things "sound" right and are often repeated as if they were true, but something does not become true simply because it is repeated.

As noted earlier in this chapter, while industry codes can *suggest* desired practices, a trade group cannot *force* any of its members to adhere to the code. So, too, with distilled products and television advertising. In reality, some distilled products had been advertised in television commercials broadcast prior to 1996, just not in the places watched by a majority of people.

On close inspection, claims by the Distilled Spirits Council to have kept members' products off U.S. television and radio for fifty years could be seen as racist, since the products were quite common on Spanish language television up until 1988.[7] If the code had kept the products off "mainstream" TV stations and networks, why didn't it do the same job for the Spanish audiences, too? While the association wouldn't assert that the code contained an "exception" for the Spanish-language stations, giving the code credit for keeping the products off television as part of desirable public service by the association's members would logically also mean that such an exception existed.

What really kept the distilled products off most of television was that very few stations considered the commercials acceptable for broadcast. And the English-language stations that were willing to carry distilled-product commercials tended to be financially weak, limited-audience vehicles in small or isolated markets.[8] Companies such as Seagrams were faced with a simple choice: make commercials for those small audiences that might see commercials on those few stations, or design campaigns that depended on print media. Given the potential for strong negative public reactions, coupled with the very limited potential marketing gain, pragmatic business decisions would logically conclude that they should stick with print advertising.

Prior to 1988, Spanish-language stations readily accepted distilled-product advertising. So, for those audiences, the manufacturers used the broadcast media for their campaigns. The English-language stations did not, so the distillers depended on print media there.

And even on some English-language stations, there were some small-scale advertising efforts. Over two decades ago, a company sold M*A*S*H Vodka, a joke product based on the popular television program. As consumed by the characters Hawkeye, Trapper John, and B.J., it came in a medical-style liter-bag container and was promoted on those few stations that would accept the commercials. For that special product, television was a necessary advertising tool, regardless of the small audiences that might have been watching each commercial.

What changed in 1988 is that the Spanish stations and networks stopped accepting the ads. What changed in 1996 is that some visible major market stations decided to accept Seagrams commercials. After the Seagrams commercials aired, and realizing that other stations and advertisers might soon follow suit, the Distilled Spirits Council quickly altered the code to say television advertising was now acceptable, probably to avoid what could otherwise have become a conflict with its major members.

After so many years of claiming market power, the Distilled Spirits Council speaker seemed uncomfortable at the press conference explaining the sudden shift in policy. Government leaders, regulators, and some public-interest groups soon proposed possible regulatory actions. In the short run, the resulting government scrutiny of all alcoholic beverage commercial practices threatened broadcasters with the possible loss of advertising revenue from beer and wine. As it developed, the actual public reaction tended toward apathy, indicating that the stations apparently did not err in gauging their audience reactions, and the government inquiries quietly ended.

Available advertising media might force a collection of firms to follow certain practices as they decide how to efficiently reach certain target audiences. And a trade association might adopt those common practices as part of a code, formally endorsing what is already done. Yet such claims can put both the firms and the association in an uncomfortable position as market and media practices change with the times.

MEDIA VEHICLES' POWER OVER ADVERTISING

What was true for distilled products is also a force affecting all other advertisers: No U.S. mass media vehicle—no television station, cable or broadcast network, magazine, radio station, or newspaper—is required to accept any commercial advertising material it does not wish to carry. And a vehicle manager's decision to reject an advertising message as inappropriate has the power to influence or alter a campaign's strategy and tactics.

Sometimes a vehicle's objections to the advertising style or content are minor, so the firm can make changes to the ad or commercial without harming the message strategy. Of course, the marketer can take the ads to another vehicle, but only if those who would accept it also fit with the media strategy.

The FTC would like to encourage vehicle managers to do more to screen and reject ads for potentially deceptive content, since every deceptive claim discouraged by attentive media managers is one less that could take up the time and attention of the Commission. In the 1990s, I participated in some seminars run by the FTC's Division of Consumer Protection for media managers around the country. The purpose of the meetings was to encourage the men and women from the vehicles to do more to screen out deceptive advertising from their broadcasts. However, a speaker at one meeting showed us that the FTC's goals were not the same as those of the media managers. When he asked how many of the people there came to the meeting to learn about ways to spot misleading claims, a couple of hands went up. When he asked how many of them were concerned with avoiding lawsuits from advertisers based on their acceptance policies, almost everyone raised a hand. They were reassured they could reject anything they did not like, so I guess they went home happy.

The primary concern for most media decision makers is how the taste or style of the advertising "fits" with the overall vehicle image, not if the claims are true or if the product works at all. Some media companies might be very concerned with potential harm to their audience members, but it would be a gross error to presume that their practices were typical. Actually, they are quite rare. More commonly, while the vehicle managers probably would not *knowingly* carry ads that actually harm the audience, their primary concern was simply to refuse to carry offensive messages or those that would cause readers, listeners, or viewers to go elsewhere.

Some might assert that it is simpler for a vehicle's time or space sales force to trust the advertisers. Yet with the Internet and other modern techniques of quickly exchanged information, the time and expense of checking out advertiser's claims are minimized. Expedience is no longer a valid reason for a manager to ignore a possibly deceptive statement.

At the same time, however, vehicle managers are evaluated by the revenue they generate and the business profitability. So even the most socially conscious manager's policy is driven by a mix of greed and fear, wanting the revenue and hoping the advertising style or content won't drive away the audience. A rejection means a direct loss of income,[9] but an ad or commercial that repels the audience could mean that the vehicle would have a hard time attracting future advertisers and would also have to charge less to those they retain. And in marketing the vehicle's image to the audience, most focus is on entertainment value, not a reputation for honest advertisers.

There are exceptions, but these are few and limited. And even the exceptions may be less consumer-protection oriented than some people think.

Contrary to many popular beliefs (and statements in many business textbooks), the *Good Housekeeping* seal of approval is not an assurance that the magazine's employees have tested the products. The seal's promise is more limited: that the magazine will stand behind consumers with complaints wanting money back from advertisers whose products do not live up to expectations. They will not accept advertising they have discovered to be false, and if readers discover the deceptions, the magazine will stand behind them and help obtain redress. You can presume that the magazine, in turn, will seek money back from the company.

Textbooks and popular wisdom paint the media as major bulwarks of consumer protection, and in the quotation at the start of this chapter, Chairman Miller accepted that perspective, too. Media standards for acceptable advertising possess a strong potential as a force for consumer protection, but not when their use is limited and misplaced as little more than another marketing tool.

BLAMING THE ADVERTISERS

Even knowing the above forces on decisions by media managers, it is hard to explain (or excuse) the large quantity of deceptive advertising that repeatedly appears in otherwise reputable vehicles. Even if people in the time or space sales departments were unable to see that the ads were misleading, people in news or other departments could have helped.

A reporter once told me that, after running his five-day news series on bait-and-switch advertising at a local retailer, the major metropolitan newspaper where he worked printed the same ads in its weekend edition. Years ago, the advertising manager of *Bicycle USA* and the publisher of *Mother Jones* seemed to care not a whit when I sent them data proving that (different) advertiser's claims were false, even though the editorial sections of both publications frequently contained critical investigations of products or businesses. Replying to my proof that the advertiser's claims were literally false, a letter from the bicycle magazine manager said readers could protect themselves. The letter from a person who was at that time the publisher of *Mother Jones*, a proud and award-winning investigative journalism magazine, said that while they reject or restrict ads from some product categories, they accepted all submissions under a policy of free speech rights to advertisers. Yet while the cover of a media kit distributed at that time proclaimed, "Readers trust *Mother Jones*," the magazine itself didn't publish any message to readers about its advertising policy that allowed advertisers to make potentially deceptive claims.[10]

When I ask journalists about this duality, they defend it. By their logic, since they don't want advertising people to intrude in the newsroom and tell them how to cover a story, they shouldn't tell the advertising department what to accept. With the plethora of examples of advertising interests directly or indirectly influencing news content, the journalists' logic is very weak, but it is still presented as a reason for not caring about potentially deceptive advertising next to their news reports.[11]

Advertisers, for their part, do not see such a duality and are very conscious about the media content that surrounds their messages. Many companies give their agencies guidelines for types of television shows or magazines that could be purchased as vehicles. Manufacturers of products as diverse as ready-to-eat cereals, candy, and toilet paper are concerned that TV programs carrying their ads reflect the positive values they feel are important for their "family-oriented" products. MCI WorldCom received praise from a few columnists when it pulled out as an advertiser of the World Wrestling Federation's highly rated "Smackdown" program on UPN, even going so far as to issue an apology, stating that it had been unaware of the "vile content" of the show. Advertisers face threats of boycotts if their commercials appear on programs with sex or violence, or a story line offends a particular religious or ethnic group.

On the other hand, the lack of concern by journalists and editors for advertising requires that their audience will blame only the advertiser for the offensive paid content. And in some cases, they might be correct. When the first Seagrams commercials appeared on television, most critical reactions were directed at the distiller and its trade association, not the television stations. When Calvin Klein places its latest advertising messages on high-profile billboards, the complaints about offensive displays are directed at the advertiser, not the outdoor company.

Repeatedly, the public outrage over advertising messages has been directed only at the advertiser, not the vehicle that accepted the materials for publication or broadcast.

In an internationally publicized case, four New York City police officers were accused of killing an unarmed African immigrant, Amadou Diallo. Before the officers were tried in court, the American Civil Liberties Union (ACLU) paid for publication of a full-page advertisement in the *New York Times* that said "Without saying a word . . . the police killed an unarmed man." Though the men had not yet testified in court as to what had happened, the ACLU advertisement presented a conclusion that the officers had not identified themselves. The trial had not begun, but the ACLU pronounced that they were all guilty.

The appellate division of the state court system cited the ACLU advertisement as a significant part of the pretrial publicity that prompted the court to move the trial from the Bronx, where Diallo was killed, to Albany in upstate New York. And Nat Hentoff, former national and New York board member of the ACLU, publicly condemned the organization for running the advertisement. To him, the major crime at that point was that the ACLU had violated one of its own official policies, number 229: "Any attempt, in any form, intended or calculated to influence a jury should be prohibited."[12]

And Hentoff was correct. The ACLU violated its policies. Yet it is unclear why his criticism left the *New York Times* blameless. Since he had written other articles about media practices for acceptance and rejection of advertising, he knew the newspaper could have rejected this ad. Even though it violated important and basic news principles, the *Times* printed it.

The news principle involved applies when a masked man goes into a bank in front of fifty witnesses, pulls out a gun, shoots into the air, and yells, "Give me your money and no one gets hurt." The guards disarm him and place him in custody while he is still in the bank. He is unmasked, handcuffed, and arrested in the bank in front of those same fifty witnesses. Under these conditions, prior to trial, any newspaper reporting the incident, arrest, or comments from the witnesses would still refer to him as a "suspect" or "alleged gunman."

Hentoff's criticisms of the ACLU were valid, but the newspaper was a "co-conspirator" by accepting and publishing the advertisement that violated its news guidelines.

In early 1999, a Toyota Corolla magazine advertisement declared, "Unlike your last boyfriend, it goes to work in the morning." The body copy noted that Corolla is "dependable, reliable and more durable than most relationships. Too bad Toyota does not make boyfriends." Toyota and the ad agency, Saatchi & Saatchi, later released a statement that the ad was meant to be humorous and targeted to all young women. However, the ad only appeared in the African-American magazine *Jet*, whose median age of readers is reported as thirty-eight.

In an outraged letter published in the trade publication *Advertising Age*, Jesse Jackson strongly condemned both the decision to run the ad and explanations given by the advertiser and its agency in response to earlier criticisms from him and other community leaders. He complained that "For far too long, African-American males have been the victims of open attacks on their manhood, their commitment to care for and support their families and their importance to the community." The Rev. Jackson said that such advertising "speaks to the critical need for the advertising agencies to hire more minorities in creative decision-making positions. . . ."[13]

Since the ad only appeared in a black-oriented publication, one could validly assert that the ad writers were insensitive to the concerns of the audience. But this advertisement did involve minorities in the decision and one has to wonder why Rev. Jackson considered the *Jet* managers blameless. The Toyota ad was published in one of the oldest, large-circulation magazines by and for African-Americans. Regardless of how racist or insensitive the Saatchi & Saatchi copywriters might have been, the magazine publisher could have rejected the ad. The *Jet* advertising manager could have explained the problem and educated the Toyota representatives.

Maybe the *New York Times* and *Jet* employees were so clueless about their audiences and relevant ethical issues that they did not know anything was wrong until someone complained. Or maybe they knew that, at least in this case, the advertiser would be blamed and not them, so they could take the money and run. In either case, even with the wisdom of hindsight, since the ads did not cause the publications to lose readers, they had no financial reason to reject it. At the same time, they had a strong financial incentive to publish all advertising for the income generated.

Overall, for most vehicles' advertising managers, violating standards of journalism or community service are less a concern than offending with pictures of nudity.

THE AMERICAN FEAR OF BREASTS

When I visited Australia for the first time, minor differences were more glaring than big ones. Numerous North American car brands are manufactured there, so they looked strange, appearing as if they did not have a driver inside (since they drive on the left and the drivers sat on the right). American actors who are never in U.S. commercials, such as Tom Selleck, repeatedly popped up in unexpected sales pitches. And in a country with numerous almost petty restrictions on consumer freedom, a television commercial showed a close and clear view of a woman's bare, bouncing breast.

The Australian commercial for a sports bra was a clear and strong statement of the product's benefit, showing the motion and tissue damage that can result from a woman not properly supporting her upper anatomy during exercise. The demonstration was in no way lewd, lascivious, or sexual, but by clearly showing a naked breast, it would never run on a major U.S. television network. And facing the prospect of having very few stations or cable networks accept the spot in that form, the advertiser would have to find another way to promote the product's benefits or forgo using the visual electronic media.

They could try to have the model wear a shirt over the unsupported breast, or maybe use a bra that failed to provide adequate support. These alternatives would be much poorer ways to show the product's in-use benefits, and even these might be rejected if the television station or network managers thought viewers would complain, seeing a bouncing breast as "suggestive," even if covered.

When I told this to Australian students or journalists, they were amazed that such would be the case. After all, theirs is a much more regulated society. They must pay a fine if they fail to vote, they are barred from driving cars while barefoot or while talking on a cell phone, and their basic laws lack any guarantees of free speech or press, as are found in the U.S. Constitution. But the limitations on potentially offensive advertising in cases such as this do not come from government. While U.S. broadcast and cable network managers do not seem concerned about deceptive commercials, they have what sometimes seems like a paranoid fear of complaints. And a direct view of a breast is not something the U.S. managers think viewers would want to see.

The contrasts get very strange.

The U.S. subscriber-only network HBO produces a provocative program called *Sex and the City*. The language and nude scenes would never appear on the nation's commercial stations, but the program appears on prime-time, ad-supported, broadcast stations in New Zealand. When U.S. stations or networks show the Mel Brooks movie *Blazing Saddles*, even if on the advertising-supported cable network Comedy Central, they usually bleep out the Madeline Kahn character's name because it translates from Yiddish into a sexual activity.[14] While shock jock Howard Stern actively talks about body parts and sex, the television network E! blocks out the breasts and buttocks when his women guests take off their bikinis or thong underwear. (However, nothing is blocked when they wear minimal or see-through clothing, so more revealing pictures are transmitted as long as a strip of cloth remains in place.)

This nearly pathological fear of naked breasts can be harmful to the viewers' best interests, as when it caused a health information program on breast cancer to be canceled. Trying to provide important guidance for women, the program included a detailed demonstration and instructions on how to conduct a breast self-examination. The demonstration was for health information, not sex appeal, yet it was dropped from being shown on Lifetime, a widely-available, women's health-oriented, advertising-supported cable TV outlet. Of course, the program could appear on pay cable outlets where all sorts of programs frequently have their characters gratuitously flashing bare breasts. But the canceled health program was important for all women, especially those who couldn't afford pay cable or other high-cost subscription outlets. Lifetime's decision was probably driven by a fear of complaints from people who would not be interested in watching any part of the program: men; women who do not want to think about needing to do self-exams; or parents whose unsupervised children are caught watching.

For the most part, magazine publishers have never possessed these fears, but they, too, might face a pragmatic distribution problem at newsstands. Nike's 1999 print advertising campaign for a sports bra showed a frontal shot of a woman without shirt or bra next to a diagram of the product. Even though all ads were to appear inside the magazines—none were to be in front or back cover positions—Condé Nast Publications requested that the nipples be covered even though some of their magazines carried graphic text descriptions of a personal nature without problems. Since some newsstand vendors would not distribute the publications if they contained visual nudity, the publisher asked that the pictures be altered to avoid having magazines pulled off newsstand shelves.[15]

These types of U.S. restrictions are not totally new. Prior to 1982, the National Association of Broadcasters' voluntary Radio and Television Codes were the basis for advertising acceptance decisions at the major networks and larger stations that accounted for (about) 80 percent of broadcast audiences. When the NAB dropped its code activity, the stations and networks continued to follow its basic guidelines for several years, including a ban on live models in underwear commercials. An underwear advertiser wishing to reach these audiences used alternatives that are recalled and well known to many people: models wearing bras outside clothes; an announcer pointing out the benefits of a product while it is strapped to a mannequin; or the "invisible woman" spots, with underwear floating down the street. Even when the so-called "jiggle-TV" was in its prime, and while many stores had women models in the underwear pages of newspaper retail ads, the women in commercials could not be seen in their underwear, even if underwear was the product being sold.

Television program producers complain about broadcasters' restrictions on their "artistic freedom" or their need to "show reality." Before the first *NYPD Blue* program was broadcast, the network was the target of critical comments from both government leaders and members of religious groups. In its first year on ABC, the show was not carried by many of the network's affiliate stations. After the show won critical praise and high ratings, more stations cleared it for local broadcast, showing that if the program attracts an audience, broadcasters manage to overcome their fears. The program is the marketed product and, as shown by some recent movie box office flops, sex and breasts alone do not make something a popular hit. But media managers are more concerned with prurient appeal in advertising, resulting in misplaced fears of audience backlash against a naked breast presented in a nonsexual way. These fears hurt not just the marketer but the consumer needing the information.

WARNING! DANGER, WILL ROBINSON!

Under public pressure from both government and consumer protection organizations, television networks use audience advisories if a program might generate complaints. In theory, the warnings discourage children from watching the programs or, at the very least, encourage parents to monitor what children watch. Adults are warned that the program contains content they might find offensive.

In theory, consumer information is presented to help people make an informed choice what they or their children should watch. And the critics of the programs hope that the information will also discourage viewing and decrease audience size.

The warnings themselves are not a modern innovation. While critics note the current proliferation of sex and violence in program content, networks have always been concerned about offending the public. Warnings were used in any instances when the material was unusually violent, contained sexual situations, or had questionable language. Even news program anchors would give a warning before showing some particularly vivid pictures; program warnings would even be noted in *TV Guide* or newspaper program listings.

As already noted, television broadcasting possesses an inherently conservative nature. While driven by greed for larger audiences, the managers are quite timid when dealing with public criticisms and complaints from viewers. The networks worry about the reactions of the managers at affiliate stations that carry the programs.

The usual and almost-standard language for warnings is logical and provides information for the audience. As far as I know, broadcasters have never conducted research to see which type of warning would be most likely to have the desired effect on the audience. On the other hand, academic research has found evidence that the most common warnings might have a boomerang effect, actually encouraging more people to watch the program.

Results of a series of experiments have shown that commonly used warning labels actually increase interest in violent programs. Comparing labels that just provided information (e.g., "This film contains violence") as opposed to labels that also had a warning (e.g., "This film contains violence. Viewer discretion is advised"), they found that the warning labels, by telling people what to do, actually increased interest in violent programs. And it is the warnings, not just information, that tend to be used by broadcasters.[16]

The researchers noted that, intuitively, parents could use the labels to screen out material they thought might be harmful to their children. Viewers could use them to help select material that fit their interests. Yet, according to the theory of "forbidden fruit," by telling the people what they should do, the warnings have the unintended consequence of actually increasing the size of a program's audience. People are more attracted to programs when they are told the presentations are prohibited for certain audiences, especially if they are a member of the audience to whom the restriction applies.

Of course, a cynical view is that the broadcasters know all this and are manipulating the audience, consciously using the warnings to attract more viewers. I am not such a cynic. It is doubtful that the executives in power are this knowledgeable about audience impact, nor are they so immoral and possessed of Machiavellian tendencies as to even consider such a route to ratings success. Still, in a world that loves conspiracy theories, it is certain that some people will think that this is what is really being done.

The more pragmatic realization is that the viewers and children are not the real target market for the warning labels. The warnings exist to give broadcast executives peace of mind because the label helps appease leaders of groups who wish government would censor the programs and those in government who wish they could. And these critics do not want people to be informed. They want them to be *warned*!

For broadcasters, the labels are a reaction to fears of potential government censorship.

In a similar vein, many television commercials contain additional information or disclaimers in either fast-talking audio or small type at bottom of the screen. Sometimes the notes are there out of concern that, without them, the government would take action against purveyors of potentially deceptive claims. Sometimes they are inserted because the broadcast vehicle feels the clarification is needed.

Sometimes they are simple ("Batteries not included"). Sometimes they are very long and detailed (such as those giving financing terms, adjusted interest rates, or stated limitations to an offer). However, academic research repeatedly finds that most of these notes are too long or detailed or confusing for the target consumer to understand. As noted in Chapter 7, some terms mandated by government are too confusing to be understood even by people with a Ph.D. and a computer. Casual observers note that you need to tape record the commercials and use a freeze frame to read many of them. Those in child-oriented commercials might be simpler, but these too are often beyond the comprehension level of the audience.[17] But the true goal of most disclaimers is to satisfy various government or private watchdogs, not to provide useful information.

THE LIMITS OF SELF-REGULATION

This chapter started with the claims of deregulation advocates implicitly accepting some "controls" on business as needed but asserting that self-regulation was enough. In reality, there are many valid reasons for deregulation and many examples of government regulations that are contrary to the best interests of consumers. However, it is not valid to assert that self-regulation alone makes government programs "unnecessary." If greater self-regulation activity is desired, increased government regulation would be needed to serve as its incentive, since the government programs set the framework for all desirable self-regulation practices. Without the threat of government action, only the most altruistic of firms would ever pay heed to self-regulation directives.

At best, all self-regulation is a marketing tool. In part, it is a minimal effort to convince various critics that government action is unnecessary. When self-regulation helps a firm sell its products to consumers, those efforts often amount to misplaced marketing, serving short-run sales needs and not those of a greater consumer protection focus.

NOTES

1. Murray L. Weidenbaum, *The Future of Business Regulation: Private Action and Public Demand* (New York: AMACOM, 1979), p. 170. Professor Weidenbaum wrote his book at the tail end of a period of strong consumer protection activity, stating that "The nearly universal adoption of and adherence to voluntary codes of business ethics should obviate the need for much of the compulsory controls over corporate governance that currently are being advocated with increasing vehemence." In addition to his presumptions about self-regulation power, he has never, then or since, provided any evidence that voluntary codes are either "near universal" or "adhered to" by businesses.

2. Show #7189, "Curbing the FTC," broadcast March 18, 1982. Transcript 1689 was purchased from *MacNeil–Lehrer Report*, Box 345, New York, NY 10101.

3. For example and review, see Patrick E. Murphy, *Eighty Exemplary Ethics Statements* (Notre Dame, IN: University of Notre Dame Press, 1998).

4. It was surreal that this man agreed to the on-camera interview in the first place. And, after agreeing to the interview, only a cerebral flat line gives such a dare to a TV journalist on a prime-time program that is probably watched by numerous government people as well as his potential customers. But then, many people like this agree to be interviewed on *60 Minutes* or other broadcast news magazines, proving that a total lack of coherent thought is not restricted to guests on *Jerry Springer*.

5. Herbert J. Rotfeld, "Power and Limitations of Media Clearance Practices and Advertising Self-Regulation," *Journal of Public Policy & Marketing*, vol. 11 (Spring 1992), pp. 87–95; Priscilla A. LaBarbera, "Analyzing and Advancing the State of the Art of Advertising Self-Regulation," *Journal of Advertising*, vol. 9 (no. 4 1980), pp. 27–38.

6. Amy Kiste Nyberg, *Seal of Approval: The History of the Comics Code* (Jackson: University Press of Mississippi, 1998).

7. Steven W. Colford, "Hispanic TV Stations Under Fire," *Advertising Age* (October 12, 1987), p. 12; Editorial, "A Liquor Ad Debate For Hispanics," *Advertising Age* (October 19, 1987), p. 16; Editorial, "Hispanic TV's New Maturity," *Advertising Age*, vol. 59 (September 19, 1988), p. 16.

8. Herbert Rotfeld, "The Real Effects of Alcohol Advertising," *Regulation*, vol. 21 (no. 3, 1998), p. 5; Herbert J. Rotfeld, "Media Standards for Acceptable

Advertising and Potentially Desirable 'Chilling Effects' on Advertising Free Speech," in *Proceedings of the 17th Annual Macromarketing Conference* (Breukelen, The Netherlands: Nijenrode University, 1992), pp. 335–356; Herbert J. Rotfeld, "Power and Limitations of Media Clearance Practices and Advertising Self-Regulation," *Journal of Public Policy & Marketing*, vol. 11 (Spring 1992), pp. 87–95; Herbert J. Rotfeld, Patrick R. Parsons, Avery M. Abernethy, and John V. Pavlik, "Television Station Standards for Acceptable Advertising," *Journal of Consumer Affairs*, vol. 24 (Winter 1990), pp. 392–410.

9. This also explains why local media vehicles sometimes carry advertising for products that are not sold in their area. When the advertiser or agency makes such a mistake, there is no reason for media people to enlighten them. Sometimes the vehicle salespeople or advertising managers don't know if the product is locally available. But even if the people working for the vehicle did wonder why they never heard of the company before, there is no reason for them to turn down the revenue source.

10. These examples and correspondence with other magazine executives are reported in Patrick R. Parsons, Herbert J. Rotfeld, and Todd Gray, "Magazine Publisher and Advertising Manager Standards for Acceptable Advertising," *Current Issues and Research in Advertising*, vol. 10 (no. 1, 1987), pp. 199–211; Herbert J. Rotfeld and Patrick R. Parsons, "Self-Regulation and Magazine Advertising," *Journal of Advertising*, vol. 18 (no. 4, 1989), pp. 33–40.

11. There are numerous examples from a wide variety of news organizations, including many large and respected broadcast and print vehicles. These were the focus of several essays and reports in the May–June 2000 issue of the *Columbia Journalism Review*. Also see, Jef I. Richards and John H. Murphy, II, "Economic Censorship and Free Speech: The Circle of Communication Between Advertisers, Media and Consumers," *Journal of Current Issues and Research in Advertising*, vol. 18 (Spring 1996), pp. 21–34.

12. Nat Hentoff, "The ACLU Violates Its Principles—Yet Again," *Jewish World Review* (March 3, 2000). Available at <http://www.jewishworldreview.com>.

13. "Jackson Cites Lessons from an Offensive Ad," letters to the editor section, *Advertising Age*, vol. 70 (March 1, 1999), pp. 22, 24. His admonition that more minorities must be involved for business decisions that target minorities makes assumptions of misplaced marketing and other social implications that will be addressed in Chapter 13.

14. Surprisingly, a cable network channel that was owned by a fundamentalist and conservative Christian religious organization did not block out the name. Or maybe it is not surprising if you realize that they would be unlikely to hire people who speak Yiddish.

15. Alice Z. Cuneo and Wayne Friedman, "Nike to Alter Sports Bra Ads For Some Magazines: Bare Breasts Are Covered to Avoid Newsstand Flap," *Advertising Age* (July 19, 1999), pp. 1, 28.

16. Brad J. Bushman, unpublished comments and research presentation at Marketing and Public Policy conference, Boston, Massachusetts, June 1997; Brad J. Bushman and Angel D. Stack, "Forbidden Fruit Versus Tainted Fruit: Effects of Warning Labels on Attraction to Television Violence," *Journal of Experimental Psychology: Applied*, vol. 2 (1996), pp. 207–226. Similar research on food information labels found an increased interest in eating the product if

consumers were given a warning instead of just information. Brad J. Bushman, "Effects of Warning and Information Labels on Consumption of Full-Fat, Reduced-Fat and No-Fat Products, *Journal of Applied Psychology*, vol. 83 (no. 1, 1998), pp. 97–101.

17. Darrel D. Muehling and Richard H. Kolbe, "A Comparison of Children's and Prime-Time Fine-Print Disclosure Practices," *Journal of Advertising*, vol. 27 (Fall 1988), pp. 37–47.

9

We'd Rather You Didn't Do That

In the long-running television program *Law and Order*, the man who died in the opening scene was revealed to have been a traveling salesman working in Europe on the eve of World War II. Selling life insurance to Jewish people in Poland, he might have been expecting the purchasers' heirs to also die so his company would not have to pay on the policies he sold. The TV drama's pivotal murder evolved from the fictional postwar company's efforts at avoiding payments to people who did survive. But decades earlier, the legal sales had immorally used people's fears of the Nazis as a misplaced marketing "incentive" to sell life insurance.

Like the Ferengi on *Star Trek*, morality or basic questions of right and wrong might never have entered the salesman's mind. Though the television show dramatized an extreme case, the goal of marketing decisions is maximizing profits. And to obtain those profits, a marketing orientation might be abused.

Chapter 8 illustrated that even when a business activity might have the illusion of a societal focus, an effective marketing perspective wouldn't require business to consider anyone's needs beyond those of the present and potential customers. This chapter deals with those times when a narrow, short-term, marketing-for-profits focus results in business activities that could not even pretend to serve society. The disservice to the greater good is obvious, and sometimes the business even fails to serve the customers' best interests. The most charitable description of some of these stories would be to say that the businesses are less than fully honest with their consumers.

Of course, the businesses described here do not have to ignore social goals to be profitable. A firm could take a broader perspective and there might be many long-run benefits to the company from doing so. Unfortunately, the more common approach is to use marketing to rationalize all sorts of less-than-desirable decisions.

DEATH, DESTRUCTION, AND POLLUTION

Most people logically associate antipersonnel landmines with images of destruction. In movies and television shows of my childhood, they frequently appeared as a constant danger, both to the military troops and to people who lived in the same area after the war ended.[1] In the 1953 movie *The Juggler*, a concentration camp survivor and a young boy are nearly killed as they wander into a postwar mine field chasing a ball. My college classmates who were not as fortunate as I was to have both a high lottery number for the military draft and a collapsed lung came back from Vietnam with stories of friends killed or maimed by the landmines that dotted the areas they patrolled. Because these weapons are a danger to civilians years or even decades after a war ends, international activists currently campaign to have them banned from future wars. A treaty to end their use was forged by the 1997 Ottawa Convention on the Prohibition of the Use, Stockpiling, Production and Transfer of Antipersonnel Mines and Their Destruction.

Major powers including the United States will not sign the Ottawa treaty, and their refusal could be seen as a misplaced marketing conflict between the needs of customers and those of society.[2] Landmines serve the needs of the military customers that buy them, protecting armies and slowing the advance of their enemies. Yet every landscape that once served as a war theater eventually pays the penalty for many years with these hidden dangers that remain buried. The new generation of modern landmines are increasing their "stealth" capability, serving a military need by making them more difficult to detect by approaching armies while increasing the societal risk for civilians who will be unable to find or remove them after the war ends. When a U.S. manufacturer of missiles and bombs receives a new contract to produce landmines, some employees might face a moral dilemma, wishing they could refuse to participate, while others would logically feel that if they did not make the product, others would.

This example might seem extreme, but the perspective applies in contexts where the threats of harm are not as direct nor as destructive per product sold.

Sales of light trucks and sport utility vehicles (SUVs) now account for more than half of all automotive sales in the United States. The vehicles are a very profitable component of the product line of any car company. When Ford Motor Company Chairman William Clay Ford, Jr., publicly admitted that SUVs produce more pollution than passenger cars and endanger drivers of smaller and lighter vehicles, he also indicated that if Ford didn't sell SUVs, another company would.[3] A couple of months later, Ford President and CEO Jacques Nasser announced a plan to produce more fuel-efficient SUVs by 2005. However, the planned five miles per gallon improvement would not eliminate the product's inherent environmental and safety problems and, at the same time, the company was rolling out a new generation of bigger and heavier gas-guzzling SUVs, such as the nineteen-foot-long Ford Excursion that weighs over 7,500 pounds.

This was not the first time Ford had sold consumers a product that they might myopically want while doing a disservice to the environment or other social goals.

During the 1970s, when Americans first encountered a problem with limited oil supplies, rationing was discussed and new laws required automakers to develop more fuel-efficient cars. In a major shift of car styling, the first step for improving fuel efficiency was called "downsizing." Where U.S. car models were previously known to grow in size and weight with each new model year, even the luxury cars were made smaller and lighter for greater fuel economy. However, Ford announced that, at least in the short run, it would sell both a downsized LTD II and the original-sized luxury LTD. A smaller version of the car was produced for the socially conscious or economically driven buyers, while the company was still providing the old "hunk of Detroit iron" for people affluent enough not to care about rising gasoline prices. Proudly selling a product to a segment that all other companies had abandoned was probably an effective sales strategy, and the distinction between the two models was even emphasized as a consumer "benefit" in some of Ford's advertising. But it was contrary to the important 1970s social goal of energy conservation.

Decades ago, a slogan frequently repeated by students protesting against both an unpopular war and corporate malfeasance was that "If you're not part of the solution, you're part of the problem."

IT'S JUST MARKETING

Even without considering these broader social concerns, serving what a market segment thinks it wants or needs might not be providing what those people should be getting. Aside from the legal products like alcohol, cigarettes, and pornography that social reformers would like to discourage or ban (discussed in Chapter 10), some products do not provide the benefits the marketing messages claims. Some of these products are of questionable value to the purchasers; some are "marginally legal" as they sidestep laws or regulations that would restrict or ban their sale. Advertising or the salespeople will tell people what they want to hear, even when the product can't or won't deliver on the promise. Sometimes the marketing information plays games with government regulations with the final result of deceiving consumers.[4]

As the marketing manager said to Dilbert in the Scott Adams comic strip, "Remember, what we do here might seem like criminal fraud but it's not. It's marketing."

In a National Public Radio "Radio Expedition," the correspondent interviewed a man who was selling unmarked acrylic sweaters to tourists by falsely claiming the products were made from wool grown and woven in nearby Nepal. When asked, the salesman said it was not deception but "just marketing." I guess his customers would not know the difference and his sales talk provided what the customers wanted—the reporter said they were good sweaters and wool-like. But marketing should not be a defense of deception and the sweater salesman was asserting that what he was doing was acceptable from a marketing point of view.

If only all such examples were so minor. Sometimes the marketing tells vulnerable or desperate people what they want to hear, even though the company does not possess a rational or reasonable basis for saying those things.

When I was living in New Zealand in 1999, the news media breathlessly reported research findings that an extract from local green-lipped mussels, called Lyprinol, had killed isolated cancer cells that were growing in a lab culture. Within days, even before animal tests were authorized and long before human tests were even considered, newspaper advertisements for Murrays Chemist announced that pills with the chemical were available for sale.[5] The top line of the ad just said "Lyprinol," with a series of terse statements in large bold print, double-spaced, with a single sentence per line:

"The sensational green lipped mussel extract.
"Each capsule contains 50mg Lyprinol.

"Dose 2 capsules 2–3 times daily.

"$49.50 bottle containing 50 capsules of 50mg.

"Mail Orders accepted. No charge for delivery."

The ad did not make any claims for the product and did not mention the research findings. As a straight announcement, it appeared to be devoid of puffery. But since the product had only been shown to kill cells in a petri dish, the chemist had no basis to assert a proper daily dosage for the worried cancer patients who were certain to be rushing to purchase it. A human body is far removed from isolated cells in a laboratory.

The advertising from Murrays should not be dismissed as an isolated aberration. New Zealand's national television and radio news programs reported Lyprinol capsules appearing on the shelves of almost all chemists in the country equally fast. Going to the largest store chain in the country to buy some antihistamines, I overheard young clerks giving customers detailed instructions on how and when to take the newly delivered mussel extract capsules. They added the guess of a "proper" dose amount because, judging from the people I heard in stores, customers would want that information before deciding to make a purchase.

I had already discovered from personal experience that many of the chemist store clerks had little special knowledge or training. For the most part, they were cashiers. When selling alternative medicines or regular over-the-counter drugs, to borrow a line by comedian George Carlin for his sports announcer persona: These clerks called it as they knew it, and if they didn't know it, they made it up. As I considered two different boxes of pseudoephedrine hydrochloride, I noticed one with thirty 60mg pills and the other with twelve 120mg pills for a negligible reduction in price and the same daily dose in total milligrams. Three different clerks argued with my choice because the 120mg pills were timed-release, which to them (and maybe their customers) carried some mystical value.[6]

The New Zealand government quickly stopped the sales of Lyprinol and ordered that the product be removed from stores. Various politicians and media commentators called for investigations, charging that a conspiracy or fraud might have prompted the initial press release about the product's research. While it could be argued that people have a right to buy a product that they think might help alleviate their medical problems, the chemists were going overboard in telling people the methods and amounts to take of a product with so many unknown properties.

When he was judging the Miss Italy pageant in 1992, the pharmacist owner of the Italian company, Medestea Internazionale, said he was approached by several contestants wanting his cosmetic company to come up with a product that would help them retain their youthful looks. Even these young and beautiful women were concerned that they were starting to develop cottage cheese thighs. As a result of this interest and eager market, he developed Cellasene, a collection of various herbal chemicals and dietary supplements claiming to be a miracle cure for cellulite.

The manufacturer says Cellasene does not just reduce the appearance of cellulite but cures the condition. And it would be an understatement to say there exists an international and intense demand for the product. When it was first sold in Australia, the first shipment of 50,000 boxes sold out within an hour. Women fought each other and assaulted store clerks in their eagerness to buy it; riots broke out when rumors of a shortage circulated.[7] In the United States, the product is fairly expensive, but sales are strong.

While the company's advertising says the product is a "safe, clinically studied dietary supplement," several U.S. and Canadian agencies were taking a close look at the product's marketing claims and its effect on users. There have been three clinical trials of the product at a hospital near Milan, Italy. However, all three studies combined involved a total of only 105 women, none of their results were assessed and published in peer-reviewed medical journals, and all three violated certain protocols for medical tests that leave them open to strong possibilities of observer error and human bias.[8] Even as an extremely small-scale (ten women), double-blind study was planned, doctors were raising health concerns about dangers from certain ingredients in the product. However, since it is sold in the United States as a dietary supplement and not a drug, it is outside Food and Drug Administration (FDA) authority and does not require research on safety and effectiveness prior to sale.[9]

Both Lyprinol and Cellasene raise questions about the medical supplement business. While cancer clearly falls into a different class of medical problems than fat thighs, these consumer groups are similar in that the afflicted will buy almost anything that seems like a cure. Some limited information exists that these products might do what customers desire, and it is possible that later research might support what the salespeople implied, but at the time of sale, no one could validly assert that they were the cures the customers sought.

The Florsheim Shoe Company has introduced a product line incorporating the old folk remedy of magnets. While magnets have long been touted as cures for everything from allergies to cancer, there is virtually no evidence that static magnets such as those in insoles could increase circulation, improve energy, reduce fatigue, or provide pain relief. In response to an inquiry from *Consumer Reports*, Florsheim acknowledged the uncertainty of the remedy but said that they are selling the shoes "in response to increasing demand from consumers who believe they benefit from this technology."[10] In these cases, misplaced marketing uses consumers' faith in the unknown to sell products.

"YEAH, WE LIED"

In the sarcastic humor of television spots for Sprite, the popular commercials for other brands as well as a variety of other products are spoofed, with a focus on the improbable doofus consumer who believes that opening a soft-drink can would cause a party to break out. "Trust your taste buds, not commercials," viewers are told, obviously because commercials lie. Yet it is strange when even large, well-known companies defend themselves against consumer criticisms by admitting that their advertising or other marketing messages are "not quite" true.

While decades of cigarette advertising promoted the brands as important personal statements for people who wish to be seen as independent, individualistic adults, product liability defenses would point to the various medical reports and package warning labels, asserting that "everyone" knew the dangers and that smokers assumed the risk. Corporate documents that are now available reveal that millions were spent by the businesses' to generate publicity as they tried to bury or denigrate evidence of the product's risks to smokers' health. Over the decades, despite their own internal research to the contrary, heads of cigarette companies were repeatedly seen on the evening news as they appeared before Congress or government agencies piously asserting that nicotine was not addictive or that they were uncertain about their product's dangers.

While it is currently fashionable to demonize cigarette makers, their efforts to protect brand names and product images are not unique. The conflict between cigarette advertising brand images and product facts are extreme, but similar conflicts occur in many other industries.

A lesser-known example would be the unpublicized case against a motorcycle company. When a purchaser lost a leg in a collision with a car, his personal injury suit charged negligence by both the motorcycle maker and the car driver, making a product liability claim that depended on some old advertising. The company's advertising since the 1930s had stated that it had safety guards positioned in front of the rider's legs that would "prevent all serious injuries," so the plaintiff logically claimed that the company was negligent because the guards were absent from the model he had bought more recently.

But the guards never were able to prevent all injuries to the rider, and the company never manufactured a product that could. The manufacturer's liability defense was that the company should not be negligent for failing to supply something that had never existed in the first place. The company distanced itself from the older promotional literature by saying that the claimed benefit of preventing serious injury was made in an earlier era of advertising expectations, indirectly and by implication, via puffery or what could be called "weasel words."[11] Given that, their defense asserted that the prior claims could not be used as evidence that such protective guards existed.

In addition, the motorcycle people said they had made these claims in an earlier period in a different business climate toward marketing. Back then, when many firms made advertising claims with conscious knowledge of their falsity, the advertiser could validly have anticipated that it would never be called to account for them.

In an advertising self-regulation case, Tropicana challenged a Minute Maid comparison spot. While most elements of Tropicana's challenge had a great deal of merit, other parts depended on an assertion that Tropicana's own promotional efforts were false. It is interesting that this latter observation came up only in the dissent written by one member of the National Advertising Review Board (NARB) panel that reviewed the National Advertising Division (NAD) of the Council of Better Business Bureau's initial decision. The dissent was written by the public member, a college professor; the four business professionals on the panel apparently did not have problems with Tropicana misleading the consumers by a "slight" misdirection.[12]

Minute Maid's advertising had claimed that its frozen, concentrated orange juice was superior to Tropicana's Pure Premium, not-from-concentrate, orange juice. While it was true that Minute Maid's taste test found that consumers preferred it by two to one over Tropicana, Minute Maid had used bottled water to mix its brand of orange juice for the test. In research to challenge that test, Tropicana used tap water. Both the NAD and the NARB panel thought that testers conducting the original Minute Maid taste test should have also used tap water unless they had evidence that significant numbers of consumers used bottled water to mix the product in their homes. No problem there, or so it would seem, and the NARB panel was unanimous on this point.

On the other hand, the other issue raised of Tropicana's "seasonality" was more vexing. Four of the five members of the NARB panel agreed with the NAD and Tropicana that the taste test was also faulty because of Minute Maid's failure to take into account that Tropicana, like all other not-from-concentrate juices, has product variations throughout the year that are discernible to consumers' taste. Consequently, products tested in October and December are not representative of the Tropicana product available to consumers in June, when the advertising ran. For the NAD/NARB majority, the applicable principle was that "for a comparison claim to be true and not misleading, it must be based on tests of products representative of those available to consumers *at the time the advertising runs*" (emphasis theirs from the case report).

There may be no problem with the principle, though (as noted in the NARB dissent) to apply it here assumes that brand advertising has a relatively immediate effect, an assumption that ignores a large amount of research literature. But at a more basic and pragmatic level, applying it here also ignores Tropicana's own, possibly misleading promotional claims. Tropicana never attempted to tell consumers about the seasonal variation, instead using the same uniform package and brand identity all year round. In fact, Tropicana always portrayed its product in advertising as "perfect." The professor's dissent noted that "Minute Maid was testing the 'same product,' at least as advertised by Tropicana."

Advertisers often say they are honest and want consumers to trust their claims. Yet they sometimes respond to charges of deceptive advertising by saying, in effect, "Well, we weren't quite telling the truth that time, but we didn't have to." Maybe such a view is ingrained in the mentality of many marketing people.

Years ago, visiting New York advertising agencies with a group of Pennsylvania State University advertising students, the creative director at one company proudly presented the evolution of its current campaign for a client's puppy food. The product was developed following an extensive survey of veterinarians as to what the dog doctors thought optimal puppy food should contain, so the first commercials said they had "the formula recommended by veterinarians." The client and agency knew that they had about six months until that formula would be studied and imitated by major competitors, and once that happened, a unique nutrition claim would no longer be legally acceptable. So from the beginning they had a second theme all set to go and the commercials were launched just prior to our visit: "Vets helped us create it. Puppies helped us sell it."

The second theme seemed innocuous enough, but we were told it was selected because the agency's research indicated that these literal statements would "trigger in people's minds" the former claim that was no longer true. In our discussions during the trip home, some of the students were a bit bothered that the agency was proudly making a claim to trigger a now-deceptive association, but others in the van were not concerned at all. Several students said that, "They're not telling lies. It's just advertising."

SELLING BY CONFUSING THE CUSTOMER

Consumer testing companies such as the Consumers Union study brands of different products and people logically expect that they will find comparable quality if they buy that brand. Brand names also assist shoppers in making price comparisons between stores. And, in theory, when products have more variations and features than canned peas, each brand's model name or number helps consumers as they hunt for their selected bundle of product features at the best price.

Intuitively, the names and manufacturers' model numbers should convey information to consumers and they may be a helpful tool for shoppers. Yet sometimes they seem to confuse instead of help.

As my birthday approached, relatives asked what I would like as a gift. At the top of the list was a new electric razor, but I wanted to specify a brand and model so they got one that would work on my beard and face. I checked with friends, read catalogs, and found a recent evaluation article in a consumer testing magazine. Armed with all this information, I wrote down a brand and alternative model numbers.

But by the time anyone got to the stores, my chosen brand had altered all its model numbers without any indication of how the new system related to the old one. Faced with confusion on what I would like, they bought something else. And when I later went to the stores, I, too, had no idea which one to buy.

This situation is counterintuitive. Basic marketing perspectives would logically require new models to have some ties to the old ones, so shoppers could use their past experiences to help them shop. With satisfied past customers, and top ratings from a respected consumer information source, logically the company should at least inform buyers of the relationship between the new numbers and the old ones, so the company could maximize sales from satisfied users and their friends. The product testing companies do not test running shoes, stereo components, or electric razors every year, so the old model numbers would also be used by many new shoppers.

But actual marketing practice is not always logical, or so it seems.

A century ago, consumer-protection activists feared the power of corporate monopolies, so laws passed at that time and currently still in force try to prevent any firm from gaining such power. Instead, in cartoonist Scott Adams's view of the future, capitalism will increasingly shaft consumers by use of "confusopolies," systems of marketing by which consumers will be unable to tell what is going on.[13]

In today's world, shopping for a new stereo component, television, VCR, or pair of running shoes can result in buying out of exhaustion instead of confidence and knowledge. Finding a store that offers "the lowest prices" is easy. Many proclaim, "We'll match anyone's price on the same model." The problem is that no two stores carry the exact same model, so direct comparisons are impossible. Even on the Internet, it is hard to find direct comparisons of the exact same product models.

The first discount store has model #755. The second store has model #756 or #755-R. To make it more confusing, each minor change in numbers does not just increase or decrease the quantity of special features, but, instead, alters the overall option bundle. There is no way to directly compare one to the other. Driving from store to store, finding the same brands but a different array of model numbers at every location, the shopper gets increasingly confused and frustrated. Choice can't be based on price comparisons since the price and feature bundles are different; no store must meet a competing price since no two stores carry the same models.

So different stores are safe making a "low-price guarantee."

Economists say that prices and transactions are set by a meeting of supply and demand. But to an economist, reality is just a concept. I have a better model. As the consumer's fuel or other shopping-time costs cut into potential savings from "smart shopping," the purchase is made at the store or Internet location where the confusion curve and the frustration curve meet at a point of relative psychological equilibrium. Instead of the power of monopoly, consumers lose to the power of confusopoly.

THAT'S INFOTAINMENT

In U.S. colleges and universities, most advertising courses are taught in the departments, schools, or colleges of "journalism and mass communications." Years ago, when I was teaching advertising in one such program at the Pennsylvania State University, a group of journalism students in my class told me that they were "grossly offended" that their news writing program shared resources with those for advertising education.

"Journalism is getting the facts and telling people," they said, "while advertising is just selling."

"On the other hand," I pointed out, "both advertising people and journalists give and hold back information as influenced by their own point of view. At least when you see that it is advertising, you know that is what they are doing."

Despite the students' idealism, journalists are people and news is a business—a competitive business. Both are open to many competitive and economic pressures, the same as other people and businesses. Chapter 8 offered many anecdotes about advertisers influencing what and how news was reported. Sometimes the pressure is direct, as when Brown & Williamson pressured CBS News' *60 Minutes* not to broadcast a story.[14] Sometimes the issues of possible influence are indirect.

As journalists criticize each other, well-known journalists periodically are revealed to have accepted "honoraria"—payments for making presentations to business groups whose members they might be covering in the future. Entertainment giant Disney owns the U.S. ABC broadcast network, so viewers can validly question the news decision whenever people from the latest Disney movies appear as interview guests on the network's television programs.

Australian talk radio host John Laws's huge national audience and political influence impel prime ministers to take his calls without advance notice. What he says (or in one case, did not say) is perceived as influencing the outcome of elections. In 1999, Australian media watchdog groups and news organizations revealed previously secret agreements between Laws and major Australian businesses in which his on-air opinions were bought in exchange for annual payments to both the radio host and his home broadcast station in Sydney.[15] Laws implemented the largest single deal that received the most media attention when he received a prearranged on-air call from the Australian Bankers Association's chief executive officer, Tony Aveling. Followed an arranged script, pretending that the call was spontaneous, Aveling "convinced" the radio star that the nation's banks had a positive story to tell. Afterward, as per the agreement from the association, Laws's negative comments about the banking business ended and he started to make regular positive comments on behalf of his paying client.[16]

Once the cash-for-positive-comment agreements became public, and when his audiences were told that his opinions were bought, Laws did not seem to care. In response, he said that he was not a journalist or public relations professional, but rather an entertainer or salesman. When a listener wrote a letter complaining about his switched advocacy on the banking industry, an unrepentant Laws thought the letter was hilarious and read it on the air. Reading the line where the listener wrote, "You're a cheap whore," he paused, then said, "I'm not cheap."[17] Of course, at this point the banking association was backing away from the deal and issuing apologies.[18]

Even if the original deal had been announced to audiences and labeled as advertising, host-read "live" radio commercials have a greater impact than those that are distinctly different and prerecorded, possibly hearing the host's reading as a personal endorsement. And, in general, consumers view any advertising content with a less trusting and more skeptical mind set. Most U.S. newspapers and some magazines require that all advertising be readily distinguished from the editorial content or carry a mark on the page clearly identifying it as "ADVERTISING."

Still, many people probably think they can look at television and readily discern what is a commercial. And maybe they now can.

Infomercials have become a common part of the television land-scape in the United States, but they are a recent development. When the programs started to proliferate less than two decades ago, viewers at that time expected sales messages to be restricted to the breaks during and between programs, and that anything longer was a program itself. The term "infomercials" was coined as a criticism of this then-new sales format that attempted to blur the boundaries between commercial and noncommercial messages.

The infomercial program length was not, by itself, what confused audiences. These sales programs were produced as talk shows, news magazines, documentaries and even investigative consumer report programs that claimed to present reports from "unbiased" tests, surveys, or endorsements. Several tried to appear as if they were giving bona fide news reports, with the sponsor as a "guest expert" who was "interviewed" by the talk show host or the self-designated investigative news reporter. And almost all programs further concealed their sales intent by having their own "commercial breaks" to enhance the illusion that the rest of the time was a regularly scheduled program.

Then and now, broadcasters are required by government regulations to identify these programs as advertising. But the regulations never applied to cable-TV networks and, until recently, many television stations were negligent in providing a clear advertising identification. Some of these cable and broadcast managers told me that they did not have to provide a note that the following program was advertising because they thought that labels appeared in the programs themselves or in the printed programs guides. And they sometimes did, but not always.[19] And some stations either did not understand or simply ignored the regulations.

In the late 1980s, a California television station promoted itself locally and on regional cable systems as "the business channel." But it was not a news channel. Instead, depositions in a lawsuit brought by a viewer revealed that it ran virtually all paid commercial broadcasting throughout the schedule. On newslike programs that were the bulk of the schedule, business people paid a fee for the privilege of being interviewed. The programs did not carry any notice that the guests paid a fee for the interview, nor did the station broadcast any viewer-oriented advertising labels that might have lessened the credibility of the newslike show. And at least one interviewer was a former reporter from another station in the Los Angeles area. Seeing a program about a way to lessen tax obligations, Hazel Nielson contacted the advertiser for more information. Believing the salespeople because the business owner repeatedly appeared on the "news" programs, she invested $100,000.[20]

In the California case, as with many early infomercials, even when there might have been an initial (albeit quick) label that the programs were advertising, they appeared in the first few seconds and were easily missed. Besides, the strong program content often outweighed any label or disclaimer.

The infomercial program *Consumer Challenge* was produced by the makers of MDR Fitness Tablets who bought the half-hour period to run the show. It began with the announcer proclaiming, "*Consumer Challenge*, hosted by Jonathon Goldsmith, the show that examines popular new products for you, the consumer, with investigative reporters Catheryn Grap and Don Hale. On today's *Consumer Challenge*, we will investigate MDR Fitness Tabs: New product or consumer rip-off?" A hair-loss program was presented as an investigative program hosted by a major television star, though the conversations with the "experts" were only the star interacting with comments from the advertiser's paid experts that were taped in advance. Erin Gray hosted an Oprah-style program on cellulite whose guests and audience testimonials all talked about the benefits of the sponsor's product, though actual sales messages were reserved for the commercial breaks.[21] During the 1990s, the Federal Trade Commission took action against a sales program for sunglasses that presented itself as an independent, investigative consumer program and against a major distributor of several infomercials.

Of course, the infomercials' use of consumer misdirection is mostly considered a problem of a decade past. Today, the television guides have become better at identifying the commercial programs in their listings, as have the television stations and cable networks. Some advertisers place their logo or commercial identification on a corner of the screen that appears throughout the program. However, there are exceptions and some on-air identifications still appear only at the start of the program so that they aren't seen by people tuning in after the first couple of minutes. Yet the viewing public has become used to these programs and recognizes them as sales efforts, so the infomercial's special ability to deceive consumers has been declining, if not lost, as the format itself is easily recognized.

But this does not mean the problem no longer exists. With other media and other formats, like the John Laws Australian opinion-for-a-price case, the merging is not always so obvious. While carrying advertising and otherwise seeming the same as other publications, many magazines actually are produced by advertisers so they could publish positive "news" stories about the products they sell. As doctors try to keep up to date on new drug research, many of the publications they receive are published by the pharmaceutical manufacturers with the "news" shaped by a staff they control. Women's magazines attract advertisers by carrying positive news stories about health and beauty products next to related advertising (though publishers will insist these are regular stories produced by their staff).[22]

More recently, a U.S. network's evening block of popular situation comedies featured interrelated crossover themes featuring Elizabeth Taylor. Her star appeal might have boosted ratings for the shows, but the real reason for her presence was that the stories all featured a new product carrying her name that was being introduced in stores.

SELLING BY OFFENDING

As already described in Chapter 5, the Breast Cancer Fund's San Francisco billboards of beautiful models with scars in place of their exposed breasts generated numerous complaints from parents saying that they did not want to explain the picture to their children.[23] But then, the campaign's goal was to get more people talking about breast cancer. Feminine hygiene television commercials are consistently cited in surveys of "most obnoxious" advertising; many men say they will quickly change the channel or leave the room when another of those ubiquitous spots appears on the screen. But then, many men are embarrassed when a wife or girlfriend asks them to pick up a box of the product at the store.

Everyone should expect to be offended by some advertising they see because not all advertising in the mass media is aimed at them. But for some strange reason, some companies set out to offend as many people as possible and do not care what noncustomers think, or so it seems.

Bad Frog Beer's label depicts a frog extending its middle finger in an apparently obscene gesture, resulting in the product being banned in Ohio, Pennsylvania, New York, and New Jersey. Maybe the company president feels the shelf visibility from the label and negative publicity is worth some state alcohol control board restrictions on sales. A car wash company in Los Angeles calls itself Hand Job, which is of questionable taste at best, but its newspaper ads rather inanely suggest that people should "give a hand job for Mother's Day." In a similar effort in Melbourne, Australia, billboards for a car wash identify it as the "best hand job in town," so the advertising's tasteless joke crosses an ocean. An Australian roadway sign for a woman's shoe brand has several versions of the product pictured, but the focus of attention is a man in his jockey shorts holding an upraised shoe at a suggestive (imitative?) angle near his groin. And U.S. advertiser Calvin Klein seems to seek headlines with fashion ads that prompt public outrage and Congressional investigations into possible child pornography in his billboard displays.

These advertisers probably believe that the lost business of offended people will be offset by the customers who remember the advertised benefit because it is so crudely conveyed. As discussed in Chapter 4, some of these advertising writers are talking to each other instead of customers; at least the car wash slogan was tied to a literal product benefit. But since these are billboards and/or product labels, to the critics these unavoidable and in-your-face questionable ads raise broader social issues.

As account executive, Bob sent commercials for the client's new Mexican-flavored potato chip to the Chicago television stations days before the scheduled broadcast dates, only to have the spots rejected by both the NBC- and CBS-owned outlets whose managers said it was "offensive to Hispanics." Bob goofed, since the policy at the ad agency where he worked required him to show both planned storyboards and rough cuts of all commercials to the networks and their owned stations to get feedback on acceptance or rejection issues. In a rush and under the gun, he showed the finished commercials to editors of the local Spanish-language newspaper. Once he acquired their written statements that the commercials were not offensive, he convinced the broadcast station managers to alter their prior decisions.

Still, Bob remained angry for several weeks. "Don't they think I would be careful not to offend a major part of my target audience?" he repeatedly asked. Not only did he forget that his chips could be successful with sales to non-Hispanics, he did not realize that the stations were concerned about offending anyone in their service area. More important, the client should have been concerned about such potentially offensive messages, too.

Even good advertising that works with a specific target audience may cause problems when it offends others who were never even intended to see the commercials. It may come close to causing an international incident.

Goodyear Tire and Rubber's Spanish-language commercial ran for five days in Peru and might have been acceptable to tire buyers in that country. A black man jokingly compares the stomach of another man to a spare tire and the fat man replies by making a similar jocular comparison to the black man's lips. However, when news of the commercial reached North America, the critical public reaction did not see any humor in commercials from a U.S. business insulting a person's racial characteristics. The Goodyear chairman and CEO issued a public apology to Kweisi Mfume, president of the U.S. National Association for the Advancement of Colored People and the company fired the Peruvian ad agency that had created the commercial. Several months later, the U.S.–based agency lost the Goodyear account.[24]

A brief magazine news note reported that makers of an unnamed brand of potato chip in South America seemed surprised at the complaint from the Israeli embassy when their commercials showed Adolf Hitler becoming a nicer person by eating their chips. To increase the insensitivity, a swastika morphed into the company logo in the final scene.

Offending the community is not a marketing abuse in the same sense as the other examples in this chapter. For the firm, it's self-destructive: The advertising agency that created "Dick" and other quirky, supposedly hip, marginally tasteless commercials for Miller Beer was eventually fired because they did not help sell the product. On the other hand, these examples are images that people can't avoid. People are sick of these ads, and maybe getting sick of advertising itself.

Advertising messages have become ubiquitous. The clutter could be call "ad nauseam."

Four decades ago, well-known San Francisco advertising man and business iconoclast Howard Luck Gossage campaigned against billboards as an intrusion into our visual field.[25] When Lyndon Johnson was the U.S. president, Congress enacted the Highway Beautification Act, an effort to restrict and control advertising clutter along the highways. Environmentalists have long complained that trees are often cut down so more billboards can be seen. But, decades later, advertising messages are virtually everywhere.

No matter what you think of the publications and what they represent, *Playboy* and *Hustler* are seen only by people who choose to buy the magazines. Advertising is becoming our culture's equal opportunity insulter.

IT'S MORE THAN "JUST MARKETING"

From deadly weapons of war to questionable cures to anthropomorphic amphibians making obscene gestures on beer labels, a segment of customers are given what they think they need. The product sells (or doesn't) based on customer demand and *caveat emptor* (let the buyer beware). Marketing people can't bend or control minds, but some marketing does come out as warfare against consumers' skepticism. And social concerns never even enter the picture.

The inside back cover of *Consumer Reports* magazine is called "Selling It," reporting in a humorous vein various twists, abuses, and "excesses in the world of marketing": multiple statements on the same package that are self-contradictory; empty product claims or brand-specific claims true for all products in the category; direct sales envelopes with misleading offers; and new packages that look to be the same size while carrying less of the product at the same old price.

Virginia Slims cigarettes has a new tag line, "Find your voice," to which the magazine adds, "OK, but can I cough first?"

For the honest marketing man or woman, as the saying goes, with friends like these you don't need enemies. After reviewing these examples, marketing professionals should not be surprised that they are accosted by strangers who learn their vocation and that they "get no respect" (to borrow a popular comedic refrain).

Because he was a known drug user, comedian Lenny Bruce (who eventually died of an overdose) was required by a judge to submit to a test for addiction. The comedian later told his audiences that, despite the negative test results, the doctor reported to the court that Bruce was really an addict who had fooled the test by going off drugs. By this view, people who drive at the speed limit are not obeying the law, but rather, slowing down to fool the police. But with modern radar detectors, this is not all that illogical. Every modern Olympics story includes allegations of athletes who train on drugs and then quit long enough before the games to both have the drug benefit and still appear clean on a medical screening.

I guess there is no reason to expect marketing people to be any different. Business leaders might wish to set a more uplifting or positive tone, but "can do" means that many firms "will do."

NOTES

1. Even with the heavy diet of war movies common for people of my generation, I can't recall any positive or useful portrayals of landmines used by movie "heroes."

2. This original example was first pointed out to me by an M.B.A. student at the University of Canterbury in New Zealand, Philippa A. Stewart, "Landmines and the Misplaced Marketing of Destruction," *Journal of Consumer Marketing*, vol. 17 (no. 3, 2000), pp. 201–202.

3. Keith Bradsher, "Ford Admits SUVs are Environmental Brutes But Profits Outweigh Social Responsibility," *New York Times News Service* (May 12, 2000).

4. Ivan Preston, *The Tangled Web They Weave: Truth, Falsity, and Advertisers* (Madison: University of Wisconsin Press, 1994). This outstanding review of the advertising law and the loopholes used by advertisers also indicates that regulations can allow companies to lie to consumers.

5. In English-speaking countries outside North America, the *chemist* is the retail pharmacy and store for over-the-counter drugs.

6. In contrast to the experiences described in Chapter 3, shopping in New Zealand stores was a joy. People were always available and ready to help shoppers, though that did not necessarily mean they were better trained in the details of the store products. And like the young people in that chapter, the clerks I dealt with in the different chemist stores were also arithmetic challenged. They had difficulty understanding that by following the label direc-

tions on daily dose and looking at the cost per pill, the bigger timed-release pills cost more per day for the benefit of not having to take them as often.

7. Hilary Bower, "Say Goodbye to Cellulite," *The (Manchester) Guardian* (March 16, 1999); Sarah Ryle, "'Miracle Cure' for Cellulite Goes on Sale," *The (London) Observer* (March 7, 1999); Thomas Jaffe, "Fat Chance," *Forbes* (May 3, 1999).

8. In one of the studies, both patients and doctors knew what products they were getting and what they were expected to do. The other two studies were single-blind, meaning the doctor knew who was getting the drug and who got a placebo. Since results involved measuring dimensions of women's soft tissue, the potential for researcher bias and simple error was very high. And bias is a danger in all areas of research, even impacting researchers' unconscious decisions and assessments, as was so clearly pointed out by Stephen Jay Gould, *The Mismeasure of Man* (New York: W. W. Norton & Company, 1996).

9. However, the Federal Trade Commission filed a complaint against Rexall Sundown, the U.S. distributor, and sought an injunction on sale of the product, *FTC v. Rexall Sundown, Inc.* (Southern District of Florida). "Rexall Sundown Charged by FTC With Making False and Unsubstantiated Claims for 'Cellasene,'" *FTC News*, released July 20, 2000. The court complaint is available at <http://www.ftc.gov/os/2000/07/rexalcmp.html>.

10. "Selling It: A Step in the Wrong Direction," *Consumer Reports*, vol. 65 (October 2000), p. 67.

11. Ivan L. Preston, *The Great American Blow-Up: Puffery in Advertising and Selling*, rev. ed. (Madison: University of Wisconsin Press, 1996). In this case, the plaintiff was drawing implied meanings from advertising claims and the manufacturer was overstating the value of a feature. The guards did not protect the rider but might have been able to limit the amount of serious damage to the motorcycle itself.

12. The following discussion and quotations are from the Report of NARB Panel 94, "Advertising by Minute Maid Company, A Division of Coca-Cola Company, for Minute Maid Frozen Concentrate Orange Juice," Panel Chairman John Moorhead, February 26, 1997.

13. Scott Adams, *The Dilbert Future: Thriving on Stupidity in the 21st Century* (New York: HarperCollins, 1997).

14. Lowell Bergman, "Network Television News: With Fear and Favor," *Columbia Journalism Review* (May–June 2000). This particular example became public when it was the basis for a big-budget movie, but other instances go undiscovered. Lawrence K. Grossman, "'The Insider:' It's Only a Movie," *Columbia Journalism Review* (November–December 1999).

15. Combined, these deals paid Laws in excess of $4 million per year. Arrogant Americans might note that this is Australian dollars. However, the sum still translates into U.S. dollars two or three times more than that for a top winner on Regis Philbin's game show.

16. Lance McMahon, "Talk Radio Advertorial Regulation: The 'Cash for Comment' Case," in *Proceedings of Marketing and Public Policy Conference* (Chicago: American Marketing Association, 2000), pp. 96–104.

17. T. Dusevic, "Ethical Cleansing: Investigations of Australian Radio King John Laws Can Only Be Good for the Media," *Time International*, vol. 154 (no. 4,

1999), p. 12; J. Lyons, "Inside the Court of King John," *The Bulletin* (July 27, 1999).

18. Apologies and "regrets" of bankers were published in *The Australian*, July 22, 1999; July 23, 1999; and September 2, 1999. However, they apparently were slow to realize they had done anything wrong, as reported in J. Kavanagh, "Bankers Fail to Tell, or Get, the Message," *Business Review Weekly* (July 30, 1999).

19. Patrick R. Parsons and Herbert J. Rotfeld, "Infomercials and Television Station Clearance Practices," *Journal of Public Policy & Marketing*, vol. 9 (1990), pp. 62–72; Rader Hayes and Herbert J. Rotfeld, "Infomercials & Cable Network Programming," *Advancing the Consumer Interest*, vol. 1 (no. 2, 1989), pp. 17–22.

20. Herbert J. Rotfeld, "Media Standards for Acceptable Advertising and Potentially Desirable 'Chilling Effects' on Advertising Free Speech," in *Proceedings of the 17th Annual Macromarketing Conference* (Breukelen, The Netherlands: Nijenrode University, May 30, 1992), pp. 335–356; Herbert J. Rotfeld, "Factors in Media Vehicles' Standards for Acceptable Advertising," unpublished presentation abstracted in *1998 Marketing and Public Policy Conference Proceedings*, vol. 8 (Chicago: American Marketing Association, 1998), p. 40. Since the man who took the money was now broke and in jail, she sued the station to recover her investment, claiming that she made it, in major part, because of the deceptive nature of the programs. That case was settled days before the scheduled trial, with Mrs. Neilson getting all her money back from the station, plus enough to cover expenses and attorney fees.

21. Obviously, the Italian company mentioned earlier in this chapter was not alone in tapping into this large market of consumer concern. In this case, the product was of questionable value and the overinflated claims (as well as the misleading infomercial format) were eventually the focus of FTC action.

22. Michael Hoyt, "When the Walls Come Tumbling Down," *Columbia Journalism Review* (March–April 1990), pp. 35–41; Gloria Steinem, "Sex, Lies and Advertising," *Ms.* (July–August 1990), pp. 19–28; Anne Cunningham and Eric Haley, "A Look Inside the World of Advertising-Free Publishing: A Case Study of *Ms.* Magazine," *Journal of Current Issues and Research in Advertising*, vol. 22 (Fall 2000), pp. 17–30.

23. Marianne Costantinou, "Shocking the City That Can't Be Shocked," *San Francisco Examiner* (January 27, 2000), p. A1; Jonathan Curiel, "Graphic Breast Ads Taken Down," *San Francisco Chronicle* (January 29, 2000), p. A13.

24. "Burnett Loses Its Goodyear Account," *Advertising Age* (December 17, 1997); "Goodyear Awards McCann $25m for Latin America/Asia," *Advertising Age International* (March 6, 1998).

25. Howard Luck Gossage, "How to Look at Billboards," *Harper's Magazine* (February 1960), reprinted in *Is There Any Hope For Advertising*, Kim Rotzoll, Jarlath Graham, and Barrows Mussey, eds. (Urbana: University of Illinois Press, 1986), pp. 109–115.

10

Fear of Marketing

Aside from the deceptions, frauds, and market abuses of Chapter 9, marketing itself, and especially advertising, possesses an image as inherently evil, even when honestly employed in connection with legal products or services that people want to buy. Public health managers in Chapter 5 had faith in the power of advertising to solve social problems, but the flip side is that the consumer fears that marketing activities cause people to act in a fashion contrary to their own self-interest.

Many people seriously believe that they are manipulated by advertising messages directed below the threshold of conscious perceptions. They can't see it, but they think the hidden messages are there and influencing them, nonetheless. Visible and obvious marketing efforts for name-brand products are seen as creating the generic consumer desires to smoke cigarettes, drink alcohol, or gamble. Numerous critics of marketing apparently believe that, without advertising, smokers would never realize how enjoyable addiction to a carcinogenic substance could be. As described in Chapter 1, even some people who understand that marketing must deal with audience predispositions believe that those all-knowing business managers know just what buttons to push to get consumers to buy products.

Many marketing educators and practitioners like to talk about their work as "marketing science." So an amusing image is formed in my mind whenever there is discussion of marketing research employed for evil purposes. It raises the specter of the "mad marketing scientist," a cross between the comic book icon of a mad scientist and Hollywood's favorite heavy—the businessperson driven by unbridled avarice.

For whatever reason, marketing decisions to serve customer demand for socially condemned yet legal products are under constant scrutiny. The advertising is under constant attack and use of any marketing tools is often called unethical. And some marketing tools are themselves accused of being destructive to society and culture.

For many, the public fear of marketing power persists. And for people with those fears, almost all marketing efforts are misplaced.

POPULAR PARANOIA AND
MYTHS OF MANIPULATION

Almost every bookstore carries materials that claim to alter your habits by use of subliminal messages over television, stereos, or home computers. Subliminal manipulation of the public is a frequent plot device in television, movies, and books, though these works of fiction all fall under the heading of fantasy.[1]

Quite simply, it is *impossible* to "manipulate" anyone by advertising messages—subliminal or otherwise. In fact, numerous mass communications and persuasion studies failed to find any support for the idea that subliminal advertising is able to control people's behavior.

Many people know about a 1950s researcher who claimed to have influenced a movie theater's Coke and popcorn sales by subliminal messages of "eat popcorn" and "buy Coca-Cola," via single frames inserted into a movie. Not consciously seen by the audience, their subconscious impact allegedly caused the sales increases reported in announcements of his "experiment."[2]

The story is repeated by many people as a fact, but it does not become true simply because it is repeated. Oh, the researcher made the claims, but people who repeat the story of the movie experiment fail to also note the events that followed the initial announcement that audience members had been manipulated.

A major research firm attempted numerous repetitions of the experiment under controlled conditions, never finding significant changes in popcorn or drink sales. Other studies by academic researchers also failed to replicate the original results. The man who conducted the first theater study eventually admitted that he had invented his experiment's results in an effort to revive his then-failing research firm.[3]

In modern times, another man points to hidden pictures in ads that he claims cause sales. He finds "S-E-X" hidden in a picture of ice cubes, and extensive lascivious imagery in the picture of clams on his restaurant placemat. He also claims to find hidden sexual pictures in the artwork of DaVinci or Michelangelo (never bothering to explain why an Italian artist would find significance in the English word S-E-X to make them worth burying in a major painting). And his ideas have obviously captured the popular imagination: He has sold many books, and he is a well-paid and well-traveled speaker on the lecture circuit.[4]

Of course, anyone might spot all types of "buried" images in pictures, but you can also find them in clouds, cow pastures, the Chicago skyline, and the dot patterns of acoustic tiles. This does not mean people intentionally put the pictures there, or that the pictures cause people to buy products. Not a single scrap of theory or research data supports the possibility of subliminal advertising playing a useful role in the advertising business. It does not influence how people make purchases.

Unfortunately, many people strongly believe that subliminal advertising messages possess massive power over their lives. I report research data to my students and, in some cases, nothing I say can shake their preconceptions.[5] Otherwise intelligent and thoughtful students tell me they are doing a term paper on this topic for an English class, saying "But I know you don't believe in it." But it is not a matter of belief, as if the topic were the best movie of the year or whether dogs are smarter than cats.

The surprising thing is that after seeing all the data and research, people still ask whether advertisers are using subliminal messages. Well, I do not know *all* advertisers, but consider the constraints of the business. The preparation of every ad or commercial involves many people, and it is difficult to imagine that any advertiser could keep the inclusion of subliminal messages secret.

The advertising managers would have to know about it. The copywriters and art directors, the people who plan the ads, would have to work out how the subliminal messages are hidden. The people who produce the ad would have to be informed, since they put it in final form and would need to make certain the hidden messages are properly reproduced. All it would take would be one person to stand up and say, "Look at what we did!" The resulting bad publicity would be incalculable.

When you consider the weak ability of any ad to communicate a message (much less persuade an audience), any advertiser would be extremely foolish to take the publicity risk of using subliminal advertising.

During the 2000 U.S. presidential campaign, a television commercial for George W. Bush had a brief flash of the word "Rats" on the screen during comments about the Democrats. Of course, the supposedly subliminal note was quickly discovered by reporters, forcing the candidate to spend time explaining how or why such an insert appeared. If it wasn't, as he said, an accident from a computer-generated graphic, then the president is really dumber than his worst detractors like to claim.[6]

If advertisers from the lunatic fringe wished to go to the effort of using subliminal messages, that is their own business. There might be someone foolish enough to waste money in this manner, but no one need care in the least.

ILLUSIONS AND DELUSIONS
OF MARKETING'S CULTURAL ROLE

There exists a body of marketing critics that view market segmentation and the demassification of media audiences as a potentially destructive force in modern society. They don't blame some amorphous business conspiracy for the increasing fragmentation of media audiences, but they present a paranoid view of our cultural future. In their view, as stated in an article in *Marketing News* (of all unexpected places), "The commercial discipline of segmentation is antithetical to a free, open and democratic society.... [The narrow and more personal messages through segmented media vehicles] separate people rather than bring people together. They kill our common dreams and aspirations, and compartmentalize the American experience."[7]

As a core area of that business, market segmentation itself has been increasingly criticized for all sorts of reasons. And while these criticisms are often voiced by people with limited knowledge or understanding of marketing theory and practice, the mere existence of the critics has influenced marketing theory and research. I address in Chapter 14 how some business critics call segmentation the "potential exploitation of vulnerable populations." To them, the research question becomes when, not if, segmentation might be unethical. And as discussed in Chapter 11, marketing might be an improper guide for the production of cultural products.

But aside from using segmentation as an abused marketing tool, the critics described here see segmentation itself as a destructive cultural force.

The basic premise is that audience segmentation—and especially the pinpoint targeting that is theoretically possible with new media technology—reinforces suspicion, alienation, and lack of empathy between people of different groups, since they have lost the shared consumer experience that the old mass media audience system provided. They condemn cable television and the Internet as the most devastating forces against people's ability to communicate with each other.

In the early days of radio, movie theaters would stop the show and play the latest episode of *Amos 'n Andy*, lest the customers stay away to listen at home. In the early days of television, it was Milton Berle or *I Love Lucy* that everyone watched. Two decades later, almost everyone on the street had the shared experience of watching *M*A*S*H* or *Dallas* or *The Brady Bunch*. The advertising on these shows would be the subject of conversation, even for people not interested in buying the products. Today, with increasing demassification of the media and the ability of marketers to target refined audiences, the ability to share a narrow, specific consumer experience is becoming the only thing linking anyone together, or so this theory goes.

These business critics *expect* marketing to provide the nation's shared culture. Maybe they are just getting old. Their complaints ignore that fact that the plethora of modern media options allow young people to share the cultural products of a generation ago. Old television programs and movies are endlessly repeated on various cable networks, finding new audiences and fans with each repetition. New delivery systems provide new and extended life for the popular music or books of earlier decades. Some of my students listen to CDs by the same groups whose music filled my apartment complex when I was in graduate school.

This critical cultural analysis and resulting view also requires overlooking so much of the modern reality, as well as ignoring a bit of the past. As one author expressed this that "[The] U.S. is experiencing a major shift in balance between society-making media and segment-making media" to our social detriment.[8] Yet he overlooks the historic nature of the advertising-supported media system that always gave primary service to those groups of people that marketers wanted to reach. Their critical analysis usually disregards the mass media icons that exist and thrive, though maybe not in a way that appeals to them.

Anyone who teaches a wide range of different undergraduate students finds the shared experiences that still exist. Traveling around the country to different schools, or even around the world, there exist popular television shows for which many people recount the same experiences. If a student in class wishes to talk about a new commercial seen the night before, it requires little explanation, since most of the class has seen it, too. And the faculty member could readily recount the same commercial or show when traveling across the country to talk to a different student group or even to a room of business executives. Young people go to school or meet people on the street and talk about interesting Web sites or popular games.

As it says in the *Talmud*, "We see not things as they are. We see them as we are." These business critics probably are noting their own disconnection from so much of the media and not necessarily that of audiences. It is akin to when syndicated columnist Thomas Sowell wrote that the diaper-changing stations in men's public restrooms were "wasted space" because he never saw anyone use them. Similarly, a city council member critical of his city's cable system suggested that it make space for WGN by removing Lifetime since he did not know anyone who watched Lifetime, not realizing that the network is oriented toward women.

This is not to deny that media are becoming demassified, or that these new media have great potential for tailoring messages to specific market segments. Yet the pragmatic reality is that this same trend also presents problems, as media buyers need to place messages in more vehicles to communicate with the target audience. The modern business problem is how to come up with a common strategic message that transcends narrow concerns of single audiences, cultures, or even nations. And as the audience for each vehicle becomes smaller and narrower, the data on that audience become less precise, *despite* what some critics like to believe.

The unremarkable and well-known fact is that U.S. media are becoming demassified, reflecting the new influxes and changes of society. And many minorities are increasingly recognized as valuable markets that buy for their own personal and diverse subcultural reasons. As they have throughout history, immigrant groups change the face of the country. New generations have their own common icons that the elders see but seldom understand.

It is strange. These critics of business expect marketing to be an institutional force responsible for giving the nation a single shared culture. To a point, it does that. But, for the most part, it is incapable of doing so and never could. As my former office mate seemed to say once a week, that's why there are so many flavors of Jell-O.

SELLING SIN

In his newspaper column, L. M. Boyd once listed the anonymous assertion that "People are more violently opposed to fur than leather because it is safer to harass rich women than motorcycle gangs." Bill Maher observed on his *Politically Incorrect* television program that laws restricting the marketing of motorcycles, booze, or bungee jumping are pushed by people who'd rather ban motorcycles, booze, or bungee jumping altogether.

As a very visible business practice, marketing often becomes the target of many public criticisms when used by firms selling certain products. Frequently, marketing tools are singled out for special negative notice by critics of firms involved in making or selling alcoholic beverages, guns, cigarettes, pornography, and legal gambling activities.[9]

The makers of any product try to find segments in which product use is either increasing or remains strong (or at least remains strong in light of decreasing per capita demand). Once finding those segments, whether for a "sinful" product or not, the marketer provides product features, designs brand names, advertises, and sells at a price that satisfies the needs of selected market segments better than other firms.

It is strange how targeting almost any group for these products other than high-income white males is criticized. A new cigarette brand aimed at office secretaries and other low-level clerical working women is condemned for targeting a "vulnerable" audience, as is another brand of menthols for urban-dwelling African-Americans. A new beer appealing to low-income black consumers generates accusations that the corporations are attempting to commit genocide, since the beer contained a higher alcohol content that these consumers preferred.

Of course, children should not be the targets of these adult products.[10] That is why people below a certain age or elderly people with impaired judgment are called "vulnerable groups." But critics of marketing practices also refer to adult women, African-Americans, Hispanics, and other minorities as "vulnerable groups," as if they were children needing protection. It is odd that only possessors of pale penises are perceived to also possess the potential to personally resist the persuasive power of marketing promotions. Adult women should resent someone else saying they are incapable of deciding to smoke or buy guns. No one has ever suggested that African-Americans should be banned from purchasing cigarettes or alcohol.

Yet, by the definitions of marketing, all elements of the marketing plan are employed to facilitate both consumer satisfaction and the organization's well-being. To put it more bluntly, efficient market segmentation and target markets are used to maximize a firm's sales or profits. They do not necessarily seek to maximize generic sales, but they do desire sales for the marketer.

Many people believe that any marketing is misplaced and should not be used for these products, but marketing is not the real problem. Their problem is with the products themselves. Critics of these products believe that no tool that maximizes a firm's sales or market share should be employed.

In reality, many nonusers of these products really wish to prevent other people from using them. But since the products are legal, the critics attack marketing, seeing it as a sales tool used to maximize sales. Critics argue that it "improperly" increases generic demand for the products, while defenders assert that it can only influence brand choice for people already predisposed to making a purchase. Yet the real issue is not demand, but sales—any sales—and company profits on products the critics view as "undesirable."

Maybe the critics dislike consumers' motives for buying or using these products. Many women buy guns out of fear and related concerns for personal protection. People play lotteries out of greed. Advertising does not create fear or greed, but it is sometimes seen as improper to use marketing tools to play on them. At best, cigarettes and pornography are described as "guilty pleasures," with varying degrees of social condemnation often admitted even by the users, who apologetically refer to their "filthy habit." Even when the strong demand segments for cigarettes, malt liquors, and other dangerous products are people of legal age, business critics still assert that they are too young, uneducated, or otherwise too naive to know the full risks.

The products are socially condemned, yet legal. Regardless of popular "appeal" or social acceptability, people want to buy these products. It is the nonusers who disapprove. Maybe the issue is not legitimacy, but, rather, the ups and downs of government or public groups that try to restrict how consumers use products—and sometimes succeed.

No one is yet asserting that cigarettes or alcohol should be prohibited in a fashion akin to marijuana or cocaine. Sales to adults of guns and pornography are protected by the first two amendments to the U.S. Constitution. And even when illegal or severely restricted, gambling thrives. But regardless of consumer demand, marketing practices are under constant attack, and their uses are often called unethical.

THE CONDOM CONUNDRUM

Since AIDS remains incurable, activists continue to pressure the mass media to accept condom commercials as a part of the campaign to slow the spread of the disease. But the condom companies have their own marketing problems, and their priorities do not necessarily mesh with those of the activists. And none of the companies have very large budgets for advertising and sales promotion.

First and foremost, the condom companies want to promote brand demand, not generic use of the product. Maybe Trojan would be happy to make generic advertising appeals, since it is the largest brand name and holds about a two-thirds market share. If you assume that brand share will remain constant, Trojans would be bought by three out of every five new users, but that is not a safe assumption. Lifestyles or Durex have much smaller market shares, so they and the other companies certainly would use their limited marketing budgets for brand demand within the group of users.

Yet it is difficult to promote any form of brand image via the mass media, since vehicles limit the form, format, and content of condom commercials. The restrictions limit the companies' abilities to promote the product to anyone, much less the targets most at risk for the disease.

As this is being written, none of the major broadcast networks have accepted a condom commercial for broadcast during their programs. The three oldest broadcast networks still state the ban on the product in their written codes, a policy that is also followed for their owned and operated stations. The Fox network has indicated that they "might" accept condom commercials, but every year has rejected all those the companies have submitted.

Actually, one condom company marketing manager told me she hopes the networks keep rejecting the spots. Every rejection generates publicity that gets the spots shown for free, but if they were accepted for broadcast, a single network placement would wipe out her entire annual promotion budget.[11]

Network affiliates and cable networks accept condom ads, but they are not free from restrictions or limitations on form or content. Some television stations accept condom ads if the message is safe sex for disease prevention, but not if the message is birth control (though, as far as I know, the product is used the same way for either goal). The station and cable network managers want to avoid complaints, and they fear that parents might object to stations broadcasting sex-related messages to their offspring. Public health appeals that discuss "safe sex" are seen by many as encouraging promiscuity.

It's not easy to "tastefully" advertise condoms or safe sex. Throughout her tumultuous time in office as Surgeon General, Dr. Joycelyn Elders continuously pressed the case for more condom advertising on television. And one of her earliest critics, Janet Parshall of Concerned Women for America, was quoted as saying, "Condom manufacturers profiteer from teenage promiscuity. The Surgeon General should be pushing for abstinence, not condoms."[12]

Yet the difficult thing for people over the age of thirty to realize is that the AIDS epidemic is no longer news. People entering college in the twenty-first century have always had information about AIDS in their environment. At various spring break activities in Florida, a condom company's marketing manager discovered that the topic of safe sex was passé. In fact, the phrase "safe sex" verges on being a joke, something today's youth have heard all their lives like "buckle your seat belt." The ineluctable impression is that, like seat belt use, if young people are engaging in unsafe behaviors, it is not from lack of information about the risks.

Condom users are predominantly eighteen to thirty-five years old. But while new users are always coming into the market, others are getting older and dropping out. It is an established product. There exist some limited demographic correlates for users of specific brands, such as Lifestyles, and the goal of the companies is to develop these market segments for brand image and brand demand. In this context, the companies are caught in a three-way conflict: the limitations of what they can say, the activists who want to see generic appeals that do not serve company goals, and the critics who feel any marketing of this product to young people is misplaced and sending the wrong message.

TO PROTECT CHILDREN

Take a child and confine him or her to a cave from age two. Better yet, keep a group of them here so they can play together and develop social skills. Teachers can come in, and books and other educational materials will be available. Television and the Internet will be commercial free. Then when they reach some age deemed to be "responsible"— thirteen or sixteen or whatever—we bring them into society, let them have jobs and money, and finally allow them to see advertising.

The result? Why, chaos, of course. They never learned how to handle advertising.

Children today have money. Even when they do not make direct purchases, they influence what their parents buy. And living in a commercial world is an important part of socialization, which, we hope, involves the parents in educating children about the limits of seeing–wanting–having.

The history of marketing over the past century is intertwined with efforts to protect children from its influences. And in the name of protecting children, all sorts of marketing restrictions are enforced. Laws on sales and product distribution also limit the market choices for adults. There also are restrictions on advertising of certain products to adults in contexts in which children "might" see them. Throughout it all, the critics are loath to admit that many adults enjoy using products that might have deadly or destructive consequences as a result of long-term use. Many people seem to hold the near-paranoid view that marketing creates almost all consumer interest in cigarettes, alcohol, gambling, and pornography.

It gets strange.

Optimally, an honestly used and properly applied marketing perspective can help satisfy marketplace concerns of many people. But instead of seeing marketing as a useful business tool, many people fear it.

NOTES

1. And I won't call these stories "science fiction" because there is no basis for the concept in science, marketing, or any other field.

2. Martin Mayer, *Madison Avenue, U.S.A.* (New York: Harper and Row, 1957), pp. 146–147.

3. Stuart Rogers, "How a Publicity Blitz Created the Myth of Subliminal Advertising," *Public Relations Quarterly* (Winter 1993), pp. 12–17; Randall Rothenberg, "How Powerful is Advertising?" *The Atlantic Monthly*, vol. 279 (June 1997), pp. 113–120; Bob Garfield, "'Subliminal' Seduction and Other Urban Myths," *Advertising Age* (September 14, 2000).

4. Juliann Sivulka, *Soap, Sex and Cigarettes: A Cultural History of American Advertising* (Belmont, CA: Wadsworth Publishing, 1998), pp. 330–331; Eric J. Zanot, David Pincus, and E. Joseph Lamp, "Public Perceptions of Subliminal Advertising," *Journal of Advertising*, vol. 12 (no. 1, 1983), pp. 39–45; Jack Haberstroh, *Ice Cube Sex* (Notre Dame, IN: Crossroads Books, 1994).

5. As summarized in Timothy Moore, "The Case Against Subliminal Manipulation," *Psychology and Marketing*, vol. 5 (Winter 1988), pp. 297–316; Timothy Moore, "Subliminal Advertising: What You See Is What You Get," *Journal of Marketing*, vol. 46 (Spring 1982), pp. 38–47; Jack Haberstroh, *Ice Cube Sex*.

6. The broadcast news reports revealed that the candidate did not know how to pronounce "subliminal," providing another example of his language-mangling for late-night comedians.

7. Robert Barash, "The Dumbing-Down of America," *Marketing News*, vol. 31 (October 27, 1997), p. 4.

8. Joseph Turow, *Breaking Up America: Advertisers and the New Media World* (Chicago: University of Chicago Press, 1997).

9. An outstanding review of the marketing problems faced by firms in these product categories is presented in D. Kirk Davidson, *Selling Sin: The Marketing of Socially Unacceptable Products* (Westport, CT: Quorum Books, 1996). I used his book as the title for this section, but I can't summarize or do justice to his full analysis. He provides a thorough review of the marketing limitations faced by firms that must deal with public criticisms, many questioning the very legitimacy of their businesses.

10. As internal company documents became public, critics claimed that segments of memoranda and research notes proved that the cigarette companies considered children a target market. The companies disputed this interpretation. See, for example, Ira Teinowitz, "Critics' Take On Tobacco Ad Documents Disputed," *Advertising Age* (February 9, 1998), p. 43.

11. As a practical matter, even cable might not be very efficient. Durex ran a spot on MTV in 1997, but, in a new campaign two years later, opted for a combination of print and radio to attain a greater frequency with the young audience. In addition, the ads were changed to a pleasure appeal instead of "safe sex," which does not promote an anti-AIDS message but raises the potential for public complaints about televised spots. David Goetzl, "Durex: Good Sex, Not Just Safe Sex," *Advertising Age* (July 5, 1999), p. 12.

12. It is somehow ironic that Dr. Elders was later accused of having stepped over the line of tasteless suggestions by advocating masturbation as a sexual outlet to help young people remain abstinent.

11 ——————————————

The "Wrong" Benefits I:
Politics and Popular Culture

When told to come up with some impressive labels for a hand cream, an advertising copywriter invented the arresting and healthy-sounding term "oxygenating moisturizers." She also wrote some promotional copy that described "tiny bubbles of oxygen that release moisture into your skin." Her work then was turned over to the client company's research and development department with instructions to come up with a product that matched the copy.[1]

This might seem like an example of a world upside down, with a product created to match the creative advertising. However, the company was acting honestly, wanting to design a new product that would truthfully deliver on the copywriter's claims. If her prose matched a consumer interest, she was providing directions for a new product designed to meet consumer needs.

On the other hand, another company once wanted to change its already-popular soft drink to fit its advertised claim: "a little bit of natural flavor in every drop." Since the best-selling flavor in the brand line did not have any natural flavoring, the company decided to add a trace amount of natural juice to the product formula. The minuscule addition would not alter the taste but it would change the product to fit the advertising theme the manufacturer wanted to use.[2] Technically, this might have made the new ad claims true, but it is a story of marketing abuse that could easily have fit with those reported in Chapter 9.

A modern marketing perspective develops new products to match consumer interests; it doesn't produce new products simply to deliver what a manufacturer wants to create. Marketing planning for a product's features is based on assessing what consumers would choose.

But if you give people the power to choose, who says they will choose wisely? Maybe some things should not be "designed" to fit a marketing plan. Marketing shouldn't be applied to everything in society; some parts of culture or public life are too important to let public opinion dictate their content or form.

In the fictional business meeting portrayed in a television commercial, executives plan for a new movie about a slug. They have already produced a prototype for a line of new slug toys. The coupons are printed and contracts are signed for slug tie-ins with retailers. They have consumer tests of a "slug on a stick" food product and actors with strong star appeal have all signed their contracts. What about a script? Writers are standing by who can produce it the following week.

One part of Chapter 10 described concerns of business critics who are upset that entertainment and other mass media products are designed to serve narrow audience segments. Their concern is that appeals to precisely defined groups take away the shared experience of the greater society. For the examples in this chapter and the next, something important for the greater good is lost when all cultural or political "product" features are designed to fit what consumers think they might want. From a societal point of view, while marketing tools could be used to sell products to the public, sometimes it should not dictate the product itself.

MARKETING AT LEADERSHIP'S EXPENSE

From the start of Jimmy Carter's run for the White House, and even after he had defeated Gerald Ford in the presidential election, news reports scrutinized the symbolism of Carter's every move. Analysts endlessly assessed Carter's image "decisions," such as carrying his own garment bag on airplanes, walking down Pennsylvania Avenue for his inauguration ceremony, and wearing a cardigan sweater for a televised speech on energy conservation. Even cartoonist Garry Trudeau's "Doonesbury" strip had a Carter staff member managing a special White House Office on Symbolism. The ineluctable impression was that everything Carter said or did was based on a marketing plan instead of political conviction.

With every major election, marketing becomes a greater center of attention in the news, with frequent headlines featuring poll results specifying who is "winning" or "losing" at a given point in time. Reporters and analysts provide more information on the candidates' marketing decisions than on their political values or proposals. And this probably is not improper when the major party candidates obviously make speeches and create advertising based on marketing plans.

The politicians have paid opinion-poll researchers on staff and changes are made in political strategy to fit the latest readings of the public mood. While there are basic differences between voters who identify themselves as Republicans or Democrats, marketing encourages candidates to appropriate each other's issues by spouting platitudes focus-grouped and tested for maximum popular appeal. As a result, the candidates often sound the same. In the 2000 election, marketing research decided exactly what voters wanted to hear and what words, phrases, or tones of voice would persuade them or turn them off. Bush and Gore were both pliable candidates, following marketing directions from their handlers, avoiding risks, and keeping on point with similar-sounding messages designed to attract undecided voters in swing states.[3]

With marketing in control, leadership is lost. Denigrating one successful candidate of several elections ago in print and on ABC News' *This Week with David Brinkley*, columnist George Will described the man's ideological icon as being a wetted finger held to the wind.

For example, Americans love the death penalty. Apart from the basic moral issues, there are numerous reasons to question its modern existence: racial and social inequities in its application; geographic disparities in its use; financial costs of appeals and prisons required to apply it; and the unavoidable uncertainties of executing someone who later could be found innocent. Yet, according to some polls, a majority of people in the United States would remain in favor of the death penalty if it were found that as many as one person in every hundred were wrongly executed. With figures like these, no politician of stature would dare stand up to such a weight of marketing opinion. The issue is not even discussed, as most candidates try to prove they are more pro-death than their opponents.

But leaders could encourage change. When West Germany outlawed the death penalty, 74 percent of people approved of it, but this proportion had slipped to 26 percent a mere three decades later. Once the leaders made the change, a generation of people who were not brought up with the death penalty came to think of it as a barbaric relic.[4]

More recently, a sudden surge in gasoline prices had politicians scrambling for solutions. Of course, the real cause of rising oil prices was a simple matter of supply and demand, as consumers love their less-than-efficient large cars, trucks, and sport utility vehicles. The best long-term solution would be for the leaders to encourage conservation, but that would not be popular in the short run. So, instead, responding to the marketing guidance of public opinion polls, President Clinton released oil from the strategic petroleum reserves, while candidate Bush recommended greater drilling in protected wilderness areas.

Years ago, politicians tried to change public opinion. With marketing, they just respond to it. Political parties once represented strongly held values of their members, but now they represent loose confederations of people seeking power. Instead of parties trying to persuade the public of the validity of a particular point of view, party leaders adapt their views to the public whim.

The successful Republican goes right during the primaries, then veers a bit left again for the general election. The Democrat goes left until the nomination is locked, then fakes right. During the election, the major party candidates slant and time the presentations of their proposals, trying to manage their press coverage to get the best marketing-derived image across to the public.

And then there is advertising.

Advertising is a strong marketing tool for politicians and, optimally, it tells the public what the candidate will do once in office. We are voting for our political leaders and the campaigns could set the tone for our national leadership.

Of course, advertising is not the only source of political information. Journalists present the candidates' records and public statements. But the news can only go so far; there is only so much "news" to report and, as already noted, most of the news amounts to the latest analysis of the candidates' marketing plans.

Candidates for public office tell us why we should vote for them. For any ad campaign to work—whether it's for a toothpaste or for a U.S. Senate candidate—it must appeal to something that a large number of people consider important. Unfortunately, possibly because people more readily know what they dislike instead of what they like, many political messages end up with a negative tone. Negative advertising supplants leadership, with candidates trying to strike negative chords that appeal to selected target audiences.

With some voters in some situations, negative ads can win an election. But, once elected, the only mandate is to not be the person everyone voted against.

From 1989 to 1992, the president of the United States was "not-Dukakis." And four years later, he unsuccessfully ran as "not-Clinton." In 1996, the primaries were filled with negative appeals, from one candidate's politics of hate to another one's unsubtle claims that votes for Bob Dole or Phil Gramm would bring nuclear terrorists into U.S. cities. In that general election, with an incumbent president and a long-time senator representing the major parties, the candidates each had a strong basis to outline the positive leadership they would provide in office. But both candidates seemed more concerned with marketing than with leadership. Once he had locked up the nomination, Bob Dole spent his time saying how he would be a great "not-Clinton." In the 2000 campaign, the candidates both said they would be positive—since the polls started to find that voters were tired of negative campaigns—but in reality they ran all sorts of negative attacks. And from the beginning, George W. Bush sounded like his father since he, too, often said he would be a good "not-Clinton," even though his opponent was Al Gore.

This points up a basic problem of negative political ads—the same problem that makes product advertisers not use them. A new toothpaste won't find success as "not-Crest."

Not long ago, basic advertising ethics called for firms to avoid making direct comparisons with competitors' products. "You should find something good to say about your brand," the textbooks said, "not try to belittle your competitors." In modern times, many firms find that they can convey more information, and convey it strongly, by making a comparison with the leading brand. But when a business names competitors in its advertising, it has to say why its product is better, not just that the other brand is bad. Years ago, an advertising battle between Tylenol and Advil was tied to claims of product superiority. Fast food chains that claim their competitors are a poor choice only succeed in lowering sales at both places.

In product advertising, there are many alternatives for every advertised brand. Negative brand advertising may cause a named competitor to lose sales, but those people may choose to purchase products from competitors other than a negative advertiser instead. For a business advertiser, the secret to success lies in saying why consumers should be customers. Unfortunately, in politics, sometimes success can come from just saying why the opponent is so undesirable.

Discussing negative political ads only in terms of what types of advertising "works" is a mistake. Some people do vote for the candidate they dislike the least. Yes, the ads can influence an election and might be good marketing, but the electorate is not served by such a result. A candidate's advertising is a statement of what voters will get for their choice, but negative advertising only says what they won't get.

Political advertising can convey information and persuade voters. But trying to persuade people of the importance of a leader's values and the merits of his or her proposals is different than gaining power by saying what people want to hear.

In an old joke, a man says, "There go my people. I must find out where they are headed so I can lead them." With political marketing, this is not a joke. It becomes reality.

ALL THE NEWS THAT TARGET MARKETS
WANT TO HEAR

At the start of the twenty-first century, the most common television programming became the so-called reality shows. Aside from the cameras on people locked in houses or trapped on deserted islands, the broadcast and cable schedules are filled with news magazines, trial coverage, talk shows, and police chases. To a casual observer, consumers can choose from a vast and diverse selection of news options. Yet ratings dictate the options, so it is important to note what is still *not* widely available.

The three main broadcast networks have stepped away from full coverage of political conventions because ratings are down. Coverage of international news is minimal, as is economic news, since it is hard to explain and boring. In the early days of the 2000 presidential election, a reporter gave a pop quiz of sorts to candidate George W. Bush, and he was unable to show a clear understanding of other countries or their leaders. But, then, he represented the popular mood.

There have been two major changes in the U.S. news media in recent decades. First, a majority of people now report that their predominant source for news and information is television. While there has been a boom in television news channels, they all run the same materials as they try to tap what people want to hear. And this is because of the second change: Broadcast news has become a business instead of a service.

In the early days of broadcasting, news was a public service. Networks did it for prestige; stations did it because it was indirectly required for them to hold a government-granted license and operate in the "public interest." News was not expected to make a profit. But now the news division is a profit center in its own right, and this influences the decisions about what and how news is covered. News channels want to maximize ratings. News divisions of broadcast networks or stations compete for dominance in their coverage areas.

A century ago, advertising-supported newspapers also derived revenue from political parties or opinion groups. Advertising and marketing plans did not dictate the news coverage, but, rather, the political philosophy of the owner. According to some, that meant more news was covered and a greater diversity of views were available to the public.[5] But when any news vehicle depends purely on public support and the need for profit maximization, news the people need takes a back seat to what they want to hear. Sometimes, instead of giving insight into an issue, television news correspondents try to turn it into an empty joke.[6] But then, as candidates made appearances on talk programs that were more social than substantive, almost half of young adults reported that they sometimes got their news on the presidential campaign from the late-night comedy talk shows.[7]

In his cinematic black comedy *Network*, Paddy Chayefsky envisioned a world in which news editors would not give people what they needed to know, but instead, what they wanted to know, assuming that those people were members of demographic groups targeted by advertisers. Supposedly, the movie gave us a nightmare world, but marketing-driven news is the modern reality. Today, if it isn't hot and popular it might not be covered. When former football hero and media star O. J. Simpson was on trial for murder, the channels were all O. J. all the time, bumping most other information off the screen in the process. And, admittedly, their ratings went up.

MARKETING POPULAR CULTURE

The differences between art and entertainment have been a point of conflict and debate for centuries, and the commercialization of culture has long been a concern of mass communications studies. According to critics of modern popular culture, in order for music, movies, or television programs to succeed as commercial products, they must favor duplication, derivations, and formula writing over artistic innovation and true quality.[8]

Intuitively, a proper application of marketing principles to any product—even products involved with entertainment—should not be a limitation. After all, if marketing delivers products that people need or want, the producers should serve the popular culture by analysis of those audience interests and desires. That is why there are so many new magazines launched every week; that is why there are so many cable networks with their own original programs.

If this intuitive logic were correct, then the criticisms of popular culture in a capitalist system could only be valid if many firms were not using marketing principles. Instead, it is conservative economic paranoia, not marketing, that blinds mass-media executives to producing something new, different, or unusual. They imitate what has worked in the past to reduce the risk of making a wrong decision. They avoid taking chances on what is unknown and new. Not knowing what works, managers rely in large measure on what has worked in the past. Therefore, television, movie, and recording executives insist that new products provide some variation on past successes.

Yet a marketing orientation also feeds the executive's cautious approach to decision making. By starting with consumer needs and wants, marketing is a conservative approach to business planning, expecting research to reveal that people "know" what they want before it is on the market. And with music and television, some research reveals that marketing actually discourages innovation because what is "wanted" is not new.

Since recorded music is a multibillion-dollar industry, it is surprising how little academic research has addressed consumers' decision-making processes when it comes to purchasing these products. A music student and performer before completing her doctorate in marketing, Kathleen Lacher found that the strongest indicator of consumer intention to make a purchase was "the need to reexperience the music."[9] At least in terms of the rock music she studied, the audience's emotional responses were not a strong factor in music consumption.

In other words, never underestimate the power of a fan.

It is not a marketing mistake for business executives to discourage innovation in television or popular music. If anything, they are overusing a narrow part of marketing.

Both purchase and rental of movie videos probably depend on a customer's need to reexperience a movie or similar types of products already enjoyed in the past. An extrapolation of Dr. Lacher's findings would also explain why critically acclaimed television programs fail to quickly attract a strong enough audience to remain on the broadcast schedule. The "consumer" audience interested in something so totally different is often too small to deliver viable early ratings.

A marketing perspective underlies a certain logic in executive decisions. This gave rise to the late radio comedian Fred Allen's sarcastic comment, "Imitation is the sincerest form of television."

Movie studios are encouraged to maximize sequels; "new" television programs are heavy with spinoffs and clones of what has worked in the past. Recording company executives try to make all new artists fit into existing formats. In the bookstores, it often seems like a majority of the science-fiction books are based on the *Star Trek* television and movie characters because of its large number of fans. (At the very least, there are usually enough of these books on the shelves that they have their own section.)

However, Dr. Lacher found that consumers' desires to repeat an experience with rock music was the "strongest" predictor of a purchase. It wasn't the only one. Many people also sought variety. And, intuitively, people have many reasons for buying different types of music or books or choosing which television shows to watch. People must first purchase a ticket to experience a play or a new movie in a theater.

Her data clearly show how to best use radio or the Internet to sell new music to consumers, but it should not be taken as a prescription for limiting the new products that should be available.

Film critic Roger Ebert has repeatedly stated that marketing experts at movie studios "are the single most negative influence on [movie] quality because they can only recommend refinements of what has been done before. . . . Marketing cannot discover original ideas."[10] And, at least with artistic products, he is correct. Misplaced marketing enhances conservative managers' desires to minimize risks. The result is that any originality and innovation in popular culture exists in spite of the system, not because of it.

For movies or television, there is no marketing guide for success. There has never really been a successful formula for artistic products. There are so many variables that prediction is impossible. A few data points from a high-grossing movie or a television program with strong ratings does not give a basis for projecting what will work in the future. The presence of well-known stars does not predict whether a movie will make money. Clones of successful television programs or spinoffs of popular characters fail as readily as any other types of new movies or shows.[11] New music stars find success when they are allowed to do things that are new, not when they duplicate the work of others.

The only generalization is that cultural products succeed in the marketplace when they resonate with an audience. But past success does not guarantee future success and, because of the large number of variables, even market research can be wrong. Many successful and lauded television programs had a tough time getting on the air because some executive said it hadn't been done before. By some reports, early tests of the first *Star Wars* movie indicated it should have been dumped from movie production and converted into a children's television program.

Morris Holbrook, a scholar of marketing and popular culture, observed this in terms of a conflict between a producer and a production company's marketing orientation to culture.[12] Benny Goodman, for example, wanted to do new music that *he* liked, while the owners of the clubs in which he played wanted him to play the standard dance tunes that everyone knew. In the end, maybe society is best served if music, movies, and other cultural products are produced following the producer orientation.

As head of MTM Enterprises and (later) president of NBC, Grant Tinker was behind many successful television programs such as *Hill Street Blues*, *Lou Grant*, *The Cosby Show*, and *Cheers*. But his formula was no formula. He simply gave creative people the freedom and support to do their best work. Marketing helped promote the creative product, but marketing did not direct what that product should be.[13] In the end, modern marketing perspectives are often misplaced when they attempt to dictate the substance of creative products.

THE REAL REASON FOR
NONCOMMERCIAL BROADCASTING

I am not a sports fan, but I was struck by the tone of a news conference after the events at the Los Angeles Olympic Games. In a typical
scene, a team was rightfully proud when they were the first-ever U.S.
contingent in their sport to get to the finals in their event, gaining a
silver medal. Yet many reporters repeatedly asked, "Why didn't you
get the gold?"

So, too, with marketing. Even among the largest firms, number two
is often seen as a weak competitor. A firm can be very successful by
serving a niche market, and a cable-TV network can reap large profits
with programming for a special but small interest, yet the predominant view is that only the largest are the "best." And even if you're not
number one, everyone tries to get an ever-larger market share.

In television, the major networks fight over who can claim the distinction of being "number one." And public broadcasting is often criticized because its ratings are smaller than even the weakest commercial
outlet. And therein lies a basic problem for the U.S. public broadcasting system.

While public criticisms of specific offensive shows are rare, members of Congress often threaten it with the loss of public funding. Their
most common criticism is that the ratings for most programs are "too
low." Public broadcasting's most popular original programs would
also be a success on commercial outlets. Some basic and pay cable
networks have picked up the same types of series that have been able
to garner the best ratings on noncommercial television, thus adding
the criticism that public broadcasting is "unnecessary."

To an extent, the failure of public broadcasting is one of misplaced
marketing, but not the one that most people presume. Even some of
its boosters assert that public broadcasting should use various marketing tools to increase ratings, but that is the job of commercial, not
public, broadcasting.

It makes sense for commercial vehicles to seek the top ratings since,
as the basis for advertising rates, larger ratings mean more income
per commercial minute. Financial caution logically drives those stations and networks to let marketing design programs, but public broadcasters should be totally free of that fear. In theory, publicly funded
radio and television should be the least likely to encounter the misplaced marketing of news or entertainment described in the prior two
sections.

Noncommercial broadcasters deserve public support specifically
because the ratings are so low. This is not because they need the money,
but because the public-supported system was created to provide pro-

gramming for audience segments that would not be well served by the commercial system. Almost everyone seems to either listen to public radio or watch public television, just not all of them at the same time or to the same programs. If public broadcasting's programs were frequently among the most popular, then it would be superfluous.

Instead, public broadcasting's marketing mandate is to provide programs that might not be commercial successes. If marketing is used at all, it should not be to seek high ratings, but to serve a diverse range of audience segments with programs and formats that commercial vehicles could or would not try.

It is a strength of an advertising-supported media system that any audience desired by advertisers might have many vehicles by which to read, view, or hear. Trade magazine *Advertising Age*'s listings of media launchings gives weekly reports of new magazines or cable networks trying to gain the attention of all types of target groups. Yet it is also a weakness of that same system that some groups would remain poorly served (if at all) if marketers found them a less desirable target for advertising messages and appeals.

In other words, some groups are overserved, while others are not served at all, and the purpose of public broadcasting is to provide programming for the latter. Commercial networks have terminated top-rated programs when the audiences were older, rural or not those primarily desired by advertisers. Newspaper sections are created and designed to attract the most advertisers, not the most potential readers; they seek to appeal to suburban, not inner-city audiences. Many magazines stop publication not because of a lack of readers, but, rather, because of a lack of interested advertisers (which is why *Ms.* dropped all advertising to become a reader-supported publication).

Some of public television's greatest success stories did not start out that way. No one knew it would become so popular, or that its appeal would cut across so many segments. And with some educational programs and with some market segments, the lack of commercials is a plus regardless of the size of ratings. When the audience is small children, the same popular programs might not be so socially desirable if they were created with advertising sales in mind.

At the 2000 Republican National Convention, former presidential candidate Senator John McCain would only tell the reporters from Public Radio, "Pay for yourself." Bystanders could be heard in the background on the NPR program as they applauded his comment, but that says that only people who can pay should be served by broadcasting.

Public broadcasting can (and must) do a better job of providing programming for audience segments not served by other outlets. And as some commercial cable networks drain what have been in the past its staple materials, the need and push for innovation is even greater. But public broadcasting managers, as well as the people in Congress, should never lose sight of its basic goal; service to its audiences shouldn't be confused with seeking the largest audiences. Public broadcasting was created to serve the smallest groups, or, at least, not have to worry if the audience for every program innovation is large enough to be a success.

THE LIMITS TO WHEN
MARKETING SHOULD BE USED

As marketing is applied to non-profit organizations, we see many ways that a marketing perspective could help groups serve their constituencies. For example, without a marketing view, libraries would be designed and run for the convenience of the librarians. It is intuitively obvious that libraries become better public centers when they focus on the interests of library users. However, there are some things in which marketing might best stay away from issues of product design.

NOTES

1. *New York Times* magazine (September 30, 1990), p. 76.
2. Clifford G. Christians, Kim B. Rotzoll, and Mark Fackler, *Media Ethics: Cases and Moral Reasoning*, 3d ed. (White Plains, NY: Longman Publishing, 1991), pp. 220–222. This case was drawn from the reported actual experiences of an advertising practitioner.
3. It could validly be asserted that this made the 2000 election "one of the closest and most boring in American history," as observed by Robert B. Reich, "The Dead Heat," *The American Prospect*, vol. 11 (November 20, 2000). Available at <http://www.prospect.org/archives/V11-24/reich-r.html>.
4. Bill Bryson, *Notes From a Big Country* (London: Transworld Publishers, 1998), pp. 283–286.
5. C. Edwin Baker, *Advertising and a Democratic Press* (Princeton, NJ: Princeton University Press, 1994).
6. Johnathan Cohn, "Sam and Cokie, This Weak. Yuck, Yuck," *The New Republic Online* (November 6, 2000). Available at <wysiwyg://11/http://www.tnr.com/110600/cohn1106.html>.
7. This is from a Medill News Service poll described by Sonia Meisenheimer, "Gen Y Gets Political News From TV and Papers—and Leno and Letterman," Medill News Service, July 24, 2000.
8. Morris B. Holbrook, "Popular Appeal Versus Expert Judgments of Motion Pictures (Statistical Data Included)," *Journal of Consumer Research*, vol. 26 (September 1999), pp. 144–155; Beverly James, "The Political Consequences of the Commercialization of Culture," *Journal of Communication*, vol. 48 (Autumn 1998), pp. 155–161.
9. Kathleen T. Lacher and Richard Mizerski, "An Exploratory Study of Responses and Relationships Involved in the Evaluation of and the Intention

to Purchase New Rock Music," *Journal of Consumer Research*, vol. 21 (September 1994), pp. 336–380.

10. Roger Ebert, *Questions for the Movie Answer Man* (Kansas City, MO: Andrews McMeel Publishing, 1997), pp. 1, 126–127.

11. Virginia Postrel, "Economic Scene: The Golden Formula for Hollywood Success," *New York Times* (March 23, 2000).

12. For example, see Morris B. Holbrook, "I'm Hip," *Advances in Consumer Research*, vol. 13 (1986), pp. 614–618; Morris B. Holbrook and Ellen Day, "Reflections on Jazz and Teaching: Benny and Gene and Woody and We," *European Journal of Marketing*, vol. 28 (no. 8/9, 1994), pp. 133–144; Morris B. Holbrook and R. B. Zirlin, "Artistic Creation, Artworks and Esthetic Appreciation," *Advances in Non-Profit Marketing*, vol. 1 (1985), pp. 1–54.

13. Grant Tinker and Bud Rukeyser, *Tinker in Television: From General Sarnoff to General Electric* (New York: Simon and Schuster, 1994).

12

The "Wrong" Benefits II: Schools and Education

Allowing parents to choose which school their children can attend is seen by many people as the solution to perceived problems with the quality of public education. In theory, competition between schools to offer quality programs would encourage school improvement, since innovative schools attract more students while poorer quality schools lose them. In the United States, school choice is already being put into practice on a limited basis with magnet schools, in which public schools with special attractive programs can draw enrollments from across a school district. There also has been some experimentation with publicly funded vouchers, which are applied toward tuition at private schools. School systems in various parts of the world are testing other forms of school choice, and interschool competition for students already exists throughout higher education.

Since school competition requires designing programs and selling them to parents and students to increase enrollments, educators around the world now attend special seminars and conferences to give them guidance in selling their schools, calling it "the marketing of education."

Unfortunately, having a choice does not mean parents will choose wisely because, while parents know that school is something that is "done," many do not really understand just what education "does."[1] In turn, to give people the benefits they want, many schools engage in practices that are actually detrimental to the education of students. To attract students, schools do things other than provide a quality education.

The stories that follow describe how the misplaced involvement of marketing in product decisions sometimes results in benefits that provide short-run satisfactions for parents or students, but harms the quality of education itself.

THE INTRINSIC FLAW IN SCHOOL CHOICE

A year after New Zealand removed all requirements for students to attend their neighborhood public schools, many people expressed surprise that the change did not result in a push to improve the "weaker" schools. Instead, the major effect was an increase in the selectivity of those schools that were already graduating students with top test scores.[2] The parents' ability to choose schools quickly became the ability of the best schools to select their students. Since claims to be "almost good" or "getting better" were not much of an attraction for parents, and since schools were reimbursed based on enrollment, many of the other schools focused on benefits other than the quality of their educational offerings.

But the New Zealanders shouldn't have been surprised. At any level of education, the better a school's reputation, the more selective it can be in accepting new students. Universities claim the top graduates, in part, because they are able to attract the top-quality students. Those schools unable to attract top students from the outset must still seek ways to fill classes.

As a result, wherever students or parents have a choice in schools, many schools are encouraged to focus attention on a school's "values" other than education, such as the availability of extracurricular activities, swimming pools or other athletic facilities, the teachers' concerns for children's self-esteem, or the school's religious environment. This is clearly seen in the fierce competition for college students in which all sorts of education-irrelevant "benefits" come to the fore: the football team's winning record, fraternity and sorority parties, or the campus presence of a nationally known researcher who never teaches. In materials selling the schools, these peripheral values sometimes are presented as if they were more important than providing a high-quality education.[3]

In theory, national testing of students would provide standards by which parents could compare the different schools. With this in mind, many U.S. school systems now require students to meet specific reading, writing, and math standards before being promoted to the next level. And as these tests or performance requirements are imposed, schools know that the real goal is to help weak students to improve, so they offer special tutorials or summer programs.

Surprisingly, instead of embracing these programs, a loud and vocal rebellion is heard from the parents. The parents do not see the tests as a guide for education, nor do they see the special programs as a benefit for their children.

"There is time enough for school later," I heard the parents complain on NPR *Morning Edition*. "Instead of summer school, I'm taking my children to the beach." While some parents welcome the special programs, others see them as punishing the whole family, taking away from vacations or other social activities. It is usually the parents who complain about too much homework, or any homework at all, and then, failing to see the connection, complain that their children can't read or write. Education is something that happens by contagion, or so it seems. To these parents, the fault for weak education never lies with their child's failure to work.

In the novel *Mazel*, a brief story within the story tells of a traveling peasant who encounters a windstorm.[4] As the peasant walks along the path afterward, he discovers that he has gained an understanding of all the mysteries of life. When he later takes off his sandals to rest, the knowledge leaves him, only to return when he puts the sandals back on. The peasant realizes that his footwear is the source of his wisdom, but he does not know that the windstorm has blown a leaf from the Tree of Knowledge out of the Garden of Eden and it has become stuck to the bottom of one sandal.

As happens in such stories, the king's daughter is ill and the peasant uses his new wisdom to provide a cure that saves the princess' life. Discovering that a pair of sandals has enabled a peasant to possess such abilities, the king exchanges half the kingdom for the footwear. But no king wants to wear dirty sandals and when cleaning the sandals, the king's servants scrape off the leaf from the Tree of Knowledge with the rest of the dirt. As a result, the footwear fails to make him a wiser or more insightful king.

He wanted the sandals, not realizing it was the dirt that carried the real value, for the leaf was buried in the dirt. In the marketing of education, faculty and administrators often are selling only the clean sandals. Admittedly, it is hard for schools to sell something as abstract as "learning," but schools often are too quick to take the easy solution and present the "benefits" of a school as things totally irrelevant to education. As a result, many students or their parents, like the king, only want the sandals, and go to great lengths to avoid all dirt, never even taking a chance on acquiring the all-important leaf.

Seeing graduation as certification, not a mark of education, students and their parents want the diploma but not necessarily the abilities or experiences education should engender. They see school as a job, with set hours for work, credited vacation time, and "paid" sick leave, telling teachers an excused absence means credit for that day, not makeup assignments for missed work. Teachers are no longer seen by students or parents as resources to tap or as mentors who can provide guidance, but, rather, as obstacles to overcome.

Since many parents do not understand the real product of an education, the marketing of education could destroy the product in order to attract customers. This is not idle speculation. The examples that follow are quite strong.

GIVING GRADES AND AVOIDING GRIEF

Once parents and students are told to see themselves as customers for education, they expect customer service with a smile.

For example, education researchers found that many math teachers, desiring popularity among their students and parents, are crippling kids with kindness. By providing too many hints to answers for all problems, they aren't helping students develop the ability to conduct analysis and draw conclusions.[5] A demanding math teacher in Georgia had her car vandalized and eggs thrown at her house after final grades were released. In Delaware, administrators decided that a high school teacher had failed too many students and directed her to change grades. When she refused, she was fired for insubordination. To the administrators, the problem was the number of low grades, not whether the students had learned anything.[6]

Until recently, many U.S. school districts had a policy of "social promotion" for every grade, a systemwide emphasis on keeping students with age cohorts instead of making certain they learned basic academic material before moving to the next class level. While many primary and secondary schools have ended social promotion, a version of it is still found in higher education. It is not overt or widespread but it exists, and many faculty feel it is growing, since politicians, parents, and higher education administrators have a primary concern that education consumers get the product they want. At many colleges and universities, administrators use their authority to waive program requirements, course prerequisites, and registration limits, all so students can graduate "on time."

No one would argue that undergraduate programs and academic plans should be unduly dragged out, yet there are many reasons that students take more than four years to graduate. Due to jobs or other responsibilities, many modern students are unable to take a full course load of demanding classes every term. Due to either laziness or the encouragement of overprotective parents, others want to minimize the work they do during any one quarter or semester. Sometimes due to personal distractions of jobs, illness, family problems, or parties, students are unable to pass key courses in sequence for completing a program. And some students are cerebrally challenged, thereby requiring more time to understand the material and pass key classes.

When administrators capriciously waive academic requirements, the beneficiary may be a starter on a major sports team. Sometimes, the waiver is a "favor" for the child of a major donor or a relative of a Board of Trustees member. But most commonly, a dean or even someone at a top level in the campus administration has a primary concern that the student be able to graduate on the date originally planned. Faculty may try to disavow the graduate, but the administration proudly bestows a degree.

And many examples are tied to grades. Grades are changed, scores are altered or failing marks are ignored. Students with low performance in prerequisite classes are allowed to take the next course in a sequence if they attended enough classes or "tried."

And then there is grade inflation.

Grades are used as part of a college's internal standards, course prerequisites, or for entrance into upper-level programs: Students must now maintain a C (or higher) average to take many required courses, to declare a major, and, once declared, to remain in the college. At one time, the catalogs at every university said that a grade of C meant "average," but many no longer do this, since they know that "average" grades are much higher.[7]

Students and many faculty believe that grades are a major factor in the job market, so some assert that a university with tough grade standards hurts its students in the job market. But employers are not idiots. They could readily recognize a program whose B+ graduates exhibit the on-the-job insight of a hamster; they know which schools have above average or B grades as a mark of accomplishment. In the long run, it hurts a university more to give many high grades to average (or worse) students.

But grade inflation is not caused just by faculty wanting to be nice. It avoids problems. To fail students, for whatever reason, or even to award more C grades, causes a faculty member to spend time fighting complaints.

With increasing frequency, if a grade is seen as low, the student complains. The student may be lazy, stupid, or just have a problem with that course's material, but anything lower than what a student desires will engender complaints. Everyone in higher education has had the student who cuts classes, rejects entreaties to come to the office for help, and, after dismally failing the final exam, snarls at the teacher, "You're making me stay in school an extra term!" The faculty member then hears from the dean about a grade complaint. And these are the nicer students, since others compel us to start checking the back seat of the car before getting in to go home.

Too many students are ignorant and proud of it. Yet few faculty members would ever say to a student, even in those cases when it is painfully obvious, "You're lazy, you're young, and you're wrong."

These student attitudes and expectations help engender decreasing expectations on the part of the faculty. Grade inflation should not be a surprise to anyone, since these student views are often supported by administrators. It is another part of marketing the schools or programs, with the competition for funding driving down academic quality while driving up grades.[8]

A department chair once told me that "We need to get enrollments in [this] program up to 400, and then we can start to worry about entrance requirements and program quality." Similarly, in the book *Generation X Goes to College*, the author watched faculty members' enthusiasm and interest for his ad hoc committee on standards and quality die when faced with potential problems of declining enrollments at the unnamed college, especially with concomitant drives by administrators for *all* students to be kept happy.[9]

Exacerbating the incentives to pander, some university administrators actively encourage faculty to give higher grades. I have seen memos from deans, associate deans, and even vice presidents at different universities, which tell faculty that they may not fail students. Department heads may be directed to "investigate" all classes and teachers that have "too many" D and F grades in any given term. Moving from one school to another, whose incoming students possessed equivalent backgrounds and abilities (as measured by admission requirements), an award-winning teacher at the first school was called on the carpet by the provost at the second. He gave "too many" C grades and "not enough" A and B marks.

Social promotion in any form can be a marketing tool to attract and satisfy customers, but grades and standards exist for a reason. They are an evaluation of work, not a marketing tool to be manipulated to satisfy the customers. Graduation should be a sign of intellectual development, not years of existence, and students should graduate educated, not on time. And the availability of high grades should not be a marketing benefit to help keep the education customers satisfied.

STAND-UP COMEDY AND HIGHER EDUCATION

A comedian told me that his job was unique, in that hecklers in the audience tried to interfere with his show. He thought stand-up comedy was the only profession where some paying customers tried to prevent him from working.

But, on campus, many faculty find that, like comedians, they are paid (in part) by the body: Student counts often determine department funding; generation of student credit hours might influence who and how many faculty get the added pay for teaching in the summer. And, like comedians, part of our pay is based on entertainment value, though we call it "teaching performance," as measured by the student responses that provide our end-of-term teacher evaluation scores.

And while comedians may have hecklers in the audience, faculty must deal with students with attitudes. Across the country, faculty report growing numbers of students who pay tuition but do not wish to learn.

Any gathering of college faculty is filled with new tales of teacher frustration. Every class has good students who are interested, seemingly motivated, there to learn, and who appreciate being treated as if they had a brain. But too many classes have a segment of slackers who, as one friend put it, "turn in crap and don't even wince doing it." Though they come to class totally unprepared and pay no attention to the class itself, they blame the teacher when they get confused.[10]

Most students aren't whiners, slackers, or lacking all respect for faculty. And some faculty care not a whit, zero, zip, about teaching and cultivate this contempt. At the same time, students' honest challenging on an intellectual basis is why many of us wanted to become teachers in the first place. And, as teachers, we want the honest questions that help us clarify material and discern where the lecture was not as unambiguous as we believed.

But while a comedian can adroitly turn a heckler into part of the act, teachers interrogate or insult the slackers at their peril.

If you have not attended a college class for the past few decades, you might be unfamiliar with the teacher evaluation forms by which students rate the courses just completed. At the end of every class, most universities require that faculty have students fill out forms to evaluate their teachers' performance.[11] At many schools, the forms are standardized universitywide and mostly consist of multiple-choice, agree–disagree questions: "Was the professor well prepared?" "Did the professor motivate you to learn?" "Would you recommend that another student take this course?" "Did you enjoy the use of class time?" "Did the exams properly evaluate what you learned?"

Such inquiries have been around for a long time, but it is only in the recent past that they have attained their current ubiquity and status in faculty work. While they started with the positive goals of helping faculty improve their classroom communications skills, the forms have supplanted all other administrative measures of teaching evaluation.

And the numbers are what matter. For retention on the staff, promotion, tenure, and merit pay raises, teachers are required to deliver strong evaluation scores.

How would Professor Kingsfield from the movie and television program *The Paper Chase* fare today? Not well, I fear.

He interrogated students in his law school classes, drilled them on the case to be discussed that day, and asked everyone to dig down deep and think about the law. Many of his students were intimidated by him, everyone was pushed to learn, and anyone who came to class unprepared was in peril. Today, students often rebel if they are asked questions before someone tells them what they are supposed to know or how they are expected to answer. On the end-of-term evaluation forms, some students complain if the exam questions were not specifically answered in class. And every student with a complaint brings down the overall scores.

Of course, the problem starts before they get to our classes. At all levels of modern education, teachers, not students, are blamed for poor grades. So classes become simple exam preparations—nothing more—with classes merely saying, "This is important," since the student "customers" will assess the class by the grade they receive. So when called on to think through a problem, some students might just reply, "I don't know. Tell me the answer." Faculty give the answers while students memorize, pass exams, get credit, and move on.[12]

No teacher should fear pushing students to think. But in these litigious times, when students sue for higher grades, when they feel that oversleeping for a 10 A.M. class is an excused absence, and when they consider cheating a normal and necessary part of academic life, it is easy to forget that the goal of teaching is education. But the need is for students to learn and appreciate learning. And in the process of a real education, not everyone will leave the class with a warm and fuzzy feeling.

With misplaced marketing dictating the educational product, teachers are told to satisfy everyone who registers for a class. The good students might be the majority, but a few academic hecklers can destroy a class and education for everyone else.

COLLEGE FOR THE SAKE OF SPORTS

Listening to many faculty and alumni, the Auburn–Alabama football game holds a special importance beyond a sports rivalry, since they believe the winner also gains a priority for state funding. In a similar vein, the chair of the University Senate at another school told me that when his faculty were shorted on their allocation of football tickets several years ago, he received more calls expressing complaints than he had on any other issue, including curriculum changes, retirement benefits, and the new campus parking plan.

Apparently, many people seem to think of their universities as sports franchises that run a school to retain their eligibility for the college athletic conference. Working "for" the teams, many faculty see football and basketball tickets as their most important employee benefit.

But this sounds so silly. Universities exist as centers of higher education. Sports are secondary activities. But imagine what a university would be like if the primary activity were sports instead of education.

Overall, university graduates would exist to provide team boosters, in hopes that some of those boosters would donate money to the school's academic programs as well as the teams. So when budgets were tight and academic programs were being cut, alumni would focus their discussions on whether a losing coach should be fired. The highest salaries on campus would go to the coaches; during campus-wide hiring and salary freezes, pay raises would still go to the athletic director, coaches, or their staffs.

If a university were a sports franchise instead of a place of education, young athletes would first be recruited and accepted for the teams and *then* "apply" for admission to the school instead of going to school and trying out for the teams. And, of course, the basis by which athletes would apply and be accepted to school might bypass concerns about educational ability. Some young men and women might first get accepted as students and then try to join the teams but, labeled as "walk-ons," they would face derision and low expectations.

Athletes would receive academic course credit for participating in their sports. While tutors would be hired to help the important team members pass courses, those recruited as students would receive no special training to help them succeed in athletics. Faculty would also be frequently asked about the academic performance of athletes in their classes so that those with problems could be spotted and helped, though seldom would such proactive aid would go to full-time students.

Athletes would have permits allowing them to park their cars anywhere they desired, sometimes taking spaces allocated for faculty or staff use, while other students would be relegated to special lots at the campus periphery.

And in all classes, academic requirements, such as exams or term paper due dates, would be worked around important athletic events. Evening basketball games would be considered valid reasons for students not to prepare for class the next day; no faculty member would dare give an exam the Monday morning after the football homecoming game. During the football season, a special televised Thursday night game would supersede anyone's ability to seriously conduct class during the latter half of the week. (And even if they wanted to, no one could find a parking space within walking distance of the classroom that day, anyway.)

Yet, despite this sarcasm, the nightmare for many faculty is that all I described is true. We like to believe that the purpose of a university is education, not athletics, but many of us are more readily asked about the football or basketball teams, and not the quality of the academic programs. I often hear even faculty and college administrators refer to the "SEC," "Pac 10" or "Big 10" conferences as comparable places for an education.

Though many people believe football or basketball programs make money for schools, very rarely do big-time sports programs operate in the black.[13] At many schools, sports programs have a separate funding system, keeping revenue from tickets, televised games, or alumni donations away from the academic needs of the university. At the same time, they take some university funds and use offices and campus property rent free. Of course, many people also believe that more donations are made to academic programs when the team wins, but, at the same time, many large donations are made to the nonacademic funds for the team. Since the potential pool of all donors is finite, what goes to the athletic programs is money that would otherwise have gone to the school.

These student activities might have once been a useful tool to spread awareness of a school name. But today, many students, administrators, and even some faculty now focus on sports teams as if they were the primary goal of the school's existence. The marketing tool has supplanted the education benefit.

MAKING IT EASY

Increasing numbers of college students attend class as if they possess photographic memories. Or maybe they all completed that memory course sold in infomercials, the one featuring what's-his-name. That must be the answer. Perfect memories would explain why these students no longer take notes during lectures. In an encyclopedia read in my youth, the entry on "college" was illustrated by a picture of diligent students, pens poised on note pads. That might have been true then, but not now. Today, students are more likely to sit with textbooks open and highliter markers in hand, coloring sentences bright colors where the instructor mentions it as important.

In part, these "new" classroom habits are encouraged by the packaged course materials provided by textbook publishers and used by many faculty.

At every college, students develop study habits in the basic courses, classes with large enrollments that, at some schools, are often taught in large lecture halls. Given the large numbers, faculty look to minimize work by utilizing prepackaged materials: sample lectures, course outlines, transparencies, and computerized exam questions based on the textbook. When many teachers of these courses use the unaltered, publisher-provided data banks for exam questions, the students learn that they only need to read the text and memorize its printed lists.

Notes are unnecessary in these classes, and lectures themselves are superfluous. And, compounding the problem, some teachers teach to these tests (that they themselves don't write). In what passes for the lecture, they do little more than read the book to the class, saying, "This is what will be on the exam!"

While it is easy to say that college faculty do not care, one must realize that the reward system of many universities encourages them not to care about teaching. It is something to be done.

It is strange sounding and hard to explain, but while college faculty are being paid to teach, how much they are paid is mostly based on what they do when they're not teaching. Overall, research is measured, committees are counted, and teaching is "done." Universities focus resources on improving their prestige, and aside from the football team, it is easiest to assess the faculty's research activity. We can count articles. We can read citations. Faculty and their departments acquire prestige by publishing academic articles and making presentations at conferences. And such things are the primary basis for starting salaries, promotion, tenure, and merit pay raises. Teaching quality is much harder to assess, so colleges do not encourage the faculty involvement that is needed to help students grow.

A place that claims to be a teaching school often is merely saying, "We don't do much research here," not that the faculty are rewarded for serious efforts in meeting with students, designing courses, providing detailed grading feedback, and developing students' abilities to write and think and grow. Instead of focusing on improving teaching, we spend time in committees, debating such trivial things as what should be described in course catalogs.[14]

Few resources (if any) are ever devoted to a teaching improvement center. A university providing such a center would provide a strong statement of commitment to teaching, a place where faculty could get assistance improving their work as educators. Conducting an extensive Internet search of schools in the United States a few years ago, I found that such centers are extremely rare; when they do exist, they are usually grossly underfunded. When funded, the centers are sometimes misdirected, focusing on providing management tools for faculty evaluation instead of helping faculty work with students.

After completing a guest lecture at another university, I found myself outside the classroom of the instructor that the students had recently voted as best teacher. As I listened in, he was reading the student newspaper to the class, using it as a springboard for personal stories and jokes, barely mentioning any course material. I was later told that his exams were all multiple-choice questions copied directly from the textbook teachers' manual. This example might seem extreme, but many universities have a popular Professor Feelgood whose courses are empty of substantive content.

In reality, a successful career in any field requires a facile and educated mind, not the ability to regurgitate specific information that any book might contain. Faculty fail to tell students strongly and repeatedly that the abilities to think and write clearly are more important than the textbook's checklists. As part of education, notes from class could be treasured and serve as a reference for many years in the future.

For the faculty, it is easier to teach from the text and use the publishers' exams. And for the students, the resulting classes are easier, not needing lecture notes. It is easier for everyone, and it makes the classes more popular among students, but no one benefits when students learn less.

MARKETING AND THE
DESTRUCTION OF EDUCATION

When I asked a student why she had missed our first ninety-minute class, she simply said that she never attends classes on the first day. "You don't miss much," she explained. "All they do is hand out the syllabus."

"Well," I said, "in our department you miss a lot. Like many of my colleagues, my syllabus is posted on the university Web pages. In our first class, I handed out a one-page note that gave the electronic address and I then lectured for the full period."

I tried to not show any emotion in my reply, but her reaction was intense. "That's not fair!" she yelled, a comment that she and a few others carried through to their end-of-term teacher evaluations. I wondered if they would skip the first few minutes of a football game, since rarely does anyone score on the opening kickoff.

Education is a strange commodity because many consumers seem to want as little of it as possible for their money. After all, a real education requires students to work, and ignorance is instantaneous. The scarecrow in *The Wizard of Oz* gets a brain by being handed a diploma, a situation that makes many young people extremely envious.

At a meeting of a university curriculum committee, an English professor asserted that majors and minors provide students with statements of job certification. "Excuse me?" another person protested, "We all know that except for some areas of engineering or education, our majors do not actually 'certify' anything on the job market."

"Of course," the English faculty member replied, "but statements of certification is what our students want and, since they are our customers, we will give it to them."

Unfortunately, this view is not unique. I have been told similar stories by faculty at many other schools. For colleges and universities, it is easier to "sell" simple job certification to get students in classes.

The marketing of education has lost track of education itself. Too many administrators have lost touch with the roles of students or teachers and want to promote the easiest features to market. Parents need to understand just what education means so they will select schools based on true academic values. And students need to be repeatedly told that the value of education to a job is not credit earned, but learning and mental abilities acquired.

The marketing of education needs to keep focused on the real product benefits of an education. If they don't, the marketing effort gets misplaced, changing the education product to make it more attractive but not a real long-term benefit to students or society.

NOTES

1. Tom Loveless, "The Parent Trap," *Wilson Quarterly* (Autumn 1999). Available at <http://wwics.si.edu/OUTREACH/WQ/WQSELECT/LOVELESS.HTM>.

2. "Multiple Choice: The Results," *The New Zealand Herald* (August 29–30, 1998), pp. H1–H2. This article was the summary centerpiece of a group of in-depth studies printed in a special section assessing the nation's schools.

3. While campus life and the environment are relevant for choosing a school, they should not supplant an assessment of educational values. Such issues are reviewed in Thomas Sowell, *Choosing a College: A Guide for Parents & Students* (New York: Harper and Row, 1989).

4. Rebecca Goldstein, *Mazel* (New York: Penguin Books, 1995).

5. Louis J. Chatterley and Donald M. Peck, "We're Crippling Our Kids with Kindness!" *Journal of Mathematical Behavior*, vol. 14 (December 1995), pp. 429–436.

6. According to the radio reports, students who failed the class knew they had earned the grades they received. Many of them reportedly picketed the school to protest the firing, carrying signs saying, "I failed [her class] and I deserved it!"

7. J. Linn Allen, "A's Near Par for Course in College," *Chicago Tribune* (April 28, 2000). The article reports that 46 percent of the grades that fall were A at Northwestern University's College of Arts and Sciences (including A–), as were 42.4 percent of undergraduate grades that spring at the University of Illinois at Urbana–Champaign. The GPA for all courses at the University of Chicago was reported as 3.26 for the prior year.

8. J. E. Stone, "Inflated Grades, Inflated Enrollment, and Inflated Budgets: An Analysis and Call for Review at the State Level," *Educational Policy Analysis Archives*, vol. 3 (no. 11, 1995).

9. Peter Sacks, *Generation X Goes to College: An Eye-Opening Account of Teaching in Postmodern America* (Chicago: Open Court Books, 1996).

10. John Leo, "No Books Please, We're Students," *U.S. News and World Report* (September 16, 1996), p. 24.

11. I am not using the term "performance" just to play on the metaphor with stand-up comedy. This is the standard term. Schools say that these student evaluations forms are an assessment of "teaching performance."

12. The logic here raises another intrinsic problem with evaluating schools by standardized tests of students, since it encourages teachers to spend time on how to answer the tests instead of how to think through problems or how to write. For example, see Jonathan Weisman, "The Texas Education Myth: Only a Test," *The New Republic* (April 10, 2000). Available at <http://www.tnr.com/041000/weisman04100.html>.

13. The extensive research on the myths and realities of the economics of college athletics are thoroughly summarized in Andrew Zimbalist, *Unpaid Professional: Commercialism and Conflict in Big-Time College Sports* (Princeton, NJ: Princeton University Press, 1999).

14. Some very humorous and insightful essays on committees and faculty are found in Jerry Farber, *The Student as Nigger* (New York: Pocket Books, 1969). See, for example, the gunfight over a basic English requirement in his story, "Gorman."

PART IV ———————————————

EXPLANATIONS AND CRITICISMS
BY MISPLACED MARKETING

"Why are you doing that?!"

Up to this point, the primary focus has been on outcomes, the consumer frustrations or social harms from misplaced marketing. Some reasons for the lack of marketing in decisions have been delved into, criticized or noted, but examples were mostly from the end results. In the next four chapters, the marketing perspective was lost due to the process or incentives faced by organizations. Misplaced marketing comes from the job itself.

In the advertising business, so-called "targeted agencies" are employed to rewrite advertising to appeal to minority groups. Yet these companies exist in a racist ghetto, which presumes that members of demographic minority groups are incapable of taking a marketing perspective and applying it to people physically unlike themselves. Some earlier chapters noted a consumer fear that marketing people were precisely targeting narrow audiences, but e-mail spam exists because decision makers using this tool find it more efficient to ignore target marketing concerns and just send messages to as many people as possible. Since modern business terms increasingly confuse the marketing guide of public relations and the communications tool of publicity, marketing perspectives get lost as the publicity tool is employed without reference to any marketing strategy or assessment of the audiences. And, finally, looking at public organizations, misplaced marketing explains decisions and adds a perspective to the issues that few would have ever considered before.

13

Hiring the Wrong "Right" Person

When I was in high school, Woody Allen's nightclub routine included a story about an advertising agency hiring him as the token Jewish employee. He read all his newspapers from right to left (even though they weren't in Hebrew) and he peppered his conversations with irrelevant Yiddish words. Eventually, they fired him when he didn't work on Jewish holidays. In a less humorous vein, I vividly recall the chapter from the advertising copywriting textbook for my college class with the sexist title, "Is there a role for women in advertising?" In short, it answered *yes* because the business needs people to write copy for lingerie and cosmetics.[1]

Both of these stories hit home to me when I graduated college and started interviewing for jobs. A group vice president at one of the largest advertising agencies in the world told me that he could not understand why I submitted an application to his company. As he explained it, "We don't have any Jewish accounts." Then and now, I don't know what would be a Jewish account. And as with any ethnic group, people are so diverse that I doubt if I would have brought anything special to such an account just because my parents are Jewish.

Managers myopically believing that their personal views were typical of their customers provided many of the misplaced marketing examples in earlier chapters. Successful advertising people know how to use consumer research data and they study the potential markets and how their target audience thinks. In a sense, regardless of the target audience, the business is like the famous advertising campaign by a son of Greek immigrants. George Lois had each print ad or billboard portray a person of a different racial group eating a slice of bread: "You don't have to be Jewish to like Levi's Jewish Rye."

A vexing problem of misplaced marketing is that when the target audiences are Americans who are black, Hispanic, or Native American, the normal course of business practice is to require that advertising decisions be made by people who are in the same demographic group. This is not just misplaced marketing, but racist, since it presumes that all people who share physical traits think alike. Even worse, with an implicit assumption that women and members of minority groups are incapable of applying a marketing orientation to different customers, these advertising people are seen as being *only* able to prepare advertising for people physically like themselves.

This problem is most clearly revealed in some common and well-accepted business practices.

The people making day-to-day decisions at advertising agencies are usually well-paid, highly educated executives, often aged twenty-five to forty and living in urban areas. Rarely is it seen as a source of concern that they often are selling to people who are less affluent, not as well educated, older or younger than themselves, and who live outside the cities in which the agency is located. Yet when the target audience consists of African-Americans or Hispanic–Latino consumers, advertising people often turn the work over to an advertising agency whose owners and employees are members of that minority group.

Some people might see this arrangement as a positive outcome because it forces a form of affirmative action on the advertising business. But while this practice ensures that some of the business from major marketing firms goes to minority-owned agencies, it also has created a professional ghetto. As a general rule, minority-owned shops often get work *only* involving minority targets. The large advertising agencies increasingly have been criticized for their terrible record of hiring and promoting African-Americans,[2] but the minority-agency ghetto allows people who manage these "mainstream" offices to rationalize discriminatory practices for hiring or promotions:

"Why would any black people apply for a job here? We don't have any black-oriented accounts."

Even in the best light, continually turning to minority-owned agencies for advertising that targets racial or ethnic minority audiences requires racist stereotyping. It assumes that all minority group members are the same. In reality, an educated and affluent executive who is a member of a racial minority might have more in common with other white agency executives than with the members of the ethnic group who are in the target audience.

With every minority group, there are more differences among the members of the groups than there are between the groups themselves. From a marketing point of view, middle-income black consumers are more like middle-income white consumers than they are like poorer or less-educated blacks. Asians and Hispanics might seem one-dimensional to people who are not members of those groups, but they all differ greatly by the wide variety of places their families lived before immigrating. There are also differences and variations that are correlated with the subcultures of the cities in which they now live.

If white executives can read data and create advertising for people unlike themselves, so can members of racial or ethnic minority groups. A few years after I read a college textbook that said women could only write ads for very personal female products, Jerry Della Femina wrote some of the first television commercials for a brand of feminine hygiene spray.

While stores have long employed women as "cosmeticians" to sell these products to customers, many people selling cosmetics to the stores were men. Despite a store manager's skepticism, I was able to show him that a young Jewish man who takes a proper marketing perspective can successfully sell retail cosmetics to older black women.[3] U.S. history is filled with stories of immigrants who made products, movies, or great advertising that had broad national appeal. Every day, advertising that "works" is created by people grossly dissimilar from the audience. Black or Hispanic agency employees are equally capable of this.

And therein lies the real unstated "problem" in depending on minority-owned agencies to sell to minorities. It presumes that, to create advertising for an audience, one must be a member of that audience group. Women could only sell "women's products"; only athletes could sell athletic equipment. It gives an absurd license for hiring discrimination because employers could state that they need employees who look like the primary purchasers of their clients' products.

Taking this logic to its extreme, ad agency staffs would have to be expanded to cover members of all possible target groups. While it is true that mass communications work must take place within a context of understanding the target audience's subculture, understanding does not require membership, just empathy.

After I had first expressed some of the above views in a national magazine, I received a lengthy and vitriolic letter from an account executive at a minority-owned agency in Chicago. Saying that ethnic marketing should be viewed the same way as advertising in another country, his comments seemed driven by a fear that I advocated an eventual loss of the specialized business that went to his shop. He misunderstood.

Spike Lee has attained great fame and success directing and producing movies. The subjects and lead characters have been black, but many of his movies have had wide appeal among members of different racial and ethnic groups. Years ago, he started an advertising agency, a creative boutique that he said would produce high-quality advertising for "urban" (which is usually a business euphemism for "black") audiences. But after years in the business, his hiring of two white men as account and creative managers prompted numerous "expert" comments in the trade press that these new hires meant that his agency might now be unable to produce persuasive commercials for urban consumers.

Unlike the person who sent me this letter, I thought Spike Lee was able to produce high-quality commercials for mainstream audiences even before he hired white men as account and creative managers. He did not lose his ability to communicate with blacks just because white people worked for him.

Without a doubt, stereotypes influence business perceptions and cause hiring discrimination. In one study, even the young college students' feminist or generally egalitarian views did not moderate the intrusion of stereotypes into how they evaluated fictitious job applicants.[4] But in a business that constantly complains about difficulties in finding talented copywriters, the continued demographic matching of writers and target audiences means a large pool of potential people are cut off from consideration.

And the matching does not always result in better insight. When a racially offensive ad appeared in *Jet* magazine, Jesse Jackson asserted the ad showed what happens when black writers or managers are left out of a company's communications decisions.[5] But as we pointed out in Chapter 8, the African-American publisher and salespeople at *Jet* apparently decided that the ad was acceptable for publication, so these experienced black business people did not anticipate Rev. Jackson's complaints.

Most universities' marketing degree programs require a course in research methods because all future managers must know how to read and use data. Every marketing course contains a significant section covering theories of consumer psychology, since that forms the basis for marketing decisions. Few marketing managers sell only to consumers exactly like themselves; many misplaced marketing mistakes come from managers who presume that they can act as a surrogates for all potential customers, instead of shifting the focus to view the world from the consumer's point of view. There is nothing inherently wrong with a firm contracting out work to other people who might possess greater empathy with the target market. But it is strange that such special outside-supplier empathy is sought only with blacks and Hispanics.

Aside from providing a small amount of guaranteed business for minority firms, the matching of minority ad writers and audiences works only to the business' long-run detriment. Talented people work in a ghetto when mainstream work is kept out of minority-owned agencies and when agencies don't hire minorities for everyday jobs.[6]

The advertising trade press reports that this racist mind set is changing, but slowly, too slowly.

NOTES

1. Even though the book was written at a time when women were doing major and noteworthy work in the advertising business, the textbook authors felt strangely compelled to also include a lengthy discussion admonishing future ad women not to cry when the (always male) supervisor critically edits their copy.

2. For example, see Lowell Thompson, "A Dirty Little Secret Lives On," *Advertising Age*, vol. 71 (June 5, 2000), p. 32.

3. The regular cosmetician took her vacation time during what she thought would be a slow period. She did not want to lose her commissions, her "push money," from the cosmetics companies, so she was extremely angry when my sales during her absence exceeded the entire prior month. Apparently, I knew her customers better than she did, even though the customers and the cosmetician were members of the same demographic group.

4. Trina Sego, "The Effects of Sex and Ethnicity on Evaluations of Advertising Job Candidates: Do Stereotypes Predict Discrimination?" *Journal of Current Issues and Research in Advertising*, vol. 21 (Spring 1999), pp. 63–74.

5. Jesse Jackson, "Jackson Cites Lessons from an Offensive Ad," Letters to the Editor, *Advertising Age*, vol. 70 (March 1, 1999), pp. 22, 24.

6. A black copywriter anonymously recounted the personal frustrations of this situation, publishing under the sarcastic name of Carbon Copywriter. This was published in "Off-Target: Ghettoizing Black Advertising," *Brandweek*, vol. 40 (December 6, 1999), pp. 28–32.

14

The Spam Incentive

Three decades ago, marketing consultants tried to convince FTC staff lawyers and economists that "market segments" and "target audiences" are core issues of consumer deception. It was a difficult job. Like the public health officials described in Chapter 5, the commissioners and staff of three decades ago had trouble with the concept, since they thought marketing and advertising influenced all "people" as part of mass markets. To the marketing researchers, it was intuitively obvious that while some audiences might be deceived by the advertised claims, other consumers didn't need help from agency regulations.

It is interesting how things change.

Today, the FTC understands target markets and audience segments. They recognize that most media vehicle audiences are smaller and more internally homogenous. And they see it as a danger, fearing that the narrowly defined audience segments of cable television and users of the Internet provide a means for deceptive advertisers or makers of questionable products to more readily deceive and defraud the most vulnerable consumers.

Telemarketers are known to make multiple repeat calls to phone numbers once the people who answer give a positive response to their appeals. New communications technologies possess the potential for even greater refinement of target audiences and this, in turn, could allow for more precisely targeted deceptive practices.

In theory, deceptive television commercials could be sent via cable to audiences who would most readily fall for such deceptive appeals. Infomercials could use cable networks to prey on the worries and fears of selected groups. And, also in theory, various vulnerable individuals could be specifically targeted, via the Internet, for deceptive messages they are prone to believe. Children, the elderly, or more gullible people would have tailor-made deceptive messages sent directly to their computer screens.

Yet sometimes concerns for misplaced marketing are misdirected. There might exist a strong, logical potential for additional deception in new technology, but there also exist inherent limitations for actual applications.

For the mass media, and even with the Internet, targeting information is not yet that precise, nor are audience data that refined. And the economics of audience research limits the precision of data that could become available in the near future. With the Internet, as with the increasing number of new cable channels, more precise data costs more, and no one yet seems willing to pay for it. Broad demographic data are still the norm for defining media audiences, and that information provides only minimal insight into how people think.

Regulations and restrictions on cigarette marketing, described in Chapters 7 and 10, ban advertising in vehicles where a large percentage of audience members are too young to legally buy the product. But no one told the antimarketing forces that available audience data lack such precise details on magazine readership. Even with the invasions of privacy made possible by on-line shopping, marketing can track consumer purchase patterns, but not audience perceptions.

Ironically, some heavy Internet users probably would prefer precise targeting to be the real "problem." While the cookies and other Internet tools theoretically allow for targeted placement of banner ads based on past purchases or browsing habits, the real problem for consumers is the growth of "spam," electronic junk mail.

Seventy-something Ethel can't understand why she started receiving a plethora of solicitations from pornographers soon after she started using an e-mail account to communicate with friends and family. Her son thinks that it might have been a result of her research on breast cancer. After I made a single visit to a toy company Web page, I was inundated with e-mail offers for a vast array of other toys, children's books, and accessories, as if I were the father of television's *Brady Bunch*. After buying his friend a video, *The Meaning of Life*, as a fiftieth birthday gift, my cousin was getting e-mailings without end for books, posters, CDs, and DVDs, as if he (and not the friend) were the fan of

Monty Python's Flying Circus. And, after a search for interest rates and other small-investor information, Ellen started receiving several e-mail messages a day for various "sure-fire," get-rich-quick schemes.

The reason people receive so many unwanted sales contacts on e-mail could best be understood by comparing the new technology with the old.

Years ago, Trina encountered the usual resistance and frustrations as she attempted to start her new direct mail advertising business. Since this was before the growth of the Internet as a direct marketing tool, her advertising medium was the postal service, what we now call "snail mail." Her prospective clients called the medium "junk mail" and would often assert that whatever advertising mail they received was thrown into the trash unread. Believing that everyone else acted in the same fashion, they resisted retaining Trina's business because they felt that direct mail was a waste of their advertising dollars.

Beyond the ethnocentrism of these managers, believing that they were typical—managers mistakenly believing their thoughts mirror those of all potential customers is the core of misplaced marketing—answering their fears was fairly easy for Trina (and straight out of any textbook).

These reluctant prospects for Trina's business threw out all that mail not because they disliked the advertising envelopes per se, but because they received information on matters that did not interest them. The mail that was headed straight for the trash bin probably was from direct mail companies that didn't maintain and monitor their lists. As Trina would assert in her efforts to attract new clients, she would be careful to keep misdirected mailings to a minimum.

Today, computers have allowed modern direct marketers to do a better job of monitoring mailing lists. Still, errors occur and marketing money is wasted. One friend has shown me the credit card offers addressed to her cats!

Nor are telemarketing companies as universally skilled at finding the prime targets as some people like to presume.

The morning radio program had great fun with a report from that morning's newspapers. Apparently, a middle-aged women traveling alone in an elevator in Melbourne, Australia, was startled when the service telephone rang. As she tentatively answered the phone, a robust voice responded with an enthusiastic, "Hello! This is your lucky day. We can clean your carpets at a special discount price."

Similar fables have been repeated in so many parts of the world that they now sound like yet another apocryphal urban legend. And yet, like the direct mail companies, telemarketing firms want to avoid such wasted calls. People making the calls are paid by the sale, and they don't want to waste time with dead ends. Mechanical, predictive dial-ers enable salespeople to optimize their time by not having to wait through ringing and unanswered calls to find a live prospect.[1] Even automatic callers with recorded messages use paid lines and waste money.

Some states have implemented mandatory "no call" lists, in which residents can register as not wanting to receive telemarketing calls. While the laws have been fought by some telemarketing firms that feared the time and efforts of implementation, the lists have also provided a service for the businesses. Having such a list reduces the profitless calls to people who are not interested in their solicitations.

Telemarketers want to avoid people who do not possess a scintilla of desire in making a phone order but will still politely listen to the entire sales pitch and then say "No, I am not interested." I have overheard many kind and sweet-natured people sound so positive while talking to an intrusive telemarketing call, then reject the offer and hang up, followed by a few muttered curses about the intrusion. Similarly, Japanese culture is extremely antagonistic to the impersonal selling style of telemarketing; most companies operating in Japan should consider that marketing tool a waste of resources because it is patently inefficient.[2]

One of my students was unable to get a credit card company to stop calling her with new offers. She kept saying she did not want any new products; she kept saying to the salespeople, "Do not call me again." Some companies explain that they are unable to stop calls, or that it takes up to ninety days to implement a stop order (as this credit card company told me in a phone inquiry). Yet computerized tracking systems make this hard to believe. If this major company cared about the money wasted on calling clearly uninterested customers, they could find ways to expedite the tracking systems.[3] With new and proposed laws penalizing companies for calls to people who do not want to be bothered, they may suddenly find ways they can stop their agents from making more calls as soon as the first complaint is received.

Yet in direct advertising by e-mail, instead of precision targeting, Internet users get spam, the ultimate in nuisance mail. A growing software business provides programs to help Internet users screen and delete unwanted e-mail advertising, and the Federal Trade Commission has taken action against firms that use scattershot messages with deceptive claims, since the firms are obviously hoping to find many potential buyers within a broadly tossed communications net. Efforts at passing antispam laws have been opposed by political action committees and lobbying groups as a limitation on their free speech rights.[4]

With traditional direct mail, waste circulation is costly. Postage and printing combine for the high cost per thousand of anything sent through a country's postal service or any alternative carrier. Therefore, it is in the firms' best interests to spend time and effort to make certain as high a percentage of people as possible who receive the mailing are in the target audience.

For direct advertising by e-mail, the immediacy and two-way nature of the Internet allow for greater monitoring of list efficiency, but the marginal costs for each additional mailing are near zero. Instead of the printing and postage costs paid by the sender, as in snail mail, e-mail printing is electronic ink with delivery costs paid by the receiver who must download and print from a service provider. The Internet direct marketers' main costs are in design of messages and computer programs for efficient sending, so maximizing efficiency comes from increasing the number of messages sent per minute.

So, on the Internet, there is no incentive to prune a mailing list. In fact, the opposite is true. By maximizing a mailing list, every possible respondent will be more likely to receive the message. More messages sent means minimal marginal cost and a great potential for additional responses. Instead of worrying about pruning lists and getting out a single good message, multiple e-mailings are sent to the same large lists in rapid succession with different subject headers in hopes that one of them will be read.

It is a great conflict of freedom of communications. The Internet is open, free, and uncensored, which is its strength. But the growing problem of that freedom is not turning out to be audience manipulation of the unwary, but a growing nuisance paid by the receivers. Those receiving the spam only wish that the Internet were used for more precise audience targeting.

No well-planned, postal-delivery direct mail should ever be called "junk mail," but almost all direct e-mail is increasingly getting labeled as spam, a nuisance. And the difference is in the basic financial incentives for the people sending the messages.

NOTES

1. These machines are causing a concern for federal and state regulatory agencies since, when the telemarketer gets more than one live contact at the same time, consumers answer the phone and find dead air. Some people receiving these calls think they are being stalked and others worry that an elderly relative is calling in an emergency and is unable to talk.

2. Discussion and comments from unpublished talk by Charles R. Taylor at the 1999 Marketing and Public Policy Conference in Notre Dame, Indiana. The research that was the basis of that talk was published in Charles R. Taylor, George R. Franke, and Michael Maynard, "Attitudes Toward Direct Marketing and Its Regulation: A Comparison of the United States and Japan," *Journal of Public Policy and Marketing*, vol. 19 (Fall 2000), pp. 228–237.

3. In addition, making unwanted calls to uninterested consumers is also bad marketing, in that it generates ill will against the company and its products or services. Repeated calls to my student only resulted in her canceling her account.

4. Maxine Lans Retsky, "Junk Faxes, Spam Subject to Telemarketing Laws," *Marketing News*, vol. 33 (April 26, 1999), p. 7. Some existing state and federal laws can restrict some spam, but the discussion here shows the misplaced marketing incentives for a company to maximize spam mailings to whatever limits the law allows.

15

The Limits of Spin

A university's students, faculty and even alumni had focused their ire on the Board of Trustees for several years. Students and faculty resented that the board was micromanaging programs and classes on campus while seeming to ignore greater educational concerns. Programs were cut, resources were manipulated, and faculty morale plummeted. Most alumni might have been oblivious to these problems, but they also heard stories of athletic coaches who were fired by the board in mid-contract, with resulting expensive settlements. As a solution to these problems, the board hired a public relations firm to improve its image.

In 1989, the oil tanker *Exxon Valdez* ran aground off the Alaska coast and spilled over 11 million gallons of crude oil that covered 3,000 square miles of Prince William Sound and blackened 1,300 miles of shoreline. A major cause of the spill was the ship's captain, a man the company knew was an alcoholic: By most reports, he was in his cabin and drunk at the time of the mishap. In addition, contrary to prior promises, the company didn't have an emergency response plan in place. The clean-up equipment, what little there was, was buried under several feet of snow. The corporate response was best described by a political cartoon I recalled that showed the tanker aground and spilling oil while two characters on the bow raised the alarm: "Emergency! Emergency! Call PR!"[1]

To viewers of either national or local news, it is not unexpected when some segment of the public responds with anger to a corporate activity. Sometimes the public is responding to news of an accident or disaster, such as an oil spill or nuclear power plant "problems." Sometimes the public is responding to real or perceived harm from a product. And sometimes difficulties are caused by interest groups or people living near the factory or warehouse, whose basic values are at odds with those of the industry.

As a response to many problems like this, several books have come out in recent years that provide business guidelines on how to handle conflicts with public groups. They provide detailed, point-by-point assessments of some corporations' past publicity nightmares, with directions for action, examples, statements of "impulses" managers should avoid, and general guidance for making business decisions.

In the dust-jacket description of each book or its preface, readers are told that these publications aim to help managers deal with the ongoing costs of doing business in response to various groups. Some say that their approach is an aid for public relations planning. Others claim to provide guidelines for making ethical business decisions. Regardless of the labels used, these books are all selling the authors as business consultants and they appeal to every firm's ongoing need to deal with critics of business activities.

As a general rule, these books are all clearly written and well organized. But I have yet to find one I like because I am bothered by their initial statements that business managers get bad advice from their "public relations" people. It is not that I think that the usual lawyerlike guidance from so-called PR consultants—to avoid talking to the public, to conceal information, and to reveal as little as possible—is good advice. But, rather, those advice givers are not really experts in public relations at all. They're publicists or publicity managers.

The general guidance found in any of these books would be nothing new or different from suggestions by a public relations manager who used a thorough marketing-oriented approach to deal with people who are angry with the firm. And that is why I dislike the books and the advice they try to give. Every example they cover is really misplaced marketing, cases where firms replace the marketing strategy-based work of public relations with tactics-driven attempts to manage a media event.

It is unfortunate that many managers have lost sight of the distinction between marketing-driven public relations and publicity, which is a communications tool. Yet, it is increasingly common for the marketing role of public relations to be misplaced. Instead of public relations being the basis for understanding and meeting the needs of potential publics and stakeholders, businesses try to manage the media. Yet if more managers understood public relations for what it should be, they wouldn't misplace marketing when dealing with the public.

In a sense, I blame how business terms have changed—a change that obscured an important difference between PR and publicity. When that distinction was lost, a tactical activity replaced a job that used to follow from a marketing strategy.

Simply stated, public relations should be a marketing-guided basis for all business decisions that might have a public impact. Publicity, on the other hand, is just a communications tool that hopes to get favorable news coverage. In other words, public relations uses publicity as one of many communications tools; efforts to generate or manage publicity are not PR. Using marketing to deal with society is the true value of public relations efforts whose focus is on strategy; publicity is just another tool for mass communications tactics.

This loss of the distinction between PR and publicity is found on the campus of many universities. Public relations today is rarely taught by marketing faculty. Instead, PR courses and programs are found in the schools or colleges of journalism and are taught from the perspective of information management. The key courses are often in press release writing or persuasion theory. Undergraduate majors in journalism are frequently told to consider entry-level jobs or careers in PR, since they might not find positions as journalists. Many independent public relations "experts" I have met over the years are former journalists or news editors. Or worse, many journalists start working in what they call PR after losing a job at a newspaper or television station.

In business, publicists and spin doctors have taken on the label of public relations consultants, and "PR" has become synonymous with news management, not the greater marketing concern of a firm's relationship with its public.

I really don't know how the distinction between publicity and public relations got lost. Years ago, many of the original public relations businesses were offshoots of advertising agencies, providing broad marketing advice for clients to guide all activities. They did not just "handle" the press, but advised the client on how all activities could be perceived by the public. At the same time, press agents would try to get placements in the news media. Corporate publicists wrote press releases and the employee newsletters from offices located in the basement, both organizationally (and, sometimes, physically).

But, over time, corporate publicity offices were renamed "public information" or "office of public relations." They were still in the basement writing newsletters or press releases, but they might have gained more prestige from the new job title. During the same time, freelance publicists started calling themselves PR agents, changing their name but not the level of their work. While taking the job title of PR, they were still publicists who attempted to manage the media.

Chapter 4 described how using "creative" as the business term for advertising-message management has encouraged many professionals to lose track of the marketing focus that should guide how advertising campaigns are conceived and produced. In this case, the change of name and confusing PR with publicity encourage the new PR professionals to undertake message tactics using publicity without reference to a marketing perspective and strategy that public relations should require.

My old undergraduate advertising textbook began the section on public relations by noting it is 90 percent doing things in the public interest and 10 percent getting the word out by using advertising, publicity, or other communications tools. I wonder if modern businesses know this. If they focus on the communications tool and not the marketing strategy, they don't.

During the first oil crisis of the 1970s, one oil company responded with frequently repeated television commercials showing that its engineers had developed the tallest-ever offshore oil rig for use off the California coast. It was true, but the company put a lot of money behind spreading the word about this single effort. Another company responded to environmental critics by heavy exposure of a television spot purporting to show the deer who lived near oil wells. Unfortunately, someone discovered that the commercials were filmed using trained deer. The company claimed that wild deer were really in the area, but that it was expedient to use a trained deer for the commercial, to get it done and get it on television.

"Action! Roll it! Cue the deer. Hey, can someone get the deer to look at the camera when it comes to center focus with the oil pump in the background?"

But then, a PR view would have anticipated such a public reaction. The issue was not deception, but rather, doing the right thing in the public interest. The company should have hired a wildlife documentary film producer and captured the wild deer on film, instead of trying to manage the bad press after the fact. If the filmed footage had showed many deer in the area, the trained deer still could have been used for the short commercial, and it could have been labeled "a reenactment."

Before the oil tanker *Exxon Valdez* ran aground, a public relations perspective would have had the alcoholic captain in a rehab program of some kind. The company would have made certain that clean-up equipment was available because accidents *do* happen. A car company spent a large amount of money on commercials showing how they had cleaned up an empty lot. But critics quickly noted that they could have used the millions of advertising dollars to clean up more neighborhoods, which, in turn, would have eventually generated more positive publicity instead of negative reactions to the advertising.

In current news, government actions forced a brief hiatus in new gene therapy research when one man died during an experiment. To show the human cost of this halt to research, a story focused on a young boy whose only hope for surviving his fatal disease was gene therapy. When the research was renewed and he traveled to another city for the injections, the story followed the family as "They stayed the night at a Ronald McDonald house." Most people might not have heard of this public service of the family-friendly restaurant chain. Still, this is true public relations, an activity to build community relations and then let the publicity happen.

But, then, McDonald's management of public relations is not always so sagacious. A leaflet was put out in the mid-1980s by London Greenpeace, titled "What's Wrong with McDonald's? Everything They Don't Want You to Know." The leaflet accused the burger chain of being responsible for a host of injustices, from starvation in the Third World to the destruction of rain forests. With the help of a trial lawyer and a British libel law that favors plaintiffs, the fast-food giant successfully sued two unrepentant and underfunded activists in English courts. However, it took eleven years and the Pyrrhic victory was a public relations disaster.[2]

The trial was the longest in English history and cost the company a reputed $16 million to pursue. The trial judge ruled that the leaflet was truthful when it accused the restaurant of paying low wages, treating animals cruelly, and exploiting children in its advertising campaigns. McDonald's won on most of the other allegations and received a judgment of $98,000, and the losers are required under British law to pay the winner's costs. However, given the defendant's financial situation, McDonald's will never collect the judgment, let alone its costs. And the bigger cost may be in damaged public relations, with the David and Goliath image of the trial participants having many a news story discussing how it was more about "McCensorship" and not "McLibel."[3]

This points out the real reason that most businesses fail to understand the difference between public relations and publicity management. Corporations and politicians often presume that the press can and should be controlled. They believe reporters must be manipulated.

Too many so-called "business leaders" see media relations as an issue of control because they do not think of honesty and "doing the right thing" as being in their best financial interest. The junior managers think that the firm probably won't be caught if they misbehave. Senior managers assess how they'll pay the costs if and when they get caught. Stockholders presume that court sanctions and drops in sales will be brief, or so they hope. In some cases, company memos have surfaced in which managers concluded that defending liability law-suits—and even losing some of them—would cost less than product recalls that would save lives.

And, in a sense, that is the most bothersome part of these guide-books for business dealing with the various disasters of public rela-tions. The authors may be established authorities in "public dispute mediation" and have given many firms their advice.[4] In the end, their approach is really an application of the basic marketing concept as a way to deal with groups possessing interest in the firm's activities. But if the firms had used marketing as a basis for making ethical and honest decisions from the beginning, the dispute mediators wouldn't have many clients.

In a public relations context, marketing could be applied to under-standing, serving, and responding to the concerns of various publics. Instead, too many firms have misplaced the marketing management role of public relations, relegating it to a group of publicists who misplace marketing as they write news releases and try to manage reporters.

NOTES

1. For example, see John Holusha, "Exxon's Public Relations Problem," *New York Times* (April 2, 1989), p. D1; Richard Mauer, "Alaska Aid Assails Oil Industry for 'Inadequate' Response to Spill," *New York Times* (June 16, 1989), p. A1; Art Davidson, *In The Wake of the Exxon Valdez: The Devastating Impact of the Alaska Oil Spill* (San Francisco: Sierra Club Books, 1990); James E. Lukaszewski, "Managing Bad News in America: It's Getting Tougher and Its Getting Worse," *Vital Speeches of the Day*, vol. 56 (no. 18, 1990), pp. 568–573.

2. Colleen Graffy, "Big Mac Bites Back," *ABA Journal*, vol. 83 (August 1997). A video of the trial, "McLibel: Two Worlds Collide," from One-Off Produc-tions, gained worldwide distribution and was also viewed for free via a popu-lar Web page. A Web page dedicated to case-related information, which is available at <http://www.mcspotlight.org/>, claimed over 40 million visi-tors by the time the trial ended.

3. For example, see Nick Cohen, "Goodbye, Mr. Chips . . . Hello, Mr. Fries," *The Observer* (June 1998); John Vidal, "It's Been the Longest Civil Trial in En-glish History," *The Guardian* (May 16, 1997).

4. For example, see Lawrence Susskind and Patrick Field, *Dealing with an Angry Public: The Mutual Gains Approach to Resolving Disputes* (New York: The Free Press, 1996).

16

Before You Decide, Get Out of the Office

One of my law professors was a passionate proponent of the first no-fault car insurance laws: He was involved with drafting proposed laws; he felt that he knew why the first laws failed to deliver as promised; and he saw no-fault insurance as a solution to many problems facing the courts. When they were unable to come up with an answer to one of his discussion questions, some students would respond by saying "no-fault insurance," regardless of the original topic, hoping that the teacher often would be inspired to start a new lecture on what may have been a previously unrelated topic.

No matter what course I am teaching, some of my students hope to do the same thing by saying "misplaced marketing." And sometimes they're right. Sometimes it works. I could almost call this penultimate chapter "Bits and pieces," a few short examples of misplaced marketing that don't really fit under the other topics or headings.

But, then, such a label would sell this chapter short. Better to think of it as misplaced marketing for the nonmarketing parts of organizations. The rationale is that many "little" activities of nonprofit organizations or even elements of everyday life could use marketing's consumer orientation. In every case, a frustrated refrain might be, "Who's in charge here?"

For many aspects of modern life, decisions by government or others do not seem to make any sense. From a misplaced marketing point of view, the decision makers are following a "production orientation," like the providers of products and services in Chapters 2, 3, and 4. In every case, a basic marketing perspective could direct someone to find out what people need, but like the organizations and people described in Chapters 5 and 7, the decision makers are engineers or lawyers or other professionals for whom a marketing orientation is a foreign concept.

SEARCHING FOR THE
GEEK-TO-HUMAN INTERFACE

At many large universities, each college or subunit developed its own Internet server system. At Auburn, the colleges of business, engineering, and veterinary medicine each chose their own e-mail programs and hired their own network administrators. But over the past few years, outside consultants or technical administrators at these schools recommended that the administration make everyone use the same centralized system. So repeating the experiences of many other schools, faculty at Auburn were told without much advance warning that all e-mail on campus would change to a new program. At Auburn, the technical people chose Groupwise.

On one hand, the shift to a centralized program makes certain that everyone on a campus has access to equal-quality Internet service. However, no one likes to change from something familiar. And a massive, systemwide change causes confusion for many people. Adding to the confusion, the usual administrative focus does not use a customer-oriented marketing perspective, focusing on the technical issues instead of the system users.

The Auburn University business faculty were blessed to have the change managed by Matt, our very customer-conscious network administrator. Even with a change of servers and programs, Matt made certain that we retained our old e-mail addresses, old mail was reliably forwarded, and he anticipated which computers and faculty would most need his personal attention. But network administrators like Matt are extremely rare in the world of computer services. More commonly, people in that job focus on the technology and fail to realize that they are serving a diverse group of human network users.

At Auburn, the Groupwise program itself was now under the control of the central office. Matt did not work there. When a few of us later compared notes, we found that all of us had some long-time correspondents who reported problems in reading or printing our e-mail from the new program. We contacted the Information Technology (IT) office's hotline and the IT answer was terse: The people at the other schools are using, in their words, "the wrong program." Once the other schools upgraded their programs, everything would be fine.

To the technical people at the IT office, this explained it. Reading the program's documentation, I found that the flaw was intrinsic to the Groupwise program; certain other programs have problems reading Groupwise mail. Once everyone else on the planet would change to the "right" program, their problems receiving our mail would end. To the faculty, our school had selected the wrong program because it had poor communication abilities. To the IT technicians, they had provided the latest and best program, so, once the rest of the world caught up, they would be able to talk to us. Never mind that the purpose of campus Internet systems is to *facilitate* communications, and that we were communicating just fine before IT "improved" things.

Some parts of campus consider the change an upgrade to a better program, but others just lamented the loss. All would have been fine if everyone had someone like Matt in control of the Internet service. He always kept in mind that the goal was serving the faculty communications needs.

The campus IT technicians' narrow vision of technology is not new, nor is it unique to the Internet.

In the 1960s, as color television was gaining in consumer popularity, advertisers judged their commercial quality by how it looked on the newest color sets. Unfortunately, many people still had black-and-white sets or color receivers that were less than perfect. On these sets, the commercials looked terrible and sometimes consumers lost the message.

Today, color television has become nearly universal, but reception still is not perfect for everyone. One-third of homes are not on cable. Since people keep old televisions in service for many years, many sets still provide a less-than-perfect picture. Yet the advertisers assess every commercial by viewing it on a large-screen, late-model set—some ad agencies use the still-rare digital high definition televisions for client screenings—never even thinking that many members of the target audience will not get to see the production under such perfect conditions.

Brad designs Web pages, and while he wants to use the newest and best software for his clients, he keeps in mind a basic limitation. If the initial page takes too long to fully appear, the audience will stop the download and move on. The techno-whiz community might criticize the slow speed of the dial-in modem, but few people have the faster (and more expensive) broadband. Many new customers have a less-than-optimal hook-up on a slightly dated machine. Consumers do not buy new computers every year, so among every Web page's target audiences, only the small groups of people using their work-based machines can be expected to always have equipment that is the latest, fastest, and best.

Yet Brad repeatedly finds himself arguing with clients. The fancy new graphics and moving pictures look so good at the home office, his clients want to load it all onto the front page. Brad knows the consumers' first contact will not be under optimal conditions. However, his clients review each new design on their local broadband, direct-line to the page and they are slow to understand that the typical consumer will download at a different speed and clarity.

We often hear that technicians will be in charge in the new century. That might be positive for the generation of new ideas, but it would be nice if they were also able to understand the more limited views of people who are not so "into" the newest and best equipment.

The Auburn provost eventually announced at the University Senate that the new campus IT administrator would make certain that the office worked from a customer focus. As a former engineering professor, he knew the change of worldview would be difficult, since it required the technical experts to think like people who didn't own the same hardware and who might not know how to use it if they did. But he said that a customer focus would help reduce many of the problems and complaints that faculty had with the system.[1]

Among Web page designers, Brad's perspective is rare. He studied marketing in college, but most Web page designers don't. He argues with many of his clients to take a customer orientation, while their competitors (as well as Brad's clients) are enamored with the wonders of a new or flashy program. To the engineers, people who can't see the initial page fast enough to stay interested are using the "wrong" equipment or program. These people do not just misplace or lose a marketing orientation. They have no idea what it is in the first place.

STORM WARNINGS

When a heavy thunderstorm or potential tornado threatens an area, people need to be warned. But the warning also needs to be heard. Unfortunately, people sending the warnings think in terms of a production orientation, focusing on what they want people to say, instead of taking a marketing orientation by first considering what would get people to listen to the messages.

There are public sirens. There are emergency broadcasts on special weather-alert receivers, as well as on regular radio and television broadcasts. On cable channels, the local systems provide a data crawl on the bottom of the screen. And . . . there is overkill.

The audience was engrossed in the story on *60 Minutes* that a storm was in the area. People could flip to the NBC affiliate and see a small, county-by-county map marking storm advisories; the Weather Channel had updates along the bottom of the screen. A weather-alert radio might even be in the next room. But the local CBS affiliate would not settle for updates at the bottom of the screen. They repeatedly cut into the program so the "news center" and the station's weather forecaster could explain things *ad nauseam*, even when there wasn't anything new to report. To many audience members, it seemed as if the storm center was saying nothing.

The weather reporter gave details on frontal systems and radar reports for 250 miles away. Eventually, she even broke into the program for a five-minute explanation of why the storm warnings had ended. But by then no one was listening. It was wallpaper. I can imagine people across the area as they pushed the button for mute.

Only a total idiot would not know there were storms in the area: Everyone could hear the thunder, the sky was dark, and trees were bending in the wind. But if a real warning did sound, if the station needed to tell the public about a tornado spotted in the area, no one would be mentally tuned in.

Sometimes, after a town is destroyed by a tornado or flood, yet another study is launched to look into how to improve warnings and save lives. Periodically, news stories report that warnings are ignored. But it is intuitively logical that many audience members probably are conditioned to ignore the local channel's so-called storm center, since the broadcasters are more concerned with showing off the forecaster and fancy technology than they are with warning anyone. Again, the marketing orientation of consumer interests is a foreign concept to the weather center managers. They are meteorologists, not marketing people, and they are focused more on speaking than communicating a warning.

BEEP!

When working with truck drivers many years ago, I wondered why some older men and women seemed to be in the way when the trucks were backing into delivery spots. At airports, as the electric carts hustle handicapped passengers or baggage to different gates, many people just amble along and pay no heed to the warning tones or lights on the carts.

My veterinarian explained both situations when he told us why our aging dog was starting to "ignore" my wife.

When people get older, like dogs, they lose their ability to clearly hear higher frequency tones. The dog did not hear my wife as clearly as she hears me; the elderly people in the airport don't hear the cart's warning tones until it is on top of them.

There exists an obvious dilemma for the selection of audible tones for back-up warnings on trucks or carts moving through pedestrian crowds. The trucks need to get the attention of people on the street but should not be disruptive to people in nearby offices. The electric carts in airports need to be noticed, but can't be so obnoxious that other people become angry.

I was told by people claiming to be experts on such things that the commonly used high frequencies were selected after careful research. Unfortunately, most research was on young people. From a marketing point of view, they failed to consider the abilities and needs of older pedestrians—those who most need a strong warning to get out of the way.

My friend always insisted his hearing was fine. His children and grandchildren just talked too quietly, or so he said. After all, he did hear some people without a problem. But in the airport, he was always being yanked out of the way of a motorized cart.

ARE ROADS DESIGNED BY PEDESTRIANS?

Traffic lanes, traffic lights' turn signals, and potential driving hazards are laid out in a way that makes sense on paper to a designer, but often they seem to miss the marketing orientation of how people actually drive in an area.

The New Zealand newspaper's headline on the Internet seemed very strange: "Counting the cost of power pole carnage." And the first few paragraphs, while very serious and alarmist in tone, seemed almost humorous, describing the death toll "caused" by power poles along that county's highways.

"Officer, I can't understand what happened. I was just driving along and this power pole just jumped out in front of me. And I couldn't swerve away because there was this pink elephant in the next lane."

It is easy to say that the accidents are self-inflicted by the drivers who are going off the pavement.[2] But talking on a cell phone, changing the music, or swerving to avoid hitting an animal in the road could cause many otherwise-safe drivers to momentarily veer off to the side. And the power poles are placed for the power companies' convenience, instead of concerns for a safe road.

Apparently, the New Zealand power companies rarely bury their cables. Instead, they are strung at the top of sturdy poles that are set very close to the road, so people who decide where to place the poles don't seem to think about how people drive.[3]

To motorists everywhere, it often appears as if the people who design roadways don't drive cars.

When I lived in Pennsylvania, I would walk to the end of the street after a snowfall to watch all the cars going sideways down the hill. The accidents would occur all over town during the two or three slippery snowfalls of the winter. For some strange reason, there was a stop sign at the bottom of every hill, forcing the drivers to use brakes, slide, and pile up as they all went into the cross street's traffic, which was not required to stop. Rain, haze, or fog also caused assorted traffic confusions, when people came upon the unexpected stop sign at the bottom of a hill.

On paper, it made sense to have the traffic always stop when crossing the streets at the bottom of the hill. And as long as the weather was nice, it worked great for slowing down traffic that might have been speeding up in an unsafe fashion on the downhill ride. But the weather wasn't always nice.

In Auburn, when city officials widened one road at a busy intersection, they didn't widen the crossing street but did create protected left-turn lanes in all directions. And some streets had two lanes marked "left turn only." It seemed to work smoothly, at least on paper as you drew lines. One busy street now had only one lane for continuing traffic, as it received multiple lanes of turning traffic from the cross street. Traffic from the newly widened road now had the left and right turning traffic both "merging" into a single lane.

Elsewhere in towns across the country, the patterns of what is "allowed" for different lanes shift and change without much sense. On one street, a lane may be for left turn only, but on the next, there is no left turn and the right lane is only for turns. Somebody drew these plans on paper. It would be nice if they drove a car, too.

CARS FOR THE FAT AND DUM

Some years ago, Tennessee adopted an alphanumeric system for auto license plates: three consonants and three letters. As they ran out of options, vowels were added. They probably screened the combinations to delete SEX or the clearly offensive words for intercourse or a breast. But no one realized that, now that vanity license plates are common, everyone reads the metal tag. Some words might not be offensive, but they aren't the types of labels the drivers would want to hang off the bumper.

No one wants to drive a vehicle that says they are DUM or a DUD. Not many people would want their car to announce that the driver's favorite word is DUH. In one news story, people descended on one county clerk's office to return tags that said the driver was FAT. When "FAT" was replaced with "FAY," a man was similarly distressed about what people would think of him once it appeared on his truck.[4] The drivers did not feel any better after being told that the label of FAT or DUM had been randomly generated by a computer.

Drivers might be concerned with tags that make a personal statement they don't want. But the primary use for the license plates is to identify cars. As states get caught up with new and interesting designs, they have to remember that the tags must be readable.

The newly designed Tennessee tag is a darkish green state outline with a mustard-colored sunrise and black numbers or letters. Apparently, no one realized that the black digits couldn't be read more than ten feet away on the dark green background. According to one press report, no one consulted with law enforcement officials prior to printing and stamping the plates. While new plates were designed, some police indicated they had given up trying to read the old ones.[5]

The late ad man Howard Luck Gossage wrote at length about his frustrations with advertising artists who only thought in terms of what looked best to them in terms of style or layout. They would insist on showing an airline's planes in stygian skies, or cut off copy in mid-sentence, thinking only in terms of aesthetic appearances, not communications. In simple terms, Gossage concluded that artists don't read. Not that they are illiterate, mind you, just that they don't see the printing as words, but as squiggly lines that mess up the pretty pictures when they don't fit in the exact font the artist wants to use.[6] Similarly, the designers of the Tennessee license tags followed a production orientation in deciding on a new design, instead of a marketing orientation that would have considered how readily they could be read by the police.

TRADEMARK DILUTION

Article 1, Section 2 of the U.S. Constitution (as changed by the Fourteenth Amendment) directs for the "actual enumeration" of the population every ten years. Counting everyone is important, since the federal census provides the basis for both congressional representation and allocation of funds for government programs.

Unfortunately, many people don't want to respond. Some U.S. residents want privacy. Others fear that honest answers will be used against them. Every ten years the government undertakes a massive advertising and publicity effort to encourage people to fill out the forms, or to answer the questions when contacted in person. They repeatedly say that all answers are confidential, but such assurances are often not believed.

During the first year that I lived in State College, Pennsylvania, a woman showed up at my door identifying herself as from "the Census." It wasn't a normal time for a federal counting, but since I knew the census people conducted annual sample surveys, I had no reason to be skeptical. I answered her questions, though it was distracting to also deal with the three dogs at my feet, mine plus those of a friend who was visiting from out of town. During the next couple of weeks, I received a bill for the local occupation tax; a person from the office of traffic safety called to ask to why I hadn't registered the bicycle I had purchased by mail order earlier that month (since I had yet to take it on the road, even my friends didn't know I had bought it); and an animal control officer came to my house "asking" if I had two unlicensed dogs living with me.

A year later I received another call from a person saying she was from the Census. Obviously, my prior experience made me suspicious. Besides, it was unlikely I'd get called as part of a sample survey two years in a row. Instead of answering her questions, I asked for an office call-back number, a common item offered by market research companies to reassure reluctant respondents.

When I called the local number, a woman answered the phone by saying, "Tax office."

Even though I moved away from Pennsylvania many years ago, I am still reluctant to answer questions for anyone saying they are from "the Census."

In our common usage, the government count is the *Census*, and everyone often uses the term as if it were the brand name for the government activity. My "deluxe encyclopedic edition" of *Webster's Dictionary* gives an initial definition for the word, "an official counting of a country's population," but it also says that it is "a similar count of items in some other field."

A *census* is a generic word for a full counting. The U.S. Constitution calls for an "enumeration," not a census.

Technically, the local census inquiry was not a lie, though a fully honest identification would be that she was from the local tax office's census.[7] And maybe municipal government was applying the same type of dishonest marketing views used by businesses in Chapter 9. By saying they were from the *Census*, they might have been hoping that residents would mistakenly think they were from the federal government and more readily respond.[8]

Regardless of the tax office's intentions, they cause problems for the federal head counters, the same problem for any business when its brand name becomes a generic term. The dishonest operators of any local census operation create ill will for the federal effort. Most people can't or won't distinguish between the two. Since the local census does not consider answers confidential and turns them over to tax collectors, citizens will logically expect the federal census to do the same thing.

Maybe the U.S. Census needs a new trademarked name.

THE BASIC IDEA

There are many areas of work or life in which decision makers are different than the people who use the product or service. A marketing perspective can help in many ways. The shift in perceptual focus might appear difficult to implement, but all they need to do is get out of the office more.

NOTES

1. Meanwhile, our program of "choice" remains the less-than-optimal Groupwise.

2. While some government agencies report problems with young, inexperienced, and reckless drivers, no one is considering a change in the situation in which the driving age is sixteen and driver education classes are optional. While government-funded traffic safety campaigns described in Chapter 5 sought to reduce problems of drunk driving by the young, the national legislature lowered the legal drinking age to eighteen.

3. In addition, a pole that gives way in a crash is safer for motorists but it would also increase the probability of a line coming down and causing power outages for customers. Since the motorists (or their heirs) are charged for replacing damaged poles, the power companies have no incentive to use breakaway poles.

4. Laura Hill, "License Tags for DUMmies," *TENNESSEAN.com*, June 7, 2000; "FAT Plates Bring Big Headache," *TENNESSEAN.com*, September 4, 2000; Duren Cheek, "Plate Shortage Blamed on Faulty Machine," *TENNESSEAN.com*, September 16, 2000. Since some judges now punish drunk drivers by requiring them to post a sign on the car about the conviction, no one would want a car saying DUI. Fortunately, this was not a problem since they did not use the letter "I" because it would be confused with a "1."

5. Leon M. Tucker, "Police Spot a Problem on New Tennessee License Plate," *TENNESSEAN.com*, February 19, 2000.

6. Howard Luck Gossage, *Is There Any Hope For Advertising?* (Urbana: University of Illinois Press, 1986), pp. 74–89.

7. The term *census* originated from a Latin word that designated a registration for taxation. In a sense, the local tax office saying it was the census would fit this ancient origin, though I doubt if the clerks at the tax office knew this.

8. Personally, I'd like to see the federal government take action for consumer deception against the local tax offices that do this, but I know that will never happen.

PART V

CONCLUDING NOTES

17

It's Just Misplaced Marketing

These adventures started with an observation at the start of Chapter 1 that marketing is the most readily criticized of all business activities. Personally, I find many of the often-repeated, publicly held views of marketing to be both strange and (sometimes) contradictory.

The job for a marketing professional is often denigrated it as mind-numbingly easy, in that most people think any idiot can do it. In comic strips or on television programs, the know-nothing son of the boss is made the vice president of marketing. Marketing experts in the popular Dilbert comics present pie charts of the intuitively obvious, mixed with words not found in any dictionary, selling products that the company doesn't make. At the same time, the public also fears the power of marketing activities that they believe are controlling their minds with all-powerful tools of persuasion used by an immoral cadre of crooks. And, if not abusive, the all-pervasive nature of modern marketing activities are seen by many people as offensive.

In reality, marketing decisions are not obvious or easy. Good work requires intelligence, and marketing persuasion tools can only appeal to consumer predispositions. The modern marketing concept is a basic perspective for business decisions that says all work must proceed from an understanding of consumer needs and wants. And a basic impediment to decisions is that the consumer rarely thinks or perceives things the same way as the marketing manager, requiring development of a sense of empathy with different marketing segments so as to best satisfy the customers' needs.

Unfortunately, the terms of the marketing concept make it seem as if marketing itself makes all modern businesses better oriented toward service to consumers. With marketing's focus on consumer satisfactions, the business world would always do a good job of making a better society, or so some business people seem to say. As marketing views are more often applied to government and nonprofit organizations, this increased application of marketing spreads its values and consumer benefits to even more people in all walks of life. Well, maybe it does, sometimes, in some cases.

This wondrous social value of marketing may be true, at least in part. Yet for many firms and many decisions by businesses, nonprofit organizations, or government agencies, a consumer focus is often lost, ignored, misused, or abused. It is hard to argue for marketing's benefits to society when its core perspectives are often misplaced.

NONFEASANCE, MISFEASANCE, AND MALFEASANCE

Abuses of corporate power can fall into three categories: nonfeasance, failure to use power that should be employed; misfeasance, an improper application of powers and resources it has; and malfeasance, employing improper power that it should not possess. And in these adventures of misplaced marketing, the stories are all examples of situations in which consumer interests are not served because of intentional or accidental abuses of marketing power.

Marketing was misplaced in the first two sections because of business nonfeasance, but probably for different reasons. Marketing requires business decision makers to recognize that the typical customer does not view the world the same way as the business manager. In these sections, that recognition is lacking.

The adventures in Part I deal with businesses—large, small, or, sometimes, almost all firms in a given industry—that have lost their marketing orientation, and instead follow a production orientation in making their decisions. They base decisions on what they want to do instead of what would satisfy consumers.

In Chapter 2, products are designed to fit what can be made without clear reference to what would best satisfy consumer needs or desires. As a result, many people end up buying products that do a less-than-optimal job of providing their desired benefits. The adventures of Chapter 3 illustrate a key problem for consumers—bad customer service or no service at all. While the marketing concept calls for companies to satisfy consumer needs, and while services marketing is a growing topic of research and teaching interest on campus, customer satisfaction remains elusive and rare at many businesses. A more widespread application of a marketing orientation would improve this. Chapter 4 describes a lot of advertising that might be attention getting and very entertaining but not doing the selling job. In most cases the advertising writers are creating advertising or commercials to say what they want instead of communicating what consumers need to hear to be interested in making a purchase.

In Part II, a marketing perspective is not lost as much as it is ignored. The public service groups, trade associations, and government agencies might think of themselves as marketing experts (or not), but they myopically believe their thinking is typical of everyone they serve. They think they know what they are doing, but they don't. They would be doing a better job of serving the public if they applied a marketing perspective, but from arrogance or ignorance, or maybe both, they don't. Maybe they can't. It would be nice if it wasn't so, but they are not the marketing experts they'd like to presume they are.

Still, even a marketing view does not solve all problems. Sometimes marketing should not be used at all. In Part III, we deal with images, illusions, misfeasance, and malfeasance when marketing is not lost. A marketing view is "properly" used and applied, but consumers or society would be better off if it weren't. Sometimes, avarice works against ethical marketing judgments. In one of his most often-repeated quotations, the late advertising man Howard Luck Gossage said that getting business people to see how ethics is in their best interests is "like telling an eight-year-old that sex is more fun that ice cream."[1] With the label of misplaced marketing in this section, I turned an analysis of the social and ethical environment of marketing into one of pragmatic concerns relating to business decisions.

Chapter 8 described self-regulation activities that have acquired a public image as serving consumers. And while self-regulation often does that job, it is an outcome, not necessarily the intent. Public service per se is not why many self-regulation activities exist, nor is it the reason why companies cooperate with self-regulation activities of a trade association. For both good and ill, self-regulation is an often-misused marketing tool, applied for purposes of generating a positive image of business activities. Sometimes that positive image is well-earned, but other times it is not. Chapter 9 gives up any effort at pretense, when marketing tools are abused for purposes of consumer deception. And yet, in some instances when consumers fear marketing abuse, the fears such as those described in Chapter 10 are grounded more in paranoia than reality.

Chapters 11 and 12 deal with products or values that are distorted or ruined by marketing. A thorough marketing application directs all stages of product design and development, but some "products" are not improved by marketing. To the contrary, marketing can validly be blamed for boring movies, uninspiring politicians, unoriginal music, and schools that seem oriented to doing everything *except* providing a thorough education to develop the minds of our young. To pander to businesses and students' desires for job training, I often hear tales of a marketing teacher who gives his students directions on *how* to give bribes. According to one such teacher, "You'll all be asked for one at some point, so you should learn how it's done to minimize problems." A friend of mine was once asked to apply for a position as department chair at another university, but the search committee later withdrew the invitation when they read some of his research articles that criticized businesses' unethical behaviors. They didn't think that someone who was critical of business should be an administrator in a college of business.

Like Parts I and II, the short chapters of Part IV are examples of nonfeasance. But instead of looking at outcomes and consumer frustrations as the basis of discussion, these adventures focus on a small number of instances in which business biases, financial constraints, or terminology explain why a marketing view is sometimes lost or ignored.

Chapter 13 describes how racism and other stereotypes direct advertising agency hiring decisions, based on a presumption that a marketing perspective requiring empathy with different consumers can't be applied by minority employees or for minority audiences. As a result, there exists the business ghetto of so-called targeted agencies, with minority employees hired for the narrow job of converting general market advertising for audiences who are members of that same racial minority.[2] Chapter 14 explains the differing cost incentives of direct mail through e-mail versus direct mail advertising through the postal service and why, as a result, spam ignores all concerns for target audiences. Marketing views get lost in Chapter 15 because of changes in business terms. Over time, the term for the communications tool "publicity" became confused with the marketing-guided "public relations." As more publicists and people oriented toward controlling the news became the predominant focus of PR agencies, production-oriented publicity decisions have come to control many aspects of the PR businesses. Instead of being guided by marketing views, too much of modern PR takes a production orientation toward what a business wants to say.

Finally, Chapter 16 does not really deal with businesses or business decisions. Marketing for nonprofit organizations is not ignored in marketing literature. In fact, there are several textbooks on the topic.

But using the simple consumer orientation as a focus, these short adventures looked at the problems, constraints, and frustrations of people who deal with decisions made by someone who often seems incapable of thinking like, for example, the typical user of the roads or the respondent to a U.S. Census Bureau questionnaire.

MARKETING PERSPECTIVES FOR
FUN AND ADVENTURE

Toward the end of the BBC science-fiction comedy series, *The Hitchhiker's Guide to the Galaxy*, the central characters find themselves on a spaceship filled with 15 million cryogenically preserved people who had once held jobs such as salesmen, management consultants, advertising and public relations executives, or telephone sanitizers. The ship's captain explains that theirs is one of three ships dispatched from a doomed planet. This is the B Ark: The A Ark carries the planet's scientists, artists, and other intellectual achievers; C is filled with the people who do the actual work. The captain and crew can't recall what calamity befell their home planet, but they are unconcerned that they haven't heard from the other arks and that they have no idea where the ship is headed.

The hitchhikers then discover that the ship is programmed not to land, but to crash. They try to tell the captain, but he already knows and doesn't seem to care. The captain says that there is a purpose for all that, but he just can't recall what it is. "What is the reason?" the hitchhikers keep yelling. "And how do we get at the controls to make the ship land?" The captain doesn't know, but is certain he will recall the reason for it eventually. Finally, in exasperation, the one of the hitchhikers yells, "You're all bloody useless."

At that the captain becomes alert. "That's it. That was the reason."[3]

I would like to think that marketing people are not useless, or at least more important than telephone sanitizers. At the very least, marketing provides an important perspective for viewing the world. And misplaced marketing offers a new view on a whole range of business practices.

When I served as a judge for an aggressive case competition for M.B.A. students, each team was to study the client company and its business, and make a set of strategic recommendations. For some reason, few teams had any members interested in marketing, and as they juggled financial statements or construction goals, they presumed a great deal about consumer responses to prices. Every group seemed to think that if they just build it, they would have customers. Even when the client was a soon-to-be-deregulated utility, an engineer from the client leaned over and wondered why none of them applied a basic marketing view to any part of the analysis.

Apparently, it is easy, too easy, for a firm to lose or ignore or abuse a marketing perspective. And, no matter what, some people will always be offended by things that businesses do. The news media and the Internet are filled with complaints about advertising or television commercials that people don't like.

An advertisement from the inside front cover of the new *TV Guide* showed three muscular men stripped to the waist. The men stood in superhero-style, muscle-flex poses, and they had three clearly different degrees of muscle bulk to "illustrate" the benefits of a new type of feminine hygiene product. I showed it to my advertising students and just about everyone in the class didn't like it. Sometimes, critics of specific messages just have to admit they are not in the target audience for the advertising, but . . .

I really hate those panty shield commercials.

NOTES

1. Gossage died in 1969. Seventeen years later, a book listing him as the author collected his various magazine and newspaper articles: *Is There Any Hope for Advertising?* (Urbana: University of Illinois Press, 1986). Death did not stop him and this book had a "second edition," published nine years after that, with the title *The Book of Gossage* (Chicago: The Copy Workshop, 1995).

2. Carbon Copywriter, "Off-target: Ghettoizing Black Advertising," *Brandweek*, vol. 40 (December 6, 1999), pp. 28–32.

3. The story of the hitchhikers was expanded to fill a series of very popular books. This part of the tale was published in Douglas Adams, *The Restaurant at the End of the Universe* (New York: Pocket Books, 1980), pp. 170–194.

Index

ABOUT THE AUTHOR

Herbert Jack Rotfeld is Professor of Marketing at Auburn University, Auburn, Alabama. Noted for iconoclastic research and his challenges to conventional wisdom and commonly held presumptions about business practices and theories, Dr. Rotfeld is a 2000 recipient of the American Academy of Advertising's Outstanding Contribution to Advertising award. He lectures widely around the world, has been a faculty visitor at universities in the United States, Australia, and New Zealand, and is a respected scholar of advertising regulation and self-regulation. He was also a columnist for *Marketing News* and is currently a contributor section editor for the *Journal of Consumer Marketing*.